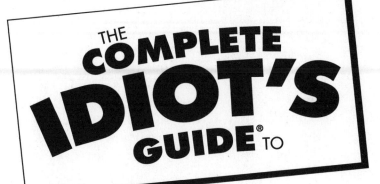

THE
COMPLETE IDIOT'S GUIDE® TO

Werewolves

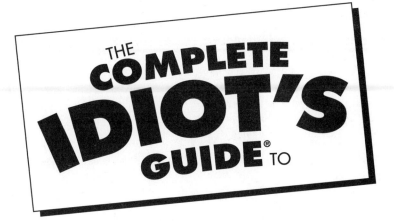

THE
COMPLETE
IDIOT'S
GUIDE® TO

Werewolves

by Nathan Robert Brown

ALPHA

A member of Penguin Group (USA) Inc.

398.45
Bro

ALPHA BOOKS

Published by the Penguin Group

Penguin Group (USA) Inc., 375 Hudson Street, New York, New York 10014, USA

Penguin Group (Canada), 90 Eglinton Avenue East, Suite 700, Toronto, Ontario M4P 2Y3, Canada (a division of Pearson Penguin Canada Inc.)

Penguin Books Ltd., 80 Strand, London WC2R 0RL, England

Penguin Ireland, 25 St. Stephen's Green, Dublin 2, Ireland (a division of Penguin Books Ltd.)

Penguin Group (Australia), 250 Camberwell Road, Camberwell, Victoria 3124, Australia (a division of Pearson Australia Group Pty. Ltd.)

Penguin Books India Pvt. Ltd., 11 Community Centre, Panchsheel Park, New Delhi—110 017, India

Penguin Group (NZ), 67 Apollo Drive, Rosedale, North Shore, Auckland 1311, New Zealand (a division of Pearson New Zealand Ltd.)

Penguin Books (South Africa) (Pty.) Ltd., 24 Sturdee Avenue, Rosebank, Johannesburg 2196, South Africa

Penguin Books Ltd., Registered Offices: 80 Strand, London WC2R 0RL, England

International Standard Book Number: 978-1-59257-985-3
Library of Congress Catalog Card Number: 2009928809

11   10   09   8   7   6   5   4   3   2   1

Interpretation of the printing code: The rightmost number of the first series of numbers is the year of the book's printing; the rightmost number of the second series of numbers is the number of the book's printing. For example, a printing code of 09-1 shows that the first printing occurred in 2009.

Printed in the United States of America

Note: This publication contains the opinions and ideas of its author. It is intended to provide helpful and informative material on the subject matter covered. It is sold with the understanding that the author and publisher are not engaged in rendering professional services in the book. If the reader requires personal assistance or advice, a competent professional should be consulted.

The author and publisher specifically disclaim any responsibility for any liability, loss, or risk, personal or otherwise, which is incurred as a consequence, directly or indirectly, of the use and application of any of the contents of this book.

Most Alpha books are available at special quantity discounts for bulk purchases for sales promotions, premiums, fund-raising, or educational use. Special books, or book excerpts, can also be created to fit specific needs.

For details, write: Special Markets, Alpha Books, 375 Hudson Street, New York, NY 10014.

Publisher: *Marie Butler-Knight*
Editorial Director: *Mike Sanders*
Senior Managing Editor: *Billy Fields*
Executive Editor: *Randy Ladenheim-Gil*
Development Editor: *Megan Douglass*
Production Editor: *Kayla Dugger*
Copy Editor: *Amy Lepore*

Cartoonist: *Steve Barr*
Book Designer: *Trina Wurst*
Cover Designer: *Rebecca Harmon*
Indexer: *Johnna VanHoose Dinse*
Layout: *Brian Massey*
Proofreader: *Laura Caddell*

This book is dedicated to a very special person, who for so long acted as my anonymous pen-pal guardian. I don't know if you will ever get to see this. Nevertheless, I want to thank you from the bottom of my heart for never abandoning me when I needed you the most … even when I behaved like the stubborn and foolish boy I for so long was.

Contents at a Glance

Contents

Introduction

Many of us remember the bedtime stories of childhood, especially the ones about walking, talking, human-eating wolves. We remember the terror of hearing how Little Red Riding Hood was devoured by the Big Bad Wolf. We remember our relief (as well as horror) when the woodsman chopped open the Big Bad Wolf's stomach to free the girl. And what about the Three Little Pigs and their well-known encounter with a Big Bad Wolf?

From a very young age, those of us in western society are introduced to the negative portrayals of wolves and werewolves. We are taught to fear them, to avoid them, and to cheer on their destruction. However, these hairy creatures of legend never die ... living forever in the immortality of myth.

For some of us, the werewolf represents the dark and savage urges within us, urges that we pretend don't exist. For others, the werewolf represents nature's dualistic potential for both creation and destruction. A select few of us, however, accept the dark side of our natures and view the werewolf as a dark sibling that should be embraced instead of feared.

In ancient times, the wolf was often revered, and ancient humans dreamed of achieving a union with the wolf's power. In medieval times, the werewolf came to be seen as the epitome of evil. Many humans were burned after being found guilty of lycanthropy. Today, the werewolf has been embraced by nearly every medium of pop culture—sometimes as a cursed human, other times as a wild antihero. For thousands of years, the werewolf has been a part of human myths, legends, and folklore. And it would seem that this rebel among rebels will not soon be forgotten because the werewolf lives within each of us.

How to Use This Book

Your appetite for werewolf lore is no doubt insatiable. So to make it as easy as possible to find exactly what you're looking for, this book has been separated into four main parts and further broken down into chapters by focus subject and type, as follows.

Where do werewolves come from? Well, you see, when a mommy werewolf and a daddy werewolf love each other very much, they sniff each other and then ... just kidding. The true theories as to when, how, and why werewolves first entered the realms of the human psyche and ancient folklore will be discussed in **Part 1, "Werewolf Origins."** This part of the text will offer in-depth explanations of the different types of werewolves, various mythological origins of werewolves from across the globe, and the werewolf's various shapeshifting relatives.

Part 2, "A History of Werewolves," picks up where the previous chapters left off. First, the text will offer summarizations of the many infamous "werewolf trials" that took place during and just following the medieval period of human history. This part will also deal with the relationship between wolves, werewolves, and organized religion, as well as providing a comprehensive treatment of various historical accounts of human encounters with werewolves.

Considering the turbulent history between humans and werewolves, how did they survive as figures in pop culture? In **Part 3, "The Modern Werewolf,"** this question will be thoroughly addressed. From literature to movies to comic books, this part will discuss the various artistic and cultural influences that have ultimately led to the popular modern perceptions of werewolves.

Werewolves have a very real relationship with humans. First and foremost, werewolves play an important role as an archetypal symbol in the unconscious of the human psyche. In **Part 4, "Of Wolf and Man,"** these man-werewolf relationships will be discussed in detail. First, there is a brief guide for what one should do (according to the available lore) if bitten by a werewolf. Also, you will be given a summary of the various methods provided by werewolf lore for how to do battle with them. Last but not least, the text offers a discussion of the potential rational explanations for the historic werewolf phenomenon.

Extras

There is a lot to be said about werewolves, and as a result some elements can easily be confused. In order to help you along the way, a number of sidebars are provided throughout the text. Here are detailed descriptions of these sidebars, which will offer you readily available explanations to the key ideas, concepts, facts, and terms related to werewolves.

Beastly Words

These sidebars offer definitions, meanings, and explanations for the various terms, words, objects, and/or names that you will encounter throughout the reading of this text.

The Savage Truth

These sidebars offer facts related to the content of the text. Some of these will simply offer interesting but extraneous side notes, while others will be directly related to the subject matter.

The Curse

These sidebars offer clarification for easily confused concepts, events, and/or words related to werewolves due to common misperceptions and/or similarities in spellings, plots, purposes, and/or actions.

Bark vs. Bite

Sometimes, especially in a discussion of werewolves, the line between reality and fiction can get a little blurry. These sidebars will act as reality checks from time to time, offering rational explanations for the many spectacular but historical situations that you will encounter throughout the reading of this text.

Acknowledgments

I would like to extend my most sincere thanks to one of my most favorite editors in the world, Randy Ladenheim-Gil. I would also like to thank Megan Douglass for being the best DE a writer could ask for. To my agent, Jacky Sach, I will always be grateful for your confidence in me. Last but not least, I extend my thanks to everyone at Alpha Books who had a part in making this project possible.

Trademarks

All terms mentioned in this book that are known to be or are suspected of being trademarks or service marks have been appropriately capitalized. Alpha Books and Penguin Group (USA) Inc. cannot attest to the accuracy of this information. Use of a term in this book should not be regarded as affecting the validity of any trademark or service mark.

Part 1

Werewolf Origins

Werewolves have existed in the lore of numerous civilizations, even when separated from one another by oceans. To Native Americans, the wolf was a wise guardian of tribal structures. Wolf rites remain sacred to the Quileute of the Pacific Northwest. European werewolves were victims of dark magic or damned by demonic pacts. The Japanese once worshipped a wolf-deity and viewed wolves as divine messengers of powerful deities. In countries where wolves are not indigenous, there are similar creatures, were-hyenas and assorted types of were-cats.

1

Werewolf Evolution

In This Chapter

◆ A discussion of lycanthropy

◆ The different potential causes of the werewolf condition

◆ An examination of the modern viral werewolf

◆ The common threads of the werewolf phenomenon

An odd howl reaches your ears from somewhere in the dark. "It's probably just some dog, howling at the moon," you tell yourself, but your words don't seem to comfort you as well as you'd like. Suddenly, something is growling just beyond sight, somewhere in the trees. Before you know it, something is behind you, breathing heavily, a savage beast ready to tear you apart without a second thought. Fear that you will soon be dead (or worse, cursed for eternity) grips your heart.

Welcome to the nightmare that is the werewolf—a frightening regression to the animal state, an often involuntary surrender to the savagery that lies within us all.

Lycanthropy and Werewolves

The state of being a werewolf is called *lycanthropy*. Stories of werewolves span the globe. However, each civilization's werewolf myth has its own unique characteristics. For example, the appearance of a werewolf's final state of transformation differs from one culture's legend/myth to another's.

> **Beastly Words**
>
> Lycanthropy is the technical term for the state of being a werewolf. In other words, it roughly means "werewolf-ism." It comes from the Greek root words *lykoi* (wolf) and *anthropos* (man/human), so it literally means "wolf-man" or "wolf-human." A person who is inflicted with or practices lycanthropy is called a *lycanthrope*.

According to some stories, a werewolf has the ability to turn from a human into a full-blown wolf, changing in both size and shape. In other stories, which have earned the most popularity in the books and films of recent times, a werewolf turns from a human into a large, wolf-like creature, as a sort of human-wolf hybrid.

You may be wondering just how, exactly, one becomes a werewolf. Well, if you would like to become a werewolf—or would simply like to avoid becoming one (which would be a more advisable course of action)—it is really rather simple. Of course, the simplest method for becoming a werewolf is to get bitten by one. Unfortunately, it would appear that few people have ever survived a werewolf attack. If you ever find yourself under attack by a werewolf, don't worry. It is far more likely that you will just be ripped to pieces and killed before the transformation ever takes place. This could be seen as good news or bad news, depending on how you look at it.

There are a number of schools of thought as to what causes a person to enter the state of lycanthropy, and these are often related closely to the beliefs of the time periods in which they were created. For example, "werewolf-ism," as lycanthropy is sometimes called, was first believed to be the result of supernatural causes such as a curse or spell. Later, it was believed to be of spiritual origin—certain people could be tricked into believing they were werewolves by some illusion concocted by the devil. Eventually, as science evolved, the cause became more scientific in nature—a rare disease, a virus, or some sort of psychological phenomenon.

The most widely recognized causes of lycanthropy are as follows:

◆ A curse passed via the werewolf's bite or through the spell of some form of dark sorcery

◆ The invocation of the wolf spirit

◆ Enchantment (usually self-induced)

◆ A virus passed by way of the werewolf's bite

The Cursed Werewolf

We will begin with the cursed werewolf, as this is the type most familiar to people. The majority of werewolf enthusiasts are already very familiar with the idea of "The Curse of the Werewolf," most likely because there is already a well-known cult classic film of the same name (see Chapter 11). Even if you have never heard of it before, you can probably figure out what it is without much trouble. In the early days of the werewolf phenomenon, it was considered a curse. The idea likely stemmed from the opinion that few people would volunteer to become savage, flesh-eating beasts on the night of every full moon. (Of course, not every werewolf myth claims that a full moon is necessary for the transformation to occur.)

The cursed werewolf is perhaps the most tragic type of all lycanthropes. It is said that they have absolutely no control over their shapeshifting abilities, and this includes their actions while in werewolf form. They recognize neither friend nor foe once the change has occurred and will attack any human who crosses their path. The human mind of the cursed werewolf is said to be completely overwhelmed, replaced by a savage and uncontrollable bloodlust. Needless to say, once a cursed werewolf begins to transform, it would behoove you to start running immediately. The last thing anyone would want to be, when dealing with a cursed werewolf that has just transformed, is the first human it sees.

The cursed form of lycanthropy commonly occurs in one of two primary ways. The first way, of course, is to be bitten by a werewolf.

The Curse of the Werewolf's Bite

The "bite curse" form of lycanthropy has some interesting folklore behind it. The usual folklore claims that if a person is attacked/bitten by a werewolf and is lucky (or, some might say, unlucky) enough to survive, then the curse passes from the werewolf to the victim. (However, this does *not* mean the curse leaves the current werewolf.) Usually, one will be able to know if this has occurred by the sudden appearance of a mark on one's palm, hand, or somewhere else on one's body. This is called the Mark of the Beast. This mark is most frequently described as an inverted pentagram and is usually said to appear on the palm of the hand.

The Curse

The Mark of the Beast that is associated with lycanthropy should not be confused with the Mark of the Beast concept that is mentioned in the biblical Book of Revelations. Of course, the folklore associated with the werewolf's Mark of the Beast may have been influenced by this part in the Bible, which might explain why it came to be described as an inverted pentagram, a symbol commonly associated with the demonic in Christianity.

Once the Mark of the Beast appears, the most common lore states that the victim will involuntarily undergo his or her first transformation when hit by the light of the next full moon (or just when the next full moon occurs, according to some). Sadly, the only known 100 percent effective cure for this sort of lycanthropy is death. Some folklore claims that the infected victim will remain mortal (and so can still be killed by normal means) until the first change occurs on the next full moon. Others claim that this isn't exactly true, that the body of a werewolf victim (if killed after the Mark of the Beast first appears) will simply reanimate and transform anyway, if it was not disposed of properly (see Chapter 16 for instructions).

The Sins of the Father

A second form of the cursed werewolf is the "familial curse" type. This is an individual who is from a family that, for one reason or another, has been marked by the werewolf's curse. Usually some tragic event, blasphemous sin, or terrible crime was committed by an ancient ancestor (or by the entire ancient clan). This led to the family being cursed with lycanthropy. Most of the time, these curses have been placed by means of either sorcery or divine intervention.

For example, some lore might claim that, long ago, the cursed clan enlisted the help of a dark sorcerer in order to secure victory in battle. When the battle was won, however, the head of the clan refused to pay the sorcerer the agreed price. (Sometimes, the popular price in such stories was the lord's loveliest daughter or firstborn child.) Sometimes these stories state that the lord betrayed the sorcerer and struck him down instead of keeping the bargain. The sorcerer then cursed the clan with his dying words and, by doing so, ensured that it could never be broken. There is one basic theme that commonly occurs in these types of stories—the clan members or leaders did not keep their contract with the sorcerer. Contracts could be seen as symbolic of civilized society. By breaking their contract, they behaved in an uncivilized manner and were therefore punished appropriately with a curse that would force them to lose their humanity completely.

In other situations, the clan commits some form of blasphemous sin against a god or some religious order. For example, a warrior of the clan might have killed a priest or perhaps made a pact with the devil in order to secure the love of a certain woman or victory in battle. As a result, a god (pagan or Christian) smote the man's entire bloodline with the cursed form of lycanthropy.

As with the bite form of cursed lycanthropy, there is only one known cure for the familial curse—quite simply, the entire bloodline has to be wiped out of existence. Usually this happens in one of two ways. Some of these werewolf clans are said to have forbidden their members from having children and then allowed nature to run its course. Others (more frequently) are said to have been hunted down and killed off by humans, who are usually more than willing to give nature a hand in such affairs.

The Spirit Werewolf

The spirit werewolf is very much the polar opposite of the cursed were-wolf in that he or she is a voluntary participant. The transformation of a spiritual werewolf is almost exclusively ritualistic in nature. The spirit werewolf invokes the spirit of the wolf, or perhaps the spirit of some type of wolf deity, and by doing so undergoes a kind of possession that leads to his or her transformation. Unlike other forms of lycanthropy, however, this transformation does not always need to be a physical one. Often the spirit werewolf primarily undergoes a spiritual or psychological transformation. At times it is said that this can lead to physical transformations in extreme cases.

Bark vs. Bite

Early explorers of certain remote regions in Africa, Australia, and New Zealand claimed they witnessed rituals in which they saw human beings change into wolves or other species of wild canine. Of course, in most cases, the transformations took place out of sight, such as behind bushes or in huts. It's likely that, in such cases, these men were victims of clever illusions. In later years, no such incredible evidence was uncovered in those regions.

For the most part, the primary legends of spirit lycanthropy come from two distinct cultures—the Native Americans (see Chapter 2) and the Norse (see Chapter 3).

The Enchanted Werewolf

Enchanted lycanthropes fall somewhere between cursed lycanthropy and spirit lycanthropy. These individuals—through the use of enchantment, sorcery, magic, and so on—have the ability to shapeshift into a wolf or werewolf. As with the spirit werewolf, some form of complex spell or ritual is frequently necessary. Sometimes, however, such spells can be condensed into a charm, talisman, or some type of worn garment (usually made of a wolf's skin) that allows the user to change shape at will.

Enchanted werewolves are said to retain a certain level of control once they have transformed. They don't immediately go on killing sprees once they have assumed this new form. However, most of the lore surrounding enchanted lycanthropy warns that there is a danger of losing control. Basically, if enchanted werewolves remain in the wolf-state for too long, they begin to lose touch with their human side. At some point, the animal nature of the wolf will overtake the human side completely, and they can lose themselves forever. Once this happens, enchanted werewolves will forget that they were ever human, causing them to permanently remain in the wolf-state. The good news is they don't even know anything has happened to them.

The Viral Werewolf

Viral lycanthropy bears a number of similarities to cursed lycanthropy. For the most part, the difference between the two is the explanation for its transmission through the bite. When science began to explain the nature of viral infections, it didn't take long for people to notice that lycanthropy behaved a lot like a virus. First, it is transmitted through bodily fluids, usually from a bite. Second, it seems to undergo a gestation period before becoming active—basically, one lunar cycle. Third, it behaves like a blood-borne virus or a sexually transmitted disease (such as HIV). This is a relatively new part of werewolf lore, the idea that lycanthropy can also be spread through sexual intercourse or other means of blood or fluid exchange. Unlike most viruses, and similar to some of the more extreme sexually transmitted diseases, however, there is no known treatment, cure, vaccine, or inoculation for viral lycanthropy. (Unless we are counting death as a cure ... in which case, there is one.)

As werewolf lore evolved into its modern form, it came to be seen in what are today considered more reasonable, or at least relatively believable, terms. As a result, the potential ways in which one could become infected with viral lycanthropy are more diverse. The accepted potential avenues of infection are as follows:

- Being bitten by a werewolf (and surviving, of course)
- Other forms of fluidic exchange, such as sexual intercourse (you get the idea)

- Ingestion of infected blood, flesh, brain matter, saliva, and so on

- Drinking from water that has pooled in a paw-print indentation of a werewolf (though this is not widely accepted)

In recent years, the pop culture lore surrounding viral lycanthropy claims that a werewolf's ability to control his or her actions or abilities is directly related to the length of time he or she has been infected. Basically, the idea is that the longer a person has had lycanthropy, the better he or she has learned to deal with it. Another point of contention in viral werewolf lore is on the subject of immortality. Some believe that lycanthropy also grants immortality, while others believe it only grants enhanced regeneration and an extended life span. A small percentage of lore insists that viral lycanthropy offers infected individuals neither immortality nor regenerative abilities, and that it only grants them the ability to transform into a wolf or werewolf.

Common Threads

Though each type of lycanthropy is unique, there are some common threads between them. These commonalities are as follows:

- The belief that one's humanity is lost, jeopardized, or at least altered by the state of lycanthropy

- The belief that (except for spirit and enchanted werewolves) lycanthropy can be spread through a werewolf's bite

- Aside from the lycanthropy of spirit werewolves, the belief that there is no known cure or remedy for werewolf-ism (unless, once again, you consider *death* to be a cure)

You may be wondering which one of the aforementioned types of lycanthropy is the "real deal," so to speak. Well, the answer to that really depends on your personal definition of "werewolf." Since there aren't exactly any werewolves available for scientific study, this is not a black-and-white issue. Some feel that the spiritual/psychological, change-of-spirit werewolves are just as real as the physical transformation of the more visually stunning werewolves of other lycanthropy types. Others believe that only those born of werewolf blood (for example, from a cursed and/or infected bloodline) are true werewolves. Still others believe that lycanthropy is an evil force or curse, a bane upon human existence, and that it would be better left to fade into the shadows of the past. Which of them is real? It would be best to decide for yourself.

The Least You Need to Know

◆ Cursed werewolves should be considered the most dangerous, as they have no control over their shapeshifting abilities or their actions once transformed.

◆ Cursed werewolves are almost never voluntary lycanthropes.

◆ Spirit lycanthropy does not require a physical transformation to occur.

◆ Enchanted werewolves may have more control than cursed lycanthropes, but a prolonged time in the wolf-state can lead them to lose their humanity.

◆ Viral werewolves are fairly similar to cursed lycanthropes, with minor differences regarding their abilities.

2

An American Werewolf in ... America

In This Chapter

- ◆ The universality of Native American wolf totems
- ◆ The significance of the wolf in Native American culture
- ◆ The skinwalkers and their relationship to lycanthropy
- ◆ The significance of the Ya Ya Ceremony of the Hopi Indians
- ◆ A closer look at the Mexican Nahual
- ◆ Discussion of the Wendigo

The Native American perception of the wolf is a vivid example of just how extremely their view of nature differed from that of the Europeans who eventually pushed them from their own lands. Native Americans have always viewed nature as a divine entity, worthy of the greatest possible respect. Anything less would be blasphemous. The incoming Europeans viewed nature as something to be conquered and exploited. To become one with the wolf, a part of the divinity of the natural realm, would be something to embrace in the Native American view. They saw wolves as wise teachers to be treated with reverence. The Europeans, on the other hand, viewed the wolf as a dangerous adversary, a savage beast that needed to be hunted down and destroyed.

Sometimes, however, those with the power to shapeshift were viewed by Native Americans as dark and evil witches, as in the case of the skin-walkers. They are thought of by most Native Americans as an ancient enemy of which only a handful remain. Nevertheless, even one of them is thought to be formidable.

Wolf Totems

The face of the wolf can be found in the totem of nearly every Native American tribe of the Iroquois, Algonquin, Pueblo, and the Northwest coastal groups. This makes the wolf one of the most universal members of Native American totems. Native American tribes credited wolves with a number of impressive powers and miracles, from the origins of certain tribes to healing the sick. Every tribe tells the stories of the wolf spirit, and the stories of his great deeds are many.

Shamans of the Crow tribe claim that a wolf skin has the power to save a person who is at the brink of death. The Inuit tell a myth about an elderly woman left to die in the freezing cold. In order to survive, she transforms into a wolf. Some Great Plains tribes claim that a deity/ spirit named "Wolf-Man" created the Great Plains especially for them. A number of tribes in the Great Plains have myths telling of how "Wolf" taught them how to hunt, as well as the importance of familial unity.

The Curse

One must understand that in the native languages, mindsets, and perceptions of the Native Americans, there is no distinction between the Wolf Spirit and an individual wolf. In their native view, all are one and the same entity. There is no need to make a distinction between the Wolf Spirit and "this wolf" or "that wolf" because they are one. They are all simply "Wolf." This concept is sometimes difficult for outsiders to grasp.

The Wolf Spirit's mythic counterpart, Coyote, is known for being frequently rash, foolish, mischievous, violent, and deceitful. However, Wolf is seen in quite an opposite way, representing the attributes of wisdom, strength, loyalty, and freedom. When Wolf speaks to a human being, Native Americans believe that he should be seen as a sacred, spiritual teacher. His words are divinely inspired and must be heeded with the utmost attention. Wolf, in some stories, has the ability to grant his powers to people.

Secret Wolf Rites of the Northwest Tribes

A number of tribes from the Pacific Northwest are of the belief that they were originally wolves and later chose to assume the human form. This is why it should not be surprising that some of these tribes have preserved their traditions of ritualistic lycanthropy. These ancient practices would more than likely fall into the category of spirit lycanthropy. Of course, one would have to know the rituals to properly categorize them ... and these tribes aren't too big on sharing this particular part of their culture.

The First Tribes of the Northwest Coast—namely the Nootka, Quileute, and Kwakiutl—are known to still actively teach certain forms of traditional lycanthropic rituals to their young men as a rite of passage. Little to nothing is concretely known about these teachings, and to this day they remain a closely guarded secret. The subject is not supposed to be discussed with outsiders, especially not whites, except in very specific wordings and in only the rarest of possible situations.

The Savage Truth

The Quileute tribe of the Pacific Northwest is small, with a population of only about 750. The tribe, however, has recently received a new swell of attention due to the presence of Quileute characters in the popular *Twilight* vampire-romance series. One of the main characters, Jacob, is a young member of the Quileute tribe. In the books, the Quileute are actually werewolves and the enemies of vampires. They have sworn an uneasy truce with the Cullens, a family of peaceful vampires who do not prey upon humans. As long as the Cullens do not come onto Quileute land, the tribe agreed not to expose what they are to the humans.

All that is known for certain about these rites is that the initiates are taken deep into the forest to a very secret and still completely unknown location (at least, it's unknown to outsiders). It is there that the initiates are instructed in the tribal lycanthropy traditions. This is thought to be a time for the elder generations to pass on their tribe's ancient heritage, which is rich with secret rites and ceremonial initiations. Most speculate that, during this time, initiates are instructed in the proper lycanthropic chants, songs, dances, and meditations.

The Ancient Enemy

According to the myths of many southern tribes, a group of powerful magic users called the *Yeenaaldlooshii*, or "skinwalkers," became a widespread terror in a time long ago. Technically, skinwalkers are not lycanthropes but *therianthropes* since they are said to be able to assume the form of many different animals (one of which, of course, is the form of a wolf or other canine). Therefore, if one were to witness a person transforming into the form of a wolf or canine, there is at least a minute possibility that one has encountered a skinwalker and not a werewolf. Unfortunately, the only way to find out would be to ask … and this is definitely not recommended.

Beastly Words

Yeenaaldlooshii roughly translates as "skinwalker" and refers to a group of powerful sorcerers who were once feared by every Native American tribe that encountered them. The term refers to their ability to assume different "skins," or appearances. In addition to animals, they were also said to be able to assume the appearance of other people.

Therianthropy is a term that is related to lycanthropy. It refers to the "were-state," in which a human assumes the form of an animal or a human-animal hybrid. Basically, lycanthropy is a specific form of therianthropy.

In certain regions of the United States (mainly in the Southwest) and in parts of northern Mexico, the subject of skinwalkers is still discussed in hushed tones. The few remaining descendents of this ancient and powerful people are believed to live in these areas and are usually either feared or revered. However, those they live among usually prefer that these skinwalkers remain anonymous.

Skinwalkers are now believed to be a part of an ancient tribal group called the *Anasazi*, which means "ancient enemy." This tribal group is believed to have been hunted down by other tribes and nearly wiped out. They were feared and hated for their powers and for the violently bloody rituals they were known to perform. These skinwalkers are believed to be all that remain of them.

Beastly Words

Anasazi has a number of possible translations, depending on an individual tribal group's usage of it. It is most commonly translated to mean "the ancient enemy." However, it can also mean, "ancient ones," or "the enemy of the ancestors." Members of this tribe are now thought to be almost extinct. However, it is believed that a small number of them remain.

Today, not all skinwalkers are considered to be inherently evil. All of them are thought to be powerful, of course, and most would rather give them a wide berth. However, the current general opinion is that their individual personalities determine whether or not a skinwalker is evil. For example, in the Navajo language, the word for skinwalker has come to simply mean "witch." One might compare the Native American view of skinwalkers to the Haitian view of a Voodoo priest or priestess or to the Hispanic view of practitioners of Santeria.

Belief in a similar figure called the *Nahual* (or *Nagual*), which is a shaman practice believed to originate from the Toltec peoples, exists among the Pueblo peoples and in rural Mexico. The relationship between the Nahual and the people they live among is similar to that of skinwalkers.

Unlike the naturally malevolent perception of skinwalkers, however, the Nahual are not often considered especially evil or unnecessarily violent. They are, however, said to be extremely lazy by nature. Having one living nearby can turn out to be a real headache, according to the lore. As a result of their laziness, the Nahual are said to misuse their powers in order to steal food or money from the homes of their neighbors. Anyone who lives alone and does not work but never seems to have trouble paying bills or getting food is often suspected of being a Nahual.

The Ya Ya Ceremony (Hopi)

At one time, the Hopi people of the Pueblo tribes took part in a ritual called the Ya Ya Ceremony. This rite was believed to grant the participants the abilities of certain animals, which commonly included the wolf. The details are not well known, but the gist of the ritual is understood. Basically, the participants would first gather a collection of skins from the animal whose spirit they wished to invoke, thereby receiving that animal spirit's abilities. Once the skins were gathered, a shaman would lead the participants through a ceremony that involved rubbing the skins on the areas of the body where the individual wanted to receive power. For example, if the speed of a wolf was desired, then the skins would be rubbed on the feet and legs. If strength was desired, then they would be rubbed on the major muscle groups. If one wanted to have the eyesight of a wolf, then one would rub the skins against one's eyes. And this was where the Hopi ran into a problem.

These days, the Hopi no longer perform the Ya Ya Ceremony because the entire group was afflicted by an eye disease epidemic that remains officially unidentified. Some Hopi believed that the animal spirits had cursed them for abusing this sacred ceremony.

> **Bark vs. Bite**
>
> The Hopi believed that the eye disease was a form of divine retribution. However, there is another, far more likely explanation. Apparently, animal eyesight was one of the more popular abilities. This meant that many participants would have been rubbing animal skins up against their own exposed eyeballs, which (as one might imagine) would have easily led them to contract any number of infectious diseases in their ocular areas.

The Ya Ya Ceremony is currently forbidden, and it appears unlikely that its practice will ever be resumed (at least, not in its original form).

Wendigo

Before you begin this section, it is very important that you understand one important fact. The *Wendigo*, technically speaking, is *not* a werewolf. The Wendigo is more like a demon or spirit than a physical creature. Of course, it *could* be a werewolf, and there are some who believe it is. However, most people are of the opinion that it is some species of Sasquatch (better known as "Bigfoot"), which is something entirely different.

Beastly Words

Wendigo literally translates as "cannibal." Originally, the term referred to those who had been possessed by the Wendigo, meaning they had resorted to cannibalism in order to survive. Over time, inhabitants of the region have claimed that the Wendigo is, in fact, a very real creature that looks somewhat like a Sasquatch with antlers.

No one is quite sure where the stories of the Wendigo first began or how the word came to be considered the name of a creature. In truth, the word "Wendigo" roughly translates as "cannibal." The native tribes of Canada and northern Minnesota created this word to refer to a person who had resorted to cannibalism in order to survive. During the winter months, they were often short on food and cut off from travel. Therefore, cannibalism became a concern, and this likely led to the creation of the Wendigo myth. When a person turned cannibal to survive, it was said that they had been possessed by the Wendigo. In such cases, these people were no longer seen as humans, and it was believed that they had the potential to undergo a physical transformation.

Over time, certain members of the tribe took on the task of being professional Wendigo slayers. The last known case of this took place in October of 1907. A Wendigo slayer of the Cree tribe by the name of Jack Fiddler had a very successful career, proudly claiming to have slain no less than 14 Wendigo. His last Wendigo slaying was of an elderly Cree woman, whom Fiddler vehemently claimed had been possessed by the Wendigo. He insisted that she had been on the verge of undergoing the physical transformation, after which there would have been no stopping her. She would have turned and, according to Fiddler, slaughtered the entire village had he not intervened. Unfortunately for him, the courts did not see the situation in the same light. Jack Fiddler and his son, Joseph Fiddler, stood trial for the woman's murder. Interestingly enough, neither man ever denied having killed her. In fact, they both pleaded guilty but claimed the killing was necessary in order to protect the rest of the village. Both men were imprisoned for her murder. Jack Fiddler was 87 years old at the time.

Over the last few centuries, witnesses have been seeing some sort of very large creature in the area, which many people claim to be the Wendigo. Descriptions vary, but it is commonly said to be about 15 feet tall, often covered in fur, with what appear to be rather large moose antlers protruded from its head. Some local lore claims that to lay eyes on a Wendigo is a bad omen and that afterward a death always occurs in the region it was sighted. Other lore claims that the Wendigo is the protector of the forests, and its wrath is reserved for those who harm the forest or do not pay nature the proper respect.

The Least You Need to Know

- The wolf stands as a universal totem spirit and is in the lore of nearly all Native American tribes.

- The tribes of the Pacific Northwest are known to still teach spirit lycanthropy, though almost nothing is known about the details.

- Skinwalkers are primarily therianthropes, not lycanthropes.

- Performance of the Ya Ya Ceremony of the Hopi is forbidden. Rubbing animal skins against your eyeballs is not a very good method for lycanthropy, but it's a very good way to contract a nasty eye disease.

- The Wendigo is not a werewolf. In fact, if it is a creature at all ... no one knows what it is.

Chapter 3

Werewolves in the Old Country

In This Chapter

- The ancient Greek myth of King Lycoan
- The hairy ritual of the Anthus clan
- The wolf-warriors of the Norse berserkers
- Sigmund's wild experience with lycanthropy
- The reason Romanians are so nice to beggars
- An Arthurian legend of lycanthropy
- Armenian lore regarding a lycanthropy curse that afflicts negligent mothers and wives who commit cardinal sins

Whereas Native Americans viewed lycanthropy as a form of spiritual or magical power, most European cultures primarily viewed it as a curse. In European werewolf lore, tales of lycanthropy are often associated with murder, tragedy, infidelity, witchcraft, curses, and the demonic. Lycanthropy was rarely portrayed as a power one should desire or pursue (except by the Norse), but as something to be avoided.

The Curse of Lycoan (Greek)

King Lycoan, according to most versions of his myth, was once a ruler of the Greek Arcadians. Lycoan is thought by many to be the first werewolf, and some werewolf enthusiasts claim that his myth tells of the origins of lycanthropy. The truth of such claims is, of course, debatable. However, his myth is definitely of significance to the body of werewolf lore. It is an example of the tragedies that befell a king who was so evil that, because of his savage behavior, the gods stripped him of his humanity.

The Curse

The name Lycoan (also spelled Lykoan, Laocan, or Lycan) is often mistakenly thought to be the origin of the term "lycanthropy." His name does, however, survive in the classification of the grey eastern timberwolf species, called *canis lupius Lycoan.*

According to Greek myth, there was a period long ago, during the times of the earliest race of men, when humanity was for the most part ignored by the gods. During this forgotten period, humans were left to their own devices without the slightest aid from divine intervention. Some humans still chose to make sacrifices and appealed to the gods for help. Other humans, primarily those with more evil dispositions, took advantage of the opportunity to commit terrible blasphemies and crimes against nature and the gods. This led to a period of untold horrors and cruelty, when most people found themselves ruled by the evilest of despots. The worst among them was a man named King Lycoan, who maintained a bloody reign over his subjects. He was bloodthirsty, twisted, psychotic, immoral, and thought nothing of taking human lives. What was worse, however, was that Lycoan considered himself above the gods.

Eventually, the terrible blasphemies of certain humans caught the attention of Zeus, lord of the Olympians and God of Thunder. He came down from Olympus and assumed the form of a man. It didn't take long for him to hear of Lycoan's terrible deeds, which led him to visit Lycoan's kingdom in Arcadia. When he arrived, the Thunder God revealed his true form to the Arcadians, who all began to bow and worship him. The arrogant king, however, doubted the power of Zeus and plotted against him. Lycoan feigned homage, inviting Zeus to stay in the palace and attend a feast in his honor. Lycoan's true plan, however, was to slit Zeus's throat that night as he slept.

After a recent victory, Lycoan had taken a hostage from the Molossians. He had the prisoner brought to him, slit the poor man's throat, and cooked his flesh. When Zeus sat down at the banquet table, Lycoan presented him with a plate of cooked human flesh. Zeus, the all-knowing god, immediately knew what had been placed before him. He was disgusted by what Lycoan has done. Enraged by this blasphemy, he brought Lycoan's entire home crashing down. Everyone within its walls was killed—all but Lycoan. Zeus had an even worse fate in store for Lycoan.

The Savage Truth

According to one guide manuscript that was written in the second century C.E. by Pausanias, a Greek travel writer, Lycoan brought a baby as a sacrifice to the altar of Zeus. As a result, Zeus cursed him for his savagery by turning him into a wolf.

The king fled from the presence of Zeus. As he ran, however, grey hair began to sprout all over his body. Zeus transformed him into a giant wolf (though some later versions claim he became half-man and half-wolf). For his violent and savage behavior, Zeus cursed Lycoan to live as a beast for the rest of his days.

The Curse

Most versions of the Lycoan myth state that Zeus transformed the cruel king Lycoan into a large wolf. However, many artistic depictions of the myth portray King Lycoan during the middle of his transformation. As a result, such depictions show Lycoan as a man with a wolf's head or in some other half-man, half-wolf state. It is not impossible that such depictions have influenced the common portrayal of the man-wolf hybrid that we now consider when we think of a werewolf.

Lycoan's Legacy of Lycanthropy

According to the writings of a Greek physician and part-time travel writer by the name of Pausanias, the Arcadian people, the descendents of Lycoan, were required to hold ritual sacrifices to Zeus for many years. However, these sacrifices were in no way designed to appease the anger of the Thunder God. Apparently, they were only designed to keep Zeus's wrath somewhat at bay. This ritual sacrifice was called *Lykaian* (also spelled *Lycaean*) *Zeus*, roughly meaning "The Lycoan to Zeus."

First the Lykaians, presumably descendents of King Lycoan, were presented before an altar on Mount Lycoan. Once certain rituals and sacrifices were completed, Zeus would show that he had accepted the offering by inflicting the curse of Lycoan upon one of the present Lykaians. Unlike their terrible ancestor's curse, however, there appears to have been a method for reversing the transformation. If the cursed individual, while a wolf, abstained from eating human flesh for no less than nine years to the day of the initial transformation, he or she would turn back into a human being.

The Anthus Family

Pliny the Elder, also known as Gaius Plinius Secundus, was a writer and Roman officer who lived from around 23 C.E. to 79 C.E. In his manuscript *Historia Naturalis*, Pliny wrote of the Anthus family, quoted from an encounter that had originally been documented by a man named Euanthes. The Anthus clan lived in Arcadia (the same home as the Lykaians), and they were the descendents of a man named Antaeus. According to one myth, Antaeus was eaten by his father's horses, which had gone mad from hunger. However, it is uncertain if this myth had anything to do with the Anthus family's cyclical lycanthropic rites.

The Curse _____

The story of the Anthus family is strikingly similar to that of the Lykaians. In truth, this may be an account of a similar Arcadian lycanthropy ritual. Some believe it is possible that Pliny, who was a Roman and thus spoke Latin, somehow confused or attempted to Latinize the name Lykaian and, as a result, landed on the name Anthus. However, it is also important to note that the two stories also bear striking differences. Therefore, it is highly unlikely that the Lykaian and Anthus clans were one and the same.

According to Pliny's tale, the male members of the Anthus family drew lots every nine years. Whoever was chosen by these lots was sent away to a nearby lake to perform a ritual that would transform him into a wolf. In this ritual, the chosen individual would first hang his clothes on the branches of an ash tree. He would then swim to the other side of the lake. By the time he reached the other side, he would be completely transformed into a wolf.

The Savage Truth

It is interesting to note that *Canis Anthus* is the proper title for a species of canine, the jackal.

He was then bound to wander in this wolf-state for the next nine years. If during nine years he did not attack a single human being, he was free to swim back across the lake. When he reached the other side, he would once again be fully transformed into a man.

The Ulfheðnar (Norse)

Among the Norse tribes, a group of warriors called the *Berserkersgang* (also called *berserkers*), or "those who act as bears," were feared for their savagery and aggression. As a result, they were coveted and hired by many of the tribal chieftains. Originally, another similar group called the *ulfheðnar* (pronounced ulf-*heth*-nar), or "Wolf wearers," were also sought out by the chieftains. Over time, the ulfheðnar merged with the berserkers and were called by the same name, despite their differences.

Unlike the berserkers, who are thought to have originated solely as a warrior group, the ulfheðnar are thought to have originally been part of some ancient religious rites. Wolves, for example, are sacred to Odin, Norse god of poetry, mead, and battle. Whereas berserkers were considered men who fought and behaved *like* bears, the ulfheðnar were considered to be men who *became* wolves. The ulfheðnar dyed their skin black and covered themselves with wolf skins. They then performed chants and dance rites that worked them into a frenzied mental state. They went completely mad and abandoned their human natures. This allowed them to fight without fear. The Norse believed that such rites also made the ulfheðnar nearly unstoppable in battle.

As a Norse conquest party approached a foreign shore, the ulfheðnar were posted at the front prows of the ships, howling and snarling. When they hit the shore, they rushed straight at the defenders, wearing no armor, carrying no shields, and wielding only basic weaponry. Their psychotic trance was so strong that they seemed to ignore even the most serious of injuries. To those they fought, death seemed the only way to stop them.

According to Norse legends of the ulfheðnar, arrows had no effect on them, swords could not wound them, and they were immune to fire. The only way to kill the ulfheðnar, claimed the Norse, was to crush their skulls in with a club. This was a scary idea indeed for those who had to battle the ulfheðnar. Crushing in an ulfheðnar's skull meant you had to engage him at close range, which meant you had to be brave enough to stand your ground and let him get near you. On numerous occasions, the initial, first-wave charges of berserkers and the ulfheðnar were so demoralizing to defending forces that they turned tail and ran, giving up ground to the main invading force that followed without so much as a fight.

Sigmund's Wild Side (Norse Legend)

In the Germanic epic the *Volsung Saga*, the main hero, Sigmund, has an encounter with lycanthropy.

Sigmund had recently come across a young and eager warrior named Sinfjötli. Though he was eager to join him, Sigmund doubted the young man's prowess and felt that he might be too inexperienced. In order to test Sinfjötli, the two went into the woods and began to pick fights with any warriors they came across, soon taking a fortune in plundered gold and other treasures. Eventually their excursion led them to a cottage where two ulfheðnar princes were sleeping. Their wolf-skin garments hung from their bedposts. Sigmund and Sinfjötli stole the magical garments and put them on. They were immediately transformed into wolves and could not figure out how to change back.

Despite this, Sigmund decided to make sport of the situation. He tells Sinfjötli that they will separate and seek to kill seven men each. When one of them came upon a group, he was to howl so that the other could join him. Sigmund was the first to come upon a group of men, and he howled out so Sinfjötli could join in the bloodshed. However, the overzealous young warrior pounced from the trees and killed the entire group before Sigmund had a chance to share in the fun.

The two separated once more. This time, it was Sinfjötli who came upon a group of 11 men. However, he did not keep to the rules of the game and failed to howl so that Sigmund might join him. He killed all 11 men on his own, then rejoined Sigmund and told him what he'd done. Sigmund was angry and asked Sinfjötli why he had not howled out. Sinfjötli arrogantly claimed that 11 men posed no challenge to him and that he didn't need Sigmund's help for such a trivial matter. Enraged, Sigmund pounced upon Sinfjötli and tore out his throat.

For the entire day, unfortunately, Sigmund could not figure out how to remove the magical garments, not from himself or the dead Sinfjötli. He dragged Sinfjötli back to the mead-hall and sat down next to him. Both men were still in wolf form. The story ends without really explaining how he returned to human form but with a somewhat comical quote from Sigmund—"Damn these wolf-forms!"

Bark vs. Bite

This particular tale of Sigmund's encounter with what appear to be princes of the ulfheðnar can tell us something about how these men were viewed. Considering the magical nature attributed to the stolen garments, this story likely illustrates that the Norse held early beliefs in the divine and/or magical powers of the ulfheðnar.

Wolf Beggars (Romanian)

In rural parts of Romania, it is customary to leave out food for wolves. It is also considered smart to give food to beggars whenever one can. This custom stems from folklore, which states that beggars are often werewolves, and for obvious reasons of self-preservation it is in one's best interest to be well thought of by both wolves and werewolves.

The reasoning behind this piece of werewolf lore is that, since a wolf is believed not to eat on a full stomach, a werewolf will probably be the same. Therefore, if one keeps full the bellies of the wolves and the beggar-werewolves, then they will not attack people or livestock. The practice seems to be effective since no one in rural Romania has been attacked by werewolves for centuries.

The Wolf-King (Arthurian)

In the tales of King Arthur, there is a little-known story about one king's experience with lycanthropy. The story is told to King Arthur by King Gorlagon, whom Arthur has sought out for wisdom. Arthur had been challenged by Queen Guinevere to discover the truth regarding the hearts, desires, and motivations of women. The king set out immediately on a quest to uncover this, vowing not to eat until he had succeeded.

The Savage Truth

Despite the fact that Arthur vows not to eat until he has found the solution to Guinevere's challenge, he lacked the resolve to follow through. On at least two occasions, Arthur is convinced to rest and eat by his hosts and attendants. Some theorize that this is why Arthur does not receive an answer from the first two men he consults.

King Gorlagon's Tale

According to Gorlagon's tale, a sapling had once sprouted on the day of a certain king's birth. By some unknown means, it came to be known that if this sapling were ever cut, and one were to be struck upon the head with it while the words "Shape of a wolf, mind of a wolf" were recited, then the person struck would transform into a wolf, both in body and mind. For unknown reasons, perhaps just intuition, the king felt that the survival of the sapling was linked directly with his own. As a result, he had a tall stone wall constructed around the garden and put its security in the charge of his closest companion, a man he had trusted his entire life. The king would visit the sapling every evening upon returning from his daily hunt, inspecting it in order to ensure that it remained alive and unharmed.

The king's wife, unfortunately, was a beautiful but rather hateful woman. She was in love with an attractive, youthful gentleman (not her husband). She wished more than anything to see her current husband dead so that she could legally marry the younger man for whom she lusted. After a time, she became suspicious of her husband's evening visits to the enclosed garden. She constantly inquired what the purpose of such visits could be. He always replied that it was none of her concern. As time passed, she began accusing him of having extramarital affairs in the garden. He simply denied her accusations and once again told her that the garden was none of her concern. Finally, the king's wife insisted that she would not eat until he had told her the truth about his visits to the garden. At first, the king stuck to his guns. After three days, however, becoming increasingly worried about his wife's health (she often feigned illness and fainting spells during her three-day fast), the king gave in. He told her about the enchanted sapling and why it had to be protected. The king's conniving wife now saw the perfect opportunity to be rid of him.

A Wife's Betrayal

The next day, when the king left on his hunt, his wife snuck into the garden, cut up the sapling, and concealed it within her sleeve. That afternoon, when her husband returned, she was waiting at the door for him. She held out her arms for him to embrace her, speaking loving and seductive words so that he would come closer. When he reached her, she flung her arms around his neck, as if hugging him. She then removed the cut sapling from her sleeve and struck him on the head. Unfortunately, she made a bit of a mistake. Instead of saying, as she'd intended, "Shape of a wolf, mind of a wolf," she accidentally said, "Shape of a wolf, mind of a man."

Immediately, the king transformed into a wolf and went running out of the castle. His wife released their pack of hunting hounds, which chased the transformed king into the woods. He narrowly managed to escape them. The king, who had the shape of a wolf but the same human mind, wandered the woods for two years. Eventually, he took a she-wolf as a mate, and she bore him two cubs. In these two years, the king never forgot what his deceitful wife had done to him. He soon decided that he would have his revenge.

The Wolf-King's Revenge

The king's former wife had now married the handsome youth she desired. In an interesting twist, she and her new husband had birthed two sons. That night, the wolf-king snuck into the village with the she-wolf and his cubs. There was an area around the castle gates where the queen would often leave her little boys unattended while she and her new husband had some "alone time." Finding the young ones unguarded, the wolf-king and his new family fell upon them with their fangs and claws. The wolves tore the two toddlers to shreds. The scene was discovered too late. The deed was already done. However, the townspeople screamed at the wolves, threw stones, and gave chase. The wolves ran into the woods and disappeared from sight.

The queen was overcome with grief at the loss of her children. Knowing that the wolf responsible was likely her vengeful ex-husband, she issued a general order to all of her serfs and knights that they were to be on the lookout for wolves. Any wolf was to be captured or killed on sight.

Though he had killed her sons, this act was not enough to satisfy the wolf-king's need for vengeance. He soon returned to the castle gates with his wolf companions. This time he found two noblemen, whom he recognized as his ex-wife's brothers, conversing there. The wolves attacked the pair, tearing out their stomachs. The men had soon been mauled to death. Once again, the ruckus caught the attention of the townspeople and the castle servants, but they all arrived too late to save the two men. They ordered the gates to be shut, and the wolf-king's two cubs were too slow to escape. The queen had the cubs hanged from a tree branch, just in view of the gate.

The wolf-king went mad with grief. First, she had betrayed him. Now she had killed his cubs. His fury became insatiable. Every night, he would prey upon the pheasants and livestock of the area. He was so successful that soon everyone feared he would bring a famine upon them. Soon, the wolf-king began to find it more and more difficult to escape the ambushes and hounds of the queen's vassals. He decided to travel to a neighboring country for a time.

Help from a Wise King

The neighboring country was ruled by a kind and wise king. That night, as the wolf arrived, he overheard a conversation that this king planned to hunt and catch the wolf-king immediately. The wolf-king was greatly troubled, as he did not wish to bring harm to so honorable and kind a man as this king was said to be. Still having the sound mind of a man, he soon came up with a plan.

The next day, the wolf-king hid as the king's hunting party passed by. Once the king was in view, he calmly walked up to him and began to circle his legs and lick him gently, as would a tamed, domesticated dog. The king was so impressed that he told his hunters and bodyguards to hold their weapons. When a large stag came into view, the king commanded the wolf-king to fetch it. The wolf-king killed the stag and returned it to the king's feet. The king, being a wise and honorable man, knew that this was no ordinary wolf and decided to bring the wolf-king to stay with him in his castle. When the king had to go away on a long journey, he left the wolf-king behind to guard his queen. The queen refused to have the wolf near her unless it was chained. Therefore, the king had a gold chain constructed and fastened to the bed-ladder. Against the king's order that the wolf only be chained at night, the queen left the wolf chained up at all times.

More Woman Trouble

Unfortunately, it would appear that both kings had the same issues with women. The king's wife was having an affair with one of the king's serfs. She brought him into their bedchamber, barely paying any attention to the wolf-king. Seeing what was happening and realizing how this woman was so much like his hated ex-wife, the wolf-king went mad, broke free, and mauled the serf, almost killing him. However, out of loyalty to the king, he did not harm the queen. Soon the ruckus brought the castle's servants to the room. The queen, not wanting to be exposed as an adulteress, claimed that the wolf had eaten her infant son and that, while trying to save the boy, the serf had been terribly hurt by the wolf. The servants took the serf to a guest room. While they were gone, the queen locked her young son away so that no one would ever know that she had lied about the infant's death.

When the king returned, the wife told him her concocted story. Being a wise man, the king refused to believe it immediately and pondered the matter for days. The whole time, the wolf-king remained calmly by his side. Soon, the king realized the wolf was nudging him a certain way, and he decided to follow. The wolf-king led him to the catacombs of the castle, where the queen had their son locked up. The king found the baby alive and well. He now knew that the queen was lying about their son's death and, therefore, likely was lying about the wolf's actions as well. The queen refused to speak, but after a bit of "coaxing," the serf was more than happy to admit the truth of their affair and of the wolf's actions.

A King Restored

One day, just by chance, the king brought the wolf with him to the neighboring country where the wolf-king had once ruled. The people now lived a wretched existence under the tyrannical rule of the foolish young man who had been made king when he'd married the wolf-king's deceitful ex-wife. There the honorable king learned the truth of what had happened to the wolf and discovered the method of his transformation. He then located the sapling and returned the wolf-king to normal by striking him on the head with it and saying, "Shape of a man, mind of a man." The wolf-king returned to his human form.

The Savage Truth

You may be wondering what Arthur's final revelation was regarding the nature of women. In true chauvinistic fashion, Arthur concluded from this story that women are evil by nature. Though the story does not confirm it, one can only imagine that King Arthur's wife, Queen Guinevere, must have been none too happy with the rather misogynistic answer he brought back from this quest.

The newly restored king divorced his wife, had her lover executed on the grounds that he was a pagan, and bestowed many gifts upon his new friend, the king of the neighboring country, before returning him to his home.

The Cursed Mothers of Armenia

There is an Armenian belief that any woman who commits a cardinal sin risks being the target of a lycanthropic curse. According to most versions of this belief, this especially applies to women who commit cardinal sins such as adultery or murder. A dark spirit will visit the woman in the night and demand that she put on a garment of wolf skin. For unspecified reasons, the woman is unable to refuse the spirit's commands. Once she has put on the garment, the curse turns the woman into a wolf for exactly seven years.

The Curse

A cardinal sin does not specifically refer to the generic sins that violate the Ten Commandments of the Old Testament. The term *cardinal sin* actually refers to one of the so-called "Seven Deadly Sins" in Roman Catholicism. These are considered the most ruinous of all sins, and include lust, gluttony, greed, sloth, envy, wrath, and pride. Also, believe it or not, there was a historical cardinal whose name was actually Sin. So try not to get the two confused.

Upon this transformation, the woman is overcome by the desires of the wolf. These animal urges take over, and her human nature is consumed by them. Desire overtakes reason, and she will first turn on her own children if she is a mother. After eating her own children, night after night she will turn on the children of her relatives. Once they have been eaten, she will make all of the other children in the village her nightly prey. Locking doors is useless, since it is said that any lock or door will magically open at her arrival.

Bark vs. Bite

The Armenian tale of the wolf's curse was likely not based on any true cases of lycanthropy. In truth, it was probably designed to ensure that women remained chaste and faithful in their marriages. The thought that one might involuntarily murder and eat one's own children, or children in general, would be horrifying to any mother. Metaphorically, it illustrates the dangers of allowing one's desires to overcome one's humanity.

On the morning of her seventh year in this state, the woman will return to her human form and is allowed to take off the wolf skin.

The Least You Need to Know

- ◆ King Lycoan of Arcadia is considered by many to have been the first werewolf.

- ◆ The descendents of Lycoan, the Lycaeans, are said to have participated in a sacrificial lycanthropy ritual called *Lykaian Zeus.*

- ◆ The Anthus clan is said to have performed its own unique lycanthropic rites.

- ◆ In their time, the ulfheðnar were considered lycanthropes.

- ◆ The Germanic hero Sigmund of the *Volsung Saga* once had an experience with lycanthropy.

- ◆ The Arthurian legend of the wolf-king is a metaphor that warns of the destructive potential of women.

- ◆ In Armenia, women who commit cardinal sins are believed to risk receiving a seven-year-long lycanthropic curse.

Chapter 4

Therianthropes of the East

In This Chapter

- The mystery of the lost people of Lou Lan
- The "fake beasts"—the therianthropes of the Filipino Aswang
- An examination of the werewolf of Banirpur
- The Layak shapeshifters of Indonesia
- The sudden extinction of the O-kami, the apocalyptic Wolf Lords of Japan

You may notice that this chapter is not entitled "Werewolves of the East." This is because true lycanthropes, as they are generally understood, are not a common part of the mythical lore of the world's Eastern regions. Wolves are not indigenous to many parts of Asia, which may at least partially explain the absence of werewolf lore in this part of the world. However, there are at least a handful of ancient legends, recent news stories, and mythical creatures from the East that bear some similarities to parts of known werewolf lore and are worth mentioning.

The Lost Wolves of Lou Lan

The fate of the people of Lou Lan is a mystery that has baffled scientists for a great many years. The ruins of this once vast and prosperous ancient city offer little to no explanation as to why the inhabitants eventually abandoned it. The city of Lou Lan is thought to have been founded sometime around 175 B.C.E., and the civilization is known to have prospered for close to eight centuries.

No one knows for certain what happened, but most evidence seems to support the fact that, sometime around 625 C.E., the entire city of Lou Lan was afflicted by some terrible, yet still unidentified, cataclysmic natural event. After well over 800 years of prosperity, the people of Lou Lan seem to have vanished overnight. The once-fertile landscape became an unforgiving desert wasteland that now bears the frightening title "Sea of Death."

Some of the artifacts uncovered in the ruins of Lou Lan have given rise to some interesting lore regarding what became of the city's inhabitants. For example, one artifact is a frightening wooden mask. It is red with a large snoutlike nose and long fanglike teeth. Such finds have led to fantastic urban legends about Lou Lan.

There are some regional legends, for example, that claim the people of Lou Lan were turned into wolves. Some legends claim the people of Lou Lan were cursed for some affront to the gods. Other stories insist that the Lou Lan inhabitants had always been wolves, but had assumed human form in order to reign over a kingdom. Eventually, these stories assert, the wolves grew tired of humans and returned to their wolf forms, taking their blessings of fertility for the land with them.

Bark vs. Bite

Did the people of Lou Lan really turn into wolves? In all likelihood, the same fate befell Lou Lan that did many other great cities of the ancient world. Too much agriculture coupled with an overconsumption of resources likely destroyed the once-fertile environment surrounding the city. A structurally strong city means very little in a world where people will die if they cannot grow food nearby. With an environment increasingly unable to continue sustaining agriculture and livestock, most of the people likely fled the city in search of greener pastures, so to speak.

The Aswang (Philippines)

As far as mythical creatures are concerned, the Filipino creature known as the *Aswang* is probably one of the most difficult for which to find a concrete description. This is probably because, in the Philippine language of Tagalog, the term Aswang has come to be used in reference to just about any evil supernatural being. For the most part, pop culture describes the Aswang as a winged, vampirelike creature. However, the original lore of the Aswang tells of one category of these creatures, referred to as "fake beasts" or "false beasts."

> **Beastly Words**
>
> **Aswang** is a term in Tagalog, the common language of the Philippines, that refers to an evil supernatural being that feeds upon human flesh. One type of Aswang, the "fake beast," is known to be an able shapeshifter.

These types of Aswang are actually pure shapeshifters and therianthropes, since they can transform into just about any shape—human, dog, cat, or any other animal. Some lore claims that an Aswang will transform into whatever living being (human included) it first encounters when it sets out for the night. Aswang live mainly on a diet of human flesh. However, they are said to have a great preference for the flesh of pregnant women and infants.

The Werewolf of Banbirpur

On the hot evening of August 16, 1996, a number of children from the village of Banbirpur, India, were going to the bathroom in an earthen toilet just outside the village proper when they claim that an unusually large wolf lunged at them from the nearby brush. The youngest child, a four-year-old boy named Anand, was dragged off screaming into the woods, trapped in the fangs of the beast. The other children returned to their village and frantically reported what had happened to their parents. The local police were notified, and a search party was immediately sent to investigate. After three days of searching, they found nothing but little Anand's severed head. The rest of his body was never discovered and is thought to have been eaten by the wolf ... if it was, in fact, a wolf.

32-40-50

Following this attack, wolf hunts were organized by both villagers and police. However, less than a dozen wolves were ever killed in these hunts (none of which were proven to be man-eaters). To make matters worse, the attacks seemed to continue as time passed. None of the wolves killed seemed to be responsible. Some residents of the area claim that this is because the attacks are not the work of a wolf ... but of a werewolf.

According to the eyewitness testimony of the 10-year-old sister of Anand, who saw the wolf that dragged away her little brother, the creature that attacked them pounced forward on all fours (which would be indicative of a wolf). Once the creature grabbed the little boy, however, she claimed that it rose back onto its hind legs and walked in a bipedal fashion (which would not suggest a wolf but a werewolf). She then claimed that the creature threw the boy over its shoulder, took the form of a man, and ran off into the woods. In some of her testimony, however, she claimed that, in its human form, the creature wore a jacket, goggles, and a helmet (which would not suggest a werewolf but a human). Some werewolf enthusiasts claim that what the girl saw was some sort of top secret "werewolf super-soldier." However, this explanation sounds highly unlikely.

Bark vs. Bite

There are many who believe that reconnaissance soldiers from neighboring Pakistan (a longtime enemy of India) are to blame for the "Banbirpur werewolf killings" that took place over the summer of 1996. This would certainly seem to fit the eyewitness accounts that the human form of the creature wore goggles (perhaps for night vision) and a helmet. During that summer, many men and police patrolled the area with clubs, sticks, and rifles—not looking for wolves (or even werewolves) but for invading troops from Pakistan.

The Layak (Indonesia)

The mythical *Layak* of Indonesia is a type of therianthrope. As with the Filipino Aswang, definitions of this being vary. Some lore claims that it is an evil spirit that has the ability to shapeshift into the form of a human or animal. The Layak will then use its form to make mischief, wreaking havoc and causing illnesses in the village of its choosing.

Beastly Words

The **Layak** (also spelled *Leyak*) is a mythical shapeshifting being in Indonesian lore. Some lore claims that a Layak is an evil spirit, while others claim that a Layak is actually a human witch with dark powers. So the next time you meet a Layak, you should ask it about this.

In other lore, the Layak is said to be a human skilled in the dark arts of poisons and black magic. According to this version of the Layak's lore, these creatures require the entrails of humans and/or the blood of unborn children for both the executions of their spells and as a source of food.

Some stories claim that, in order to shapeshift, a witch-type of Layak is required to leave its human body and possess the body of the form it wishes to assume. If one is able to find the human body of a Layak while it is not occupying it, then one has a chance to kill it. First, a sharp object must be stabbed upward through its head. Once this has been done, the Layak will be trapped in its alternate body. If it stays out of its human body for a period of time, it is said that the Layak will eventually die.

The O-kami (Japan)

The Japanese word for wolf, *O-kami*, has a double translation. In general, the word can be used to mean "wolf." Literally, however, the term means something like "great deity." This term is not surprising when one considers that the wolf was long revered as a god, *O-Guchi no Magami*, the "Great-mouthed Pure-Kami," in the *Shinto* nature religion of Japan.

Beastly Words

The word **O-kami** is a combination of the Japanese *O-*, which means "great" or "superior," and *Kami*, which roughly translates as something like "god," "demigod," or "deity," though there is no true English equivalent for this word. O-kami is generally used to mean "wolf." Literally translated, however, it actually means "great deity."

Shinto is the indigenous nature religion of Japan. For a time, it was the officially recognized state religion.

In later Shinto belief, wolves were said to be the divine messengers of the popular Sun Goddess, Amaterasu. It was even believed that a white wolf was the goddess Amaterasu in physical form. For centuries, wolves were viewed as divine beings and as the friends of humans for a number of reasons. As a result, they were often protected from humans. During some periods of Japanese history, harming or killing a wolf was considered a serious crime, one that could result in strict punishments for perpetrators. (Sometimes this included the death penalty.)

In addition to their religious status, wolves were beneficial to the agricultural environment of Japan. The worst enemies to the livelihoods of Japanese farmers were deer and wild boars. The wolf was the natural predator of both, and farmers would often pray and make sacrifices to the O-kami in order to ask for assistance in the protection of their crops. In areas where farming was a common occupation, it was not uncommon to find shrines and temples dedicated to the O-kami. Unfortunately, however, the noble status of the Japanese wolves eventually came to an end.

By the eighteenth century, Japan had entered a period now referred to as the Meiji Restoration. This was an era of sudden and extreme modernization for Japan. The reinstated Meiji imperial rulers feared that Japan was too far behind technologically and sought to catch up to the West as quickly as possible. This meant a sudden increase in urbanization, the spread of new technologies, and the creation of railroads. During this period, the O-kami ceased to be viewed as the noble messengers of the Kami or as themselves divine. They now came to be viewed as obstacles to progress, which led the government to portray these animals as vicious, man-eating devils that threatened human existence.

In 1868, bounties began to be offered for dead wolves, and many men started to make their living by hunting the animals down. Widespread, government-organized wolf hunts were held in order to "purify" the land of wolves, and the once-revered animals were now commonly referred to as *bakemono*, meaning "demons/monsters."

By the end of the nineteenth century, the former wolf lords of Japan were all but extinct. Today, the Japanese wolf is believed to have been wiped out. They have not been seen by anyone for nearly 150 years.

The Savage Truth

To this day, many scientists make camping trips to the mountainous regions of Japan in hopes of finding evidence of wolves. They often bring cameras and listening devices meant to capture the slightest evidence that even a handful of these animals survive. Unfortunately, no such evidence has yet been found.

There are some who still believe, however, that the O-kami wolves were divine beings. There is an obscure legend among the Japanese that the wolves were not wiped out, but just left the earth and returned to the paradise reserved for them by the gods. Some versions of this legend claim that, when the age of men is about to end, the O-kami will return to Japan. They will come to witness the destruction of the human race that once dared to hunt them and will lead those who remember them to a paradise where the earth will once again be reborn.

The Least You Need to Know

♦ The people of the ancient Chinese city of Lou Lan mysteriously disappeared, and some say they transformed into wolves.

♦ The Aswang is more a basic shapeshifter than a werewolf or therianthrope, though it is said to at least be able to assume wolf form.

♦ The Layak of Indonesia may be an evil spirit or human witch, according to lore.

♦ Japanese wolves were once worshipped in Japan and were later considered the divine messengers of the Shinto deities, called the Kami.

5

Relatives of the Werewolf

In This Chapter

◆ The various African legends regarding the nature of were-hyenas

◆ The bruxsa/cucubuth, the unique vampire-werewolf hybrid of Portugal

◆ The significance of were-cats in the consideration of lycanthropy

◆ Legends regarding the were-lions of Africa

◆ The many legends about the deadly were-tigers of India and Asia

While the presence of werewolves is widely common in folklore, it is not universal to all parts of the globe. In places where wolves are not a part of the indigenous wildlife, this is especially true—no wolf = no werewolf. However, this doesn't mean that cultures who do not have werewolves did not create their own unique breeds of similar were-creatures and shapeshifters. From were-hyenas to vampire-werewolves to were-cats, these creatures represent the many diverse and furry relatives of the werewolf.

The Power of the Were-Hyenas

Were-hyenas are most commonly found in Africa, which is not surprising. Hyenas are very common to the wildlife of the continent, so it would appear that they have taken the place of wolves as a canine therianthrope. These African were-hyenas are often referred to by the term *bouda* (sometimes spelled *buda*). This term has spread to many African languages and has come to mean "were-hyena" (though its original meaning was probably different).

Many aspects of the African were-hyena legends bear some striking similarities to parts of werewolf lore. For example, the two primary ways for a person to become a were-hyena are either by being bitten (which is the most common) or through the powers of magic. Also, hyenas run in packs the same as wolves. Unlike wolf packs (which are led by male *alpha* wolves), hyena packs are matriarchal, meaning that their alpha members are females. This has led some to assert that there are more female than male hyenas (though this remains unproven). As a result, many elements of these legends state that tribes who possess were-hyena powers can be identified by the fact that they have more females than males.

Beastly Words

In the animal world, an **alpha** animal is the animal in charge of a social group (such as a lion pride or wolf pack).

In Borno, a northeastern state of the Federal Republic of Nigeria, a country located on the western coast of the African continent, there is also a legend about were-hyenas. In the Borno dialects, were-hyenas are not referred to as bouda, but as *bultungin*, which literally means, "I turn into a hyena." According to local legends, there were once two tribes in the Borno region that were entirely comprised of were-hyenas.

In the African country of Sudan (located in a northwestern area of the continent), the were-hyena is viewed rather negatively as a monster that stalks the night and preys upon human flesh. This creature, in its Sudanese version at least, is also said to have a special taste for the flesh of lovers. It stalks the night and is happiest when it comes upon a loving couple and can tear them apart. These were-hyenas are said to be identifiable in human form because their bodies remain unusually hairy, they have a reddish-tint to their eyes (or red eyes), and their voices are commonly said to sound a bit off. (Some legends say they sound "nasally," like a person who speaks through the nose.)

In Ethiopia (which runs along the lower western border of Sudan), all blacksmiths are commonly said to be were-hyenas. In that country, the occupation of blacksmith is widely a hereditary one. The close relation-ship between blacksmiths and the elements of fire and Earth led people to believe that they possessed magical powers, namely to heal (because they are seen as able to work with fire yet not burn) and shapeshift (because of their apparent ability to change the shapes of things, such as turning a piece of iron into the shape of a tool). While Ethiopian blacksmiths are not necessarily treated badly because of this, they are regarded with a certain amount of suspicion and caution.

Many of the people who brought the knowledge of blacksmithing skills to the lands of Ethiopia were ethnically Jewish. Today, most of the blacksmiths in Ethiopia practice the Jewish religion. As a result, the term "bouda" has also come to be used by some Ethiopian Christians as a generic term for Ethiopian Jews. However, it would appear that, in these particular cases, the term is not always meant to imply that Ethiopian Jews are all "were-hyenas" but that they come from blacksmiths.

Which Came First, the Werewolf or the Vampire?

While in Portuguese a werewolf is referred to as a *lobis-homen*, they also have another werewolf-related creature—*bruxsa*. A bruxsa, sometimes also referred to by the term *cucubuth*, is a creature that has the combined powers of both a werewolf and a vampire.

Most versions of this legend state that a bruxsa is a werewolf who dies but is left under the light of the moon and is thereby resurrected. If the creature is allowed to return to life (or … un-death?), it will possess both werewolf and vampire powers and attributes. Some legends flip the process and claim that a bruxsa is a vampire that dies and, because it is resurrected by the moon, takes on the additional attributes of a werewolf. However, it is possible that a bruxsa can be created in either of these fashions. Nobody really knows, and the bruxsa aren't really available for comment.

The fact that these creatures are both werewolf and vampire is doubly scary because, according to many of the legends, this means a bruxsa will both drink your blood as well as eat your flesh. The bruxsa are popularly known in Portuguese folklore for having a taste for the warm flesh of children, and it is said they will even eat their own offspring because of this.

Were-Cats

Were-cats are sometimes referred to in pop culture as *bastets*. The word "were-cat" was only coined little over a century ago (though the credit for its creation frequently varies from one source to another). *Bastet*, also spelled *Bast*, was originally the name of a feline-headed goddess from the mythic pantheon of the ancient Egyptians.

Were-cats are similar to werewolves in that they are often said to be humans who possess the power to change into animal form. However, much unlike werewolves, were-cats transform into large (often predatory) cats or into a form that more resembles a human-cat hybrid. Interestingly enough, were-cats are almost entirely absent from the folklores of Europe.

Perhaps the were-cats became wary of the region, at some point, because of all the werewolves?

Were-Lions of Africa

African folklore is full of legends about were-lions. Since the lion is a very significant member of the continent's wildlife, this would stand to reason. Much like the negative European view of the werewolf, African were-lions are primarily seen as evil. The African were-lion is usually an evil sorcerer who assumes the shape of a lion to commit terrible deeds against humans (such as eating people). Were-lions also played a part in the recent history of at least one African region.

In Tanzania, a country on the western coast of Africa, during the early twentieth century, a mystical lion-rite cult violently rose to power. This cult would purchase mentally disabled children and hold them in complete social isolation until they reached adulthood. Needless to say, this caused the children to grow up with extremely savage and sociopathic tendencies. Once adults, these prisoners would be dressed from head to toe in the skins of lions in order to give them a frightening appearance. They were regarded with fear throughout the region and were referred to as "The Lion Men." The cult then sold these Lion Men to local tribal leaders, usually as war-slaves. They were also used at times as assassins because their savagery often allowed their attacks to be dismissed as committed by lions or some other wild beast.

The Curse

Some people attempt to draw parallels between the Lion Men of Tanzania and the wolf-skin wearing ulfheðnar warriors of the Norse. While members of both groups were formidable fighters and both wore animal skins, this is where the similarities between them end. The ulfheðnar were neither mentally disabled nor slaves, but were voluntary warriors who used the widespread fear of their wolf rites to gain fame and fortune for themselves on the battlefield. The Lion Men, sadly, were the involuntary victims of a cruel and greedy religious cult.

The western world first came to know of Tanzania's Lion Men in the early 1920s. At that time, Tanzania was a colony of the British. Colonial authorities began receiving reports that hundreds of people in the Tanzanian region of Singida had been killed in what appeared to be lion attacks. However, more detailed examinations of the corpses later proved this was not the case, and it was discovered that the bites and scratches from these attacks were more likely from humans.

The British colonial authorities, during the official investigation, learned of the Lion Men that were hired as mercenaries. They discovered that the cult had been using their Lion Men in order to extort the villages of the area (many of which had little with which to pay for their safety). If a village did not pay the cult, then the Lion Men would be unleashed upon them.

Were-Tigers of Asia and India

In regions of the Far East, tigers are perhaps the most feared animal in the eyes of the people. The Chinese once believed that all other races were actually tigers that had disguised themselves as humans. In Chinese myths, it is sometimes said that a person who is killed by a tiger will later haunt the living as an evil spirit. Some were-tiger myths from China even claim that were-tigers are created whenever a human being becomes possessed by the evil spirit of someone who was killed by a tiger. However, a vast majority of the Chinese were-tiger legends also claim that the condition is a familial trait and therefore one that must be inherited.

In Hindu legends, were-tigers are almost always portrayed as evil sorcerers. These dark wizards often use their powers to steal or kill livestock. If these were-tiger-sorcerers spend a little too much time in their tiger form, many of the Hindu legends claim that they will become overcome by twisted bloodlust. This will soon cause them to desire human flesh, and they will turn cannibal. If they feast upon enough human flesh, they will forget that they are humans and will permanently remain in tiger form. It was commonly believed that tigers that turned to man-eating had originally been human sorcerers.

The Least You Need to Know

- In Africa, the word "bouda" has come to mean "were-hyena."

- A bruxsa, or cucubuth, is a creature that is both werewolf and vampire, though opinions differ on which came first.

- Were-cats, popularly referred to by some enthusiasts as bastets, have some things in common with werewolves, but the two are not at all the same.

- The Lion Men of Tanzania were the unfortunate victims of a religious cult.

- In Asian lore, were-tigers are often believed to be evil sorcerers.

Part 2

A History of Werewolves

Werewolves have a long, turbulent history. In the eyes of the
medieval church and other religions, wolves became the epito-
mic symbol of evil. They were mercilessly hunted, and when they
could not be caught, innocent people sometimes paid the price as
"werewolf scapegoats," executed to appease the mob. In France,
werewolves were long considered a very real threat to human existence, agents of evil whose sole purpose was to bring harm.

Chapter 6

Werewolves on Trial

In This Chapter

◆ The crimes and execution of convicted werewolf Peter Stubbe, also known as the Werewolf of Bedburg

◆ The presidential decree that saved the "seventh sons" of Argentina

◆ The famous werewolf trials of Gilles Garnier and Antoine Leger

◆ The trial of the Gandillon family, also known as the "Werewolves of St. Cloud"

◆ The unusual Benandanti tale that was told to the courts by Theiss, an accused Russian werewolf

The idea of a person being placed on trial for being a werewolf may sound rather ludicrous. However, just a few centuries ago this was a real part of the human world. Between the eleventh and nineteenth centuries, a number of people were tried for, and found guilty of, lycanthropy. Most of them were executed, often in terribly gruesome ways. Many today believe that these werewolf trials of the past were nothing more than cases of murder or undiagnosed madness. Some believe that, in the minds of medieval people, branding a criminal a werewolf was simply a way of explaining how a human being could be capable of committing the most unspeakable of crimes such as rape, murder, infanticide, incest, and cannibalism. What follows is a basic collection of the most famous—or, rather, infamous—accounts of these werewolf trials.

Peter Stubbe: The Werewolf of Bedburg

Among the multitude of so-called "werewolf trials" that occurred between the fourteenth and nineteenth centuries, perhaps the most well known is the 1589 trial of a German farmer named Peter Stubbe. (His first name is sometimes seen spelled Peeter and his last name Stub, Stumpf, or Stump.) Much of what is currently known about this alleged incident of lycanthropy is based on a combination of hearsay and a lone secondary account published in a London pamphlet (likely based on information gleaned from the tattered remains of the official documents, most of which were lost when many German church registers were destroyed between 1618 and 1648 in the violence of the Thirty Years War). However, Stubbe is known to have spent the majority of his life as a farmer somewhere near the village of Bedburg, just outside Cologne, Germany.

The Savage Truth

The only surviving documentation of the Peter Stubbe incident is a pamphlet published in England on June 11, 1590. The story was transcribed by George Bores. The pamphlet proclaims that Bores "did both see and hear the same" as what is in his account. Considering that the date of publication predates the Thirty Years War (when the German records were destroyed), it's entirely possible that Bores's work is based on the lost church registers. However, this cannot be verified.

Little can be confirmed regarding just *how* Stubbe found himself in the position in which he was apprehended. According to the record of the incident, a werewolf (or an unusually large wolf) was sighted wearing a belt (though some sources call it a girdle) around its waist. How it was discovered or why it was in the area is not explained in any detail. The available account makes it seem as if the wolf was just strolling through the town and then it was caught (which doesn't make a whole lot of sense). Authorities gave chase, apparently knowing that this was actually a werewolf. Once they had the creature cornered, they removed the girdle, and it immediately transformed into the human form of Peter Stubbe. He was dragged before the church courts, where he soon confessed to a laundry list of extremely heinous crimes.

It is unclear whether Stubbe gave his confession as a result of torture, just confessed under the threat of torture, or first confessed and then was tortured. Regardless of how the confession came about, Stubbe eventually took the rap for the killing of 14 children, 2 pregnant women, and a good number of assorted livestock. In addition, he also confessed to having partially eaten the flesh of the children and livestock, as well as the fetuses of the pregnant women he'd slain. The court also got him to confess to having sex with his own teenage daughter (which added the charge of incest to the list), to having sexual intercourse with a *succubus*, and to committing adultery. (Stubbe kept a mistress, who was also the mother of his daughter.) Apparently, these crimes are alleged to have occurred over a span of about 25 years.

Beastly Words

A **succubus** (the plural form is *succubi,* sometimes spelled *succubae*) is a female demon commonly known for seducing men as they sleep. This likely originated from a demonic female figure from Judaic folklore, known as Lilith. In the Judaic tradition, men are not supposed to sleep alone in order to avoid encounters with Lilith.

The truth regarding whether or not Stubbe really committed any of these crimes can no longer be verified with the surviving documentation (though it is probably safe to say that at least the one about him keeping a succubus as a sex slave can be dismissed). He may indeed have been a demented serial killer. Then again, there is a possibility that he was merely a scapegoat for unsolved crimes that were committed by more elusive criminals or animals.

Having confessed, Stubbe was convicted of murder, cannibalism, incest, rape, infanticide, adultery, killing livestock, keeping a demon *familiar,* and (of course) lycanthropy. His execution was scheduled for October 31, 1589, and it would be remembered as one of most brutal in history.

> **Beastly Words**
>
> The term **familiar** refers to an idea, widely from church propaganda, that witches (and, in this particular case, a werewolf) kept demonic spirits to assist them in their work. In order to avoid being discovered, church authorities claimed that these demon servants remained invisible in the presence of others, assumed the forms of household animals (the most popular being cats, especially black cats), or just possessed the bodies of animals/pets that were already in their masters' homes.

Stubbe was first stripped almost naked before being lashed to a large wooden wheel. A pair of large iron pincers was applied to a fire until red hot and then was used to rip the flesh from 10 places on his body. As if this were not bad enough, a heavy wooden axe (a few alternate accounts claim it was just the blunt side of an axe) was taken to each of Stubbe's limbs, one by one, until every major bone had been broken. He was then beheaded and his mangled corpse burned to ashes. Sadly, his daughter and mistress were tried and convicted of being accessories to Stubbe's long list of heinous crimes. Both of them were burned alive at the stake soon after his execution.

What about the belt that Stubbe was said to be wearing when he was apprehended? Well, in his confession, Stubbe claimed to have received the belt, which gave him magical powers in addition to lycanthropy, as part of a pact with the devil. According to the surviving account, all later attempts to locate the belt were unsuccessful. As for the official explanation for the missing belt, provided by the presiding German authorities? Well … they decided that the devil must have taken it back.

The Seventh Sons (Argentina)

In the countries of Argentina, Portugal, and Brazil, there was once a firmly held belief that if one's seventh child turned out to be male (especially if preceded by six female offspring), he would be cursed with lycanthropy and referred to as *El Lobizon* (spelled *lobis-homen* in Portuguese). In Argentina, this belief was so ingrained in the culture that these "seventh sons" were almost always abandoned (or, at best, given up for adoption or sold) by their parents soon after they were born.

Beastly Words

The term **Lobizon** is actually a Spanish transliteration of the Portuguese term **lobis-homen,** from which it originated. The word is a combination of the terms *lobos,* meaning "wolves," and *homen,* which is most commonly translated as "men/males" but can also be read as meaning "son." So the term could be considered to mean something like "sons of the wolves."

Just giving birth to a Lobizon often caused a family to be stigmatized by the village community (causing social expulsion and financial hardships). In such cases, these newborn babies would be immediately abandoned, "discarded" into a river (meaning murdered by drowning), thrown off of a cliff, or suffocated before the truth of the child's sex could be discovered by anyone outside the family. This grew into such a widespread practice that Argentinean orphanages were often overcrowded, and acts of infanticide were becoming frighteningly commonplace.

The Savage Truth

Seventh sons were not as uncommon as one might initially expect. At this time in Argentina, especially in rural or agricultural communities, it was often beneficial for couples to have as many children as they could. More children meant more hands to help with the large amount of work farming required. More work meant more income, and this often meant a better standard of living for the entire family.

In 1920, Dr. Juan Hipolito Yrigoyen, the president of Argentina, came up with a most ingenious plan to bring an end to the superstitious stigma of evil that had long been associated with his country's outcast seventh sons. He officially declared that he would now be the legal godfather of any seventh son born in Argentina. In addition, Yrigoyen also decreed that a gold medal would be awarded to parents at the baptisms of all seventh sons in Argentina.

Furthering his generosity, Yrigoyen also put into law that all seventh sons would receive full educational scholarships until they reached 21 years of age. As one might imagine, the occurrences of abandonments and infanticides soon decreased dramatically. As a result of President Yrigoyen's brilliant plan, the birth of a seventh son now came to be seen by parents as a blessing instead of a curse. Having a seventh son now provided unprecedented opportunities to many rural and lower-class families, giving them a chance to have well-educated children, which in turn enabled them to improve the conditions of their families' lives.

The Burning of Gilles Garnier

Something terrible was happening to the children of Dole, France, in the summer of 1573. The children of the area were vanishing one by one and with astonishing frequency, never to be seen alive again. Sadly, many of these missing little ones would later be found in the woods … dead. Their bodies were often mutilated beyond recognition, and large sections of their flesh appeared to have been torn from their limbs as if by some powerful animal. It didn't take long for the people of Dole to realize that their children were not just being murdered by this blood-thirsty creature. They were also being eaten by it. With every passing week, the terrible situation only grew more and more desperate.

As the seasons changed, the situation did not. In early November, a boy inexplicably disappeared from the area. Shortly thereafter, the bodies of three other missing children were discovered. In December of that same year, the French authorities in Dole officially declared that these murders were the work of a werewolf. A hunting warrant was immediately issued for the child-killing beast, and a large number of hunting parties were formed to track it down.

This is where things get a little difficult to follow when it comes to the information available. According to the official records of the incident, the werewolf was soon caught in the act of attacking another child. However, the locals in the hunting party testified that they recognized this werewolf as Gilles Garnier (because it would seem that, even though in werewolf form, he retained enough of his human features to be recognizable). Garnier was well known by the villagers as a local hermit.

According to the official account, Garnier immediately returned to his human form upon being apprehended. The local hermit did not deny any of the accusations brought against him. In fact, it would appear that he openly admitted to the killings. (Of course, his confession could still have been the result of torture or coercion.) He even offered a grue-some account of how he'd murdered and eaten some of the children. He was sentenced to death for his crimes.

On January 8, 1574, Gilles Garnier, the long hunted "Werewolf of Dole," was tied to a stake and burned alive for committing crimes related to the forbidden practice of lycanthropy.

The Werewolf Family of St. Cloud

The Gandillons of St. Cloud, France, might have been one of the most unusual families in history. No one can say for certain what criminal actions, if any, they truly committed before their apprehensions. The case first began in 1574, when two children were savagely attacked by a woman named Pernette Gandillon. Pernette appeared to have been the violent matriarch of her own "werewolf pack," which included her brother, Pierre, and his two children (a son and daughter).

In her attack on the two children, she killed the younger. The older child managed to escape and reported the attack to authorities. Pernette Gandillon was soon located, and the surviving child identified her as the attacker. There wasn't really a trial. Apparently, a lynch mob had formed and immediately fell upon the crazed woman, who is said to have snarled and howled at them as she walked around on all fours. The mob, according to accounts, tore Pernette Gandillon to pieces on the spot. They more than likely believed that she was a werewolf, if her behavior was truly as accounts describe.

The Savage Truth

In the 2007 werewolf-themed, horror-romance film *Blood and Chocolate*, the female lead character's name is Vivian Gandillon. This name refers to the most famous family of alleged werewolves in history, the infamous Gandillon clan, which was known as the "Werewolves of St. Cloud."

Pernette's brother Pierre was soon arrested, along with his son, under the suspicion that he was also involved in lycanthropy. Officially, he was accused of being both a werewolf and a witch. While in custody, both Pierre and his son confessed to using a special ointment that, when rubbed on their bodies, gave them the power to shapeshift. It is written that both men removed their shirts to expose a multitude of scars, which they claimed to have received in fights with other canines while in the form of werewolves.

When the two men were placed in a cell, they began to walk around on all fours, howl, and growl at their jailors. The two men were sentenced to hang. However, before their executions, authorities also arrested and tried Pierre's daughter. She was accused and quickly convicted of being a witch and was sentenced to hang alongside her father and brother. All three were executed by hanging, and their remains were then burned to ashes. The entire family was executed, it would appear, for the crimes of one. Only Pernette Gandillon, when all is said and done, could be proven guilty of murder. She remains the only member of the family, which from that day came to be called the "Werewolves of St. Cloud," known to have ever killed anyone. It would appear that Pierre Gandillon, his son, and his daughter were executed for nothing more than being related to Pernette.

The Trial of Theiss

Of all the werewolf trials discussed in this chapter, this one is by far the most unique (not to mention creative). In 1692, in the village of Jurgenburg in Livonia, which is today a part of Russia, an 80-year-old man by the name of Theiss was put on trial as a werewolf. As seems to be the norm in these cases, Theiss did not try to deny that he was indeed a werewolf. However, he did offer to the presiding authorities what was then an unprecedented (and exceedingly brilliant) explanation for what he claimed werewolves truly were. His argument was so convincing, in fact, that he was temporarily set free and later avoided execution.

He may have been old, but Theiss wasn't at all feeble or weak. Under threat of torture, he refused to confess to having committed any crimes against human beings. However, he fully agreed with the accusation that he was a werewolf. This is where this particular story gets *really* interesting.

Theiss explained that human beings did not understand the truth regarding the natural role of werewolves in the whole "good vs. evil" dynamic. Werewolves, Theiss explained to the court, were actually the servants of almighty God himself. Apparently, his story was so convincingly told that, when he was sent back to his cell, authorities did not immediately sentence him. In fact, some folklore accounts claim that his jailors (probably not wanting to risk the wrath of hell's army) actually turned him loose. If this is true, Theiss did not appear to have stayed free. He was soon brought back to the court for further questioning.

Theiss elaborated further that he was a member of a pack of holy werewolves called the *Benandanti*. Interestingly enough, during this same time period, a group of men in Italy also confessed to being the werewolf servants of God, members of the same Benandanti, and they also claimed that their role was to battle witches and demons. (They, however, did not manage to escape their execution.) You see, Theiss testified that ever since God had given Lucifer domain over the earth, the demonic legions of hell had been relatively free to cross over into the human world (though only on certain nights of the year), and werewolves were the only ones capable of guarding the gates. Both the witches of Earth and the demons of hell, he explained, were stealing grain from farms (which he offered as the cause of a recent famine) and bringing it into hell. If not for werewolves, he told the court, the armies of hell would soon starve out and then overrun the area and soon after all of humankind.

Beastly Words

History explains that the **Benandanti** were originally an ancient religious order of northern Italy, primarily responsible for performing rites that ensured agricultural fertility. This might explain why Theiss and the members of the Italian werewolf pack picked the name since they were claiming to protect farms from thefts by witches and demons.

The old man explained that, many years ago, he'd become a part of this battle when a dark sorcerer named Skeistan (who was well known in the region, especially for being *long dead*) had broken Theiss's nose with a broom handle wrapped in hair from a horse's tail. In a chance encounter, Theiss had stumbled upon their dark scheme. He was saved by werewolves, given an iron bar (the primary weapon against the forces of evil), and initiated by the Benandanti werewolves. Theiss told the court that the gates opened their widest on the three nights of the year that marked the changing of the seasons—the eves of Pentecost (winter to spring), St. Lucia (spring to summer), and St. John (summer to winter).

The local church authorities, it seemed, were completely dumbfounded as to what they should do. If Theiss was lying, of course, then it would be no harm, no foul on their part. However, if Theiss was telling the truth … by executing him, they would be personally responsible for unleashing hell on Earth (not to mention killing a divine servant of heaven). Apparently, this wasn't a risk they were willing to take. Rather than execute Theiss for openly confessing to lycanthropy (which, according to church law, was a capital offense), they sentenced him to receive 10 lashes. For a charge of lycanthropy, this was a *very* lenient punishment for the time period.

Antoine Leger

In June of 1823, a 29-year-old Frenchman by the name of Antoine Leger decided to separate himself from the world. Leger had once been a soldier, after which he had worked briefly in a vineyard as a vine-dresser. He journeyed into the woods to assume a life as a hermit and even took up residence in a natural cave. His choice may have been influenced by the common occurrence of famines in France (the country had already been experiencing frequent and extreme famines for nearly 1,000 years), and Leger may have thought that he could live off the land by foraging and hunting. There are some who now firmly believe that Leger may have been exhibiting symptoms of a delusional mental disorder, such as schizophrenia, and that this is what led him to take up a life in the woods.

By the year 1824, however, something went terribly awry with Antoine Leger's new lifestyle. Some believe he went stark raving mad as a result of his long solitude. Others theorize that hunting and foraging ceased to offer a plentiful-enough bounty to sustain him. Whatever the case, it is safe to say that something in the mind of Antoine Leger had altogether snapped.

Leger somehow snatched a little girl who had wandered near the edge of the woods from a nearby village and dragged her to his cave. Once there, he killed the child, drank her blood, and ate some of her flesh. Some believe he tore her body apart using only his teeth and bare hands, while others say he used a blade or some other edged weapon. The records are sketchy on the details. When the girl did not return home, a search party combed the woods and happened upon Leger's cave. At the ghastly sight of the girl's mutilated corpse, the mob immediately fell upon Leger and handed him over to the Versailles magistrates.

Leger was tried for the girl's murder. In the magistrate's investigation, it was discovered that Leger had eaten of his victim's flesh. Leger admitted that he'd long supped on the raw flesh of rabbits, but that he had become consumed by an urge to taste human flesh. He also openly admitted to every gruesome detail of his crime. He was sentenced to death for crimes associated to lycanthropy (which was still considered an actual crime in France at the time).

After his execution, Leger's corpse was handed over for scientific examination. His head and brain were thoroughly examined, and the acting physicians discovered that he had in fact suffered from an unidentified brain disorder that had caused extreme deterioration of his neural tissue. This is significant because it marked the first occurrence in a werewolf trial where the beliefs offered by traditional superstitions were challenged by new advances in the arenas of science and medicine.

Bark vs. Bite

In all actuality, Leger likely exhibited symptoms of what is now referred to as "clinical lycanthropy." A century and a half later, in 1975, there would be another case strikingly similar to Leger's. In that case, the affected man was also suffering from an unidentified condition of brain deterioration, simply labeled "walnut brain." For more information on this case and clinical lycanthropy, see Chapter 18.

The Least You Need to Know

◆ History is full of documents that record the trials of alleged werewolves.

◆ Many convicted werewolves were more than likely just scapegoats, serial killers, or the mentally ill.

◆ An old man named Theiss, possibly one of the greatest geniuses of his day, is the only confessed werewolf ever to have talked his way out of being executed.

Chapter 7

Werewolves, Wolves, and Religion

In This Chapter

◆ The historic account of one priest's conversation with a man turned wolf

◆ The Vargamor, the frightening wolf witches of Scandinavia

◆ The significance of wolves in the demonology of the Christian church

◆ The widespread perceptional shifts that led to a reversal of wolf symbolism

◆ King John's personal crusade to destroy any wolves found within the borders of his empire

Both werewolves and wolves alike have had a long but turbulent relationship with the organized religions of humanity. While they have at times been worshipped, they have far more often been persecuted by the religions and governments of the past. In many religions, wolves are associated with certain demonic figures, quite often portrayed as shadowy and deceptive agents of evil or as symbols of violence and greed. Wolves had little to redeem them from such views in the medieval world. They were neither beasts of burden nor a source of food and therefore had no value to humans. They were seen as a burden and a threat to livestock, so most farmers were more than happy to participate in the Christian church's demonization of the wolf, which had once been highly revered by a number of European cultures.

The Priest and the Wolf

In 1187, Giraldus Cambrensis provided an account of one priest's rather unusual encounter with a wolf. According to the story, the priest was traveling from Ulster to Meath. When the hour grew late, the priest and his young attendant set up camp for the night in the woods along the road. They had no sooner built a fire than a wolf stepped calmly into their campsite from the surrounding woods.

Needless to say, the priest and his attendant were terrified by the sight. The wolf then began to speak in a male human voice and told the men they had nothing to fear from him (which does not seem to have helped very much). Trembling, the priest begged the wolf in the name of God not to harm them. The wolf replied with words of a Christian nature, which seemed to at least somewhat convince the priest that he was not evil.

The wolf explained that he was a member of a clan from Ossiry that was cursed to follow a particular ritual. He went on to say that every seven years two members of the clan, one man and one woman, were chosen by lots and sent into the woods to live as wolves. If they managed to survive this period without doing evil to humans, then they would be allowed to return to human form, and two new clan members would again be chosen to take their place in the woods. However, the wolf told them, his female counterpart was in the woods, very near to death. Being that they were Catholics, the wolf begged the priest to follow him to the she-wolf and perform the proper religious rites.

The Curse

You may have noticed the similarity between this story and the seven-year "wolf period" of the Greek Lycaeans. It is entirely possible that this story of the priest's is a fabrication. It may have been written in an attempt to integrate the preexisting myth into a more "Christian-friendly" form. Then again, maybe the priest really did have a conversation with a pair of talking wolves.

More out of fear than any sense of spiritual obligation, the priest followed the wolf into the woods. They soon came upon the form of a dying she-wolf, who was moaning and sighing with the voice of a human woman. Upon seeing them, she greeted the priest in a polite human fashion. The priest then began giving her the rites of a last communion. When she asked the priest to place the Eucharist wafer in her mouth, he told her he did not come equipped with any. The priest apparently lied because he was afraid to put his hand near her mouth, out of concern that she might bite him.

The male he-wolf, however, now approached the priest and pointed with his muzzle to a small missal book the clergyman carried. Somehow, perhaps by scent, the he-wolf knew that the priest had several wafers in this book. The he-wolf then reached toward the she-wolf with his paw and pulled back her wolf-skin from her head to her navel, which exposed the torso of a human woman (basically, exposing her breasts). He again implored the priest not to deny her the gift of Heaven by failing to administer the proper death rites. He then returned the wolf-skin, and she resumed her beastly form. Finding himself rather disturbed by this, and being out of excuses, the priest now removed the wafer and completed the final rites for the she-wolf. They then left her and returned to the campsite.

The he-wolf remained with the priest and his attendant through the rest of the night. In the morning, he escorted them to the road and pointed them in the proper direction. The he-wolf then returned to the woods to complete his seven-year trial.

It would seem that this account sparked some debate as to the nature of certain living things. The question was raised by some as to whether or not these particular wolves should be thought of as humans or as beasts. For example, if a hunter was to kill one of these human-wolves, would he have committed murder in the eyes of God? It was partially concluded that since these wolves were intelligent, then at the least they could not be considered "brutes." However, since it was also believed that God himself had imposed these wolf-forms upon them, they could not be considered fully human in their form either.

Wolfy Witches

One of the primary reasons that wolves and werewolves became targets of the Christian church was that both eventually came to be associated with witchcraft. What the medieval church called "witchcraft," however, was usually nothing more than the traditional practices of Europe's pre-Christian nature religions. In order to speed the acceptance of Christianity throughout the region, the Christian church actively demonized such practices by denouncing them as devil worship. Suddenly, the practice of any religion aside from Christianity would make one an outlaw. In Scandinavia, for example, women who practiced wolf rites (likely of a pre-Christian nature religion) were called *Vargamor*, meaning "wolf-crones."

After the rise of Christianity, the Vargamor were labeled a coven of devil-worshipping witches. The folklore soon changed to fit this new label, and it came to be said that the Vargamor would first lure unsuspecting men into their dens with promises of sex, then feed them alive to their demonic wolves. Some lore claimed that the Vargamor served these wolves, while others claim that they had the power to command the wolves at will.

In the myths of the Norse (which includes the ancestors of the Scandinavians), female warrior spirits called *Valkyries* were often depicted as riding on the backs of wolves. The Vargamor may have been responsible for some form of religious rite that meant to invoke the powers of the Valkyries. When this idea later encountered Christianity, however, it probably gave rise to the view that the Vargamor were witches. In much of Europe's later "pro-Christian" folklore, witches are often described as riding through the night on the backs of wolves (just as the Valkyries once were).

Beastly Words

In Norse myths, **Valkyries** were beautiful, female warrior spirits tasked with retrieving from battlefields the souls of fallen warriors who had died bravely and with honor. They would then escort the soul to Valhalla, a heavenly utopia of food, drink, sex, and battle, which was reserved only for the brave.

Demon Wolves

A number of religions, not just Christianity, have their own demonic or negative wolf figures. In the dialects of the Hindus, for example, the word meaning "wolf" is used interchangeably to also mean "criminal/ outlaw." From the Hindus to the Europeans to the ancient Aramaeans, they all have their own forms of such wolf-demons.

In Romanian folklore, the wolf-demon Varcolac may have been a reinvention of older Norse myths of the titanic wolf Fenrir (who was believed to be able to trigger the apocalypse called *Ragnarok* by swallowing the sun). Varcolac is said to be the eternal enemy of light, and he seeks to devour the moon and sun. There are rare times when he nearly succeeds, causing solar and lunar eclipses. In some legends about Varcolac (namely those that claim he is a wolf-demon), it is said that he takes physical form by emerging from the corpse of any infant that has not been baptized.

Bark vs. Bite

The Romanian myths about the wolf-demon Varcolac were also likely an attempt to reshape a pre-Christian myth into a more church-acceptable form. For example, there is the claim that Varcolac can assume a physical form by emerging from the corpse of a baby that isn't baptized. This element would have encouraged the uneducated peasantry to have their children baptized into Christianity at birth. Since infant mortality rates were very high, a good many infants did not survive their first year of life.

The demon named Managarm is also likely to have been a redevelopment of the pre-Christian Norse myth of Fenrir. The name "Managarm" roughly translates as "moon hound." This demon is said to have been born in the trunk of an Ironwood tree that was tended closely by an ancient witch. Managarm has a taste for the flesh of the dead, and so he is often found visiting graveyards. Like Varcolac, some legends say that one day Managarm will swallow the moon and cover the heavens with so much human blood that it will block out the light of the sun.

Mammon was originally an Aramaic word for "riches" and is thought to have been somehow associated with wolves (though the nature of this association is unclear). Whether or not the Aramaeans actually considered this to be the name of a certain demon, however, remains a matter of some debate. Regardless, the concept was eventually personified in both Judaism and Christianity, and the word Mammon came to be thought of as the name of a wolf-demon of wealth, greed, dishonest business, and envy.

The Church's Persecution of Wolves

In 870 C.E., the archbishop of Mainz gave a sermon that denounced the Saxon belief in shapeshifters. Little could he have known that his own church would later claim that a shapeshifter, the werewolf, was the devil incarnate. In fact, by the year 1270 C.E., the church considered it a crime of heresy if someone did *not* believe in the existence of werewolves. This was a rather strong paradigm shift, to say the least.

However, the relationship between wolves and Christianity was not always thus. At one time in church history, wolves were believed to be the holy protectors of the tomb of St. Vincent. So this presents an important question: just when, where, and (perhaps most importantly) *how* did things go so horribly wrong in the relationship between wolves, werewolves, and the Christian church?

Anyone who has read the New Testament of the Christian Bible would agree that it is full of *pastoral* metaphors that discuss the relationship of predator-sheep-shepherd. In fact, the clergy title of *pastor* originally meant "shepherd." Jesus and God (as well as the clergy, in some

churches) are seen as the "divine shepherds" of Christians, who are
the "sheep." The "predators," in this relationship are the devil and his
assorted agents of evil. Whereas the shepherds of biblical times often
had to fend off lions in order to protect their flocks, the shepherds of
Europe were more often fighting off wolves. So even before the arrival
of Christianity, wolves were seen by shepherds and farmers as a nui-
sance. This metaphor of the new religion of Christianity, however, now
allowed Europeans to label the animals as the embodiment of evil.

Beastly Words

The word **pastoral** means something related to the lifestyle, work,
and activities of shepherds and their livestock. The word **pastor,**
which is now a popular religious title, originally referred to a shepherd.

The term **inquisitor,** as it is used here, was a church title for an official
member of the Ecclesiastical Court of the Inquisition, which was supposed to be charged with rooting out enemies of Christianity, such as
heretics, witches, devil worshippers, and quite often just about anyone
else that the church deemed undesirable.

By the fifteenth century, however, the idea of physical lycanthropy
found itself under attack by new discoveries in the developing sciences.
In 1486, German clergyman and *inquisitor* Heinrich Kramer discussed
the issue of werewolves in his text *Malleus Maleficarum,* or "The
Hammer of Evil/Witches." According to this work, no human could
physically assume the shape of a wolf (except by the power of God, of
course). Therefore, the text explained, werewolves had to exist on one
side of two polar opposite groups. They could be either the servants of
God or the agents of the devil. (The book leaves absolutely no room for
middle ground in this regard.)

If the werewolf was of the latter group that served the devil, then the
book would appear to claim that he or she was not actually a real werewolf at all. The manuscript explained that witches who believed they
could shapeshift into wolves were actually being fooled by a trick of
their devilish master. Kramer insisted that this only happened because
the devil had created a convincing illusion that easily made his witches
believe they had changed their shapes, when in fact they had not.

Sadly, it was this issue that placed werewolves in the path of the Inquisition. This led to a new rise in werewolf trials, which briefly became almost as common as trials for witchcraft. In all honesty, it would have been slightly better to be found guilty of being a witch than a werewolf in those times. Whereas witches of this period were executed by hanging, convicted werewolves were not. Werewolves were still generally believed to have certain protective attributes. Therefore, it was ultimately decided by Inquisition authorities that any convicted werewolf be burned alive.

King John's War on Wolves

King John, ruler of the British Empire from 1199 to 1216 C.E., is one of the most severely disliked monarchs in human history. In fact, he was so highly despised by the masses that a number of negative rumors about the king began to spread among the people. One such rumor claimed that King John was actually a werewolf. This concept followed the king to his grave despite his best efforts. It is said that, shortly after his death, a number of monks reported hearing strange sounds coming from inside his tomb. Not wanting to have his unclean corpse on such sanctified grounds, they actually exhumed King John's corpse and relocated it to a patch of land that was not consecrated.

Perhaps as a result of the werewolf rumors, King John seemed to develop a strong hatred for wolves. He was responsible for placing a 5 shilling bounty on wolves. He claimed that they were creatures that should be removed from any truly civilized Christian empire. He also endorsed the church's claim that wolves were the embodiment of evil and should be wiped from existence. This practice, or others like it, would continue for centuries after the death of King John—the despised, wolf-killing king who was thought of as a werewolf by his own people.

The Least You Need to Know

- The historical account of one priest's encounter with a man and woman who'd transformed into talking wolves may have been a reinvention of the Greek Lycaean legend.

- The so-called "wolf witches" of European lore were likely not witches at all, but priestesses of a pre-Christian Valkyrie cult.

- Christianity once saw wolves as protectors of saintly tombs but later saw them as the embodiment of evil.

- Many of the medieval church's negative claims about both wolves and werewolves were probably caused by the campaign meant to demonize preexisting nature religions.

Chapter 8

Werewolf Hysteria in Medieval France

In This Chapter

◆ The role of the werewolf in the history and folklore of the French

◆ The frightening and bloody killing spree of the "Beast of Gevaudan"

◆ The lycanthropy trial of Frenchmen Pierre Burgot and Michael Verdun

◆ A discussion of the werewolf of Caude

◆ The terrible killings of the infamous "Demon Tailor of Chalons"

◆ Francois Bertrand's obsession with the dead

◆ The unusual trial and unique sentence of confessed lycanthrope Jean Grenier

The werewolf has long been a major player in the folklore, superstitions, history, and culture of France. Beginning sometime during the Dark Ages and continuing through the Age of Enlightenment, the entire country of France seems to have been overwhelmed by a widespread obsession about (and extreme fear of) werewolves. Historically speaking, far more people have been tried and convicted of lycanthropy in France than any other country on Earth (not to mention cases that never made it to court, often due to the swift and violent actions of frantic mobs).

The Werewolf of Medieval France

The French word for a werewolf is *loup-garou*, which is in itself difficult to explain fully. In general, the word has come to mean "werewolf." The term is a combination of the French word *loup*, which means "wolf," and another term of uncertain origins, *garou*.

The word "garou" seems to have entered the French language sometime during the fourteenth century. The exact origins of the word cannot be concretely verified. There are some who believe the word to be a trans-literation of an obscure Frankish term, *gerulf*, which roughly translates as something along the lines of "shapeshifter."

A loup-garou, in the French view, could take any number of forms. Most generically, it was thought of as a wolf or wolflike evil entity that was strongly associated with the devil. This meant that the term could be applied to both men and beasts. Sometimes the word was applied to human beings who had committed such terrible crimes that it was difficult to reconcile how they could be humans. In other cases, a particularly violent dog, wolf, or similar animal might have been dubbed a loup-garou, often to explain why it had attacked humans or to explain why it was so difficult for even the most skilled hunters to kill or capture it.

The Beast of Gevaudan

On a sunny afternoon in June of 1764, a young girl in southern France was in a pasture, tending to her family's cattle herd. When a number of the animals became unusually restless (including a few of her family's faithful herding dogs that she'd brought for protection), she raised her eyes to the nearby tree line. She immediately saw that a giant wolf was charging across the pasture toward her. According to the girl's account, this wolf stood nearly as high as the cows.

Apparently, her dogs didn't feel up to the task of defending the girl. Seeing the monstrous wolf coming at them, the dogs immediately ran away with their tails between their legs. Believe it or not, the girl claimed it was the cows that saved her. A number of horned cattle took positions between the girl and the wolf and tightly closed ranks. When the giant beast approached, the cows managed to fend it off by stabbing at it with their horns. Though the girl believed the cows were protecting her, they may have just assumed that it was after them. The girl returned home and reported the incident to her father, who passed the information on to the authorities in Gevaudan. It would later be realized just how fortunate she had been. This girl would be one of few human beings to encounter the "Beast of Gevaudan" and survive.

The Carnage Begins

After this initial encounter, the bodies of the dead began piling up with increasing frequency. At first, it was mainly killing livestock. In July, however, the beast claimed its first known human victim. In the woods near Gevaudan, a very young village girl was killed by the beast. Reports of the incident claim that her flesh had been horribly mangled, and that her heart had been torn completely out of her chest (and presumably devoured by the beast). Another little girl also soon fell victim to the beast, but all that was ever found of her was her shoes and a few bloody shreds from her clothing.

Soon enough, the shredded and partially devoured bodies of a good many more humans would start to be discovered. With each attack, the animal seemed to grow increasingly bold. In the month of August, the beast attacked a group of travelers consisting of men, women, and children (killing several people). By September, it is said to have even been attacking groups of armed men. Many survivors from these groups claimed that they had shot or stabbed the creature. However, the killings kept right on. Rumors began to spread that conventional weapons could not kill this beast. The commoners of the region were now convinced that it was not a giant wolf carrying out the attacks, but a loup-garou.

The Beast That Would Not Die

Summer gave way to autumn, yet little else changed. The beast was still out there, still killing. In October, a pair of local hunters came upon the beast in a small clearing. It immediately came at them, all claws and teeth. When the beast was less than 10 paces away, claimed one of the hunters, he'd fired his musket and scored a square shot that seemed to slow it down. The other hunter fired and hit the beast, which ended the attack. The beast turned around and limped back into the shelter of the woods.

The hunters headed back to report what had happened to authorities (who ultimately proved that they were completely incapable of protecting the people from this violent creature). Since these men (both experienced marksmen) were so certain that their shots had hit the beast in the chest and that the beast had appeared hurt when it retreated, many assumed it had gone somewhere to die (as many canine species are known to do). However, just a few days later, the killings and attacks resumed.

The Beast Marks Gevaudan

By this time, stories of the beast attacks in Gevaudan had spread to Paris. Media outlets were publishing stories of the encounters, some of which were purely spectacular works of fiction. However, most seemed to have agreed on what the beast looked like, based on eyewitness testimonies. It was far larger than any known species of European wolves, with an especially large head and snout. The hair on its front was grey, while the hair on its back was black. The teeth were also said to be especially wide, so much so that they could be seen from a good distance when exposed (which is an unusual trait, one that is uncommon to today's living wolf species). Also, the beast's gigantic paws were said to be equipped with long and sharp claws (another trait uncommon to canines, one that is usually found on large predatory cats).

Some papers of the period even tried to say it was some unusual mating between a wolf and a large cat (or some thought a wolf and jackal). Regardless of what the beast actually was, the region of Gevaudan was now completely at its mercy. Unfortunately, it does not seem to have had any. Needless to say, the people of the area avoided the woods that winter and kept their children in the safety of their villages.

As winter neared its end, the Beast of Gevaudan had begun attacking people in their own villages. The most incredible attack was upon two children who were in the presence of their parents and a fair-size group of other villagers. The beast pounced upon the children, and the adults came to their aid with pitchforks, knives, rocks, and just about any weapon they could lay their hands on.

Unfortunately, their blows did almost nothing to stop the wolf. When the dust had settled, one of the boys lay terribly wounded. The beast managed to sink its enormous fangs into the neck of the other poor child and fled. The parents and villagers stood helpless as the beast dragged the screaming child into the woods. The boy was never seen alive again.

Soldiers in Pretty Dresses

The authorities of Gevaudan seemed powerless to stop the beast that now threatened the people of the region. They decided to send a request for assistance to French Royal Court in Versailles. King Louis the Fifteenth was appalled by what he heard and immediately mobilized an entire unit of cavalry and infantry soldiers. The unit was made up of 57 skilled French *Dragoons* (40 foot-soldiers and 17 cavalry) and was led by a captain by the name of Duhamel, who was briefly seen by some as a legendary wolf-killer for his role. Later, this view would change.

Beastly Words

Dragoons are specially trained soldiers that were once a common element of European armies. They were trained to fight on foot as well as horseback and were schooled in cavalry tactics. In the beginning, members of such units were commonly armed with "dragon" muskets.

Duhamel, after realizing that most of the beast's victims had been women and children, decided that dressing in drag was the answer to cornering the beast. He ordered a certain number of his Dragoons to dress in women's clothing as they rode into the area. He had hoped that this trick might lure the beast out into the open since it did not seem to have any fear of humans whatsoever. This ruse, however, did not succeed in causing the beast to attack them.

Once Duhamel and his band of merry, cross-dressing Dragoons reached Gevaudan, he immediately assumed command of just about everything—the magistrates, villagers, livestock, farmers, etc. Whatever he thought he needed to stop the carnage, he took it. Captain Duhamel organized the villagers and armed them with heavy sticks. He placed his horsemen on line behind them and recruited the best of the hunting marksmen from among the local woodsmen. He then moved the entire group across the area. The villagers were put out in front with orders to beat at brush and vegetation with the sticks (and probably also as bait) in order to flush out the beast from any hiding place. The hunters were placed among the villagers, and the armed Dragoons followed in line formation behind them.

This plan did produce some results. Sadly, close to about 100 normal wolves are also thought to have been killed that day. However, the beast finally did show itself on multiple occasions during the execution of Duhamel's bold maneuver. The hunters and soldiers opened fire whenever it appeared. A number of shots were seen hitting the beast in vital areas. Eventually, it ran back into the woods and did not come out again.

A Foolish Assumption

A group of local hunters were sent in to track the dying animal down and confirm the kill. However, they were never able to find the beast's body. Regardless, Duhamel was absolutely certain that no living creature could have survived such obviously fatal wounds. Believing he had succeeded in bringing down the Beast of Gevaudan, Captain Duhamel returned to Versailles like a conquering hero. However, the celebration would be a short one.

Only days after Captain Duhamel marched his men out of Gevaudan, the killings resumed. The beast had returned and continued its killing spree with renewed fervor. By the summer of 1765, the beast wrought terror upon the children of Gevaudan. This time, it was not bodies that were found but scattered pieces. Strewn about arms and legs soon became almost a commonplace sight, according to some sources.

Captain Duhamel was shamed by the beast's return. The resumption of the killings made him appear either a fool or a liar. Needless to say, King Louis relieved Duhamel of his position and sought out the greatest known wolf hunters in all of France—the d'Enneval clan. The hunt would now be led by the father-son team of Jean-Charles and Jean-Francois d'Enneval.

The Beast Hunters

While the d'Enneval team had many close encounters with the beast and managed to wound it on several occasions, they never succeeded in capturing or killing it. Jean-Charles was the first to despair and returned home. The younger Jean-Francois remained, however, but to no avail. By early June 1767, near the three-year anniversary of the beast's first known attack, Jean-Francois d'Enneval was forced to abandon the hunt and return home.

King Louis now replaced d'Enneval with his chief gunner, a man named Antoine de Beauterne (who had learned much about hunting from his friends, the d'Enneval family). Beauterne very quickly succeeded in killing a gigantic wolf that was recorded as being over 6 feet long. Much like Duhamel, Beauterne returned to Versailles and reported that he had killed the Beast of Gevaudan. Also like Duhamel, however, it proved not to be the case. The wolf he killed, while abnormally large, was not the beast he sought. The killings continued.

Some locals now believed that only God could save them, and many made pilgrimages to the holy site of Notre-Dame. One such person was local hermit Jean Chastel, who took with him to the cathedral a rifle and three bullets. According to the legend, while there he had these armaments properly blessed.

Bringing Down the Beast

Enraged at having been made to look foolish, Beauterne now took drastic measures. He recruited some of the best hunters of France and returned to Gevaudan, where they were joined by scores of local hunters. In total, it is recorded that the hunting party consisted of approximately 300 men. The enormous group now relentlessly combed the countryside for the beast.

On June 19, 1767, as the sun descended into the horizon, the beast charged toward a group of hunters. Among these men was Jean Chastel, with his blessed rifle and bullets. He took aim at the beast and fired. The beast went down and stayed down. Apparently, Jean later told people that the bullets were more than just blessed—they were made of silver.

In order to confirm that this was the beast, Beauterne had the animal's belly cut open. Human remains were found inside of it. This was the man-eating terror known as the Beast of Gevaudan. The reign of terror had ended. This time, the killings did not resume.

In the end, the beast took the lives of 60 people and wounded countless others. The hunt for the creature had cost the French government a small fortune. So perhaps it is not surprising that the beast's corpse was hung up at night and paraded through the streets during the day. When it began to give off the stench of decomposition, however, it was buried.

Bark vs. Bite

There is no doubt that the Beast of Gevaudan existed. But what was it? Descriptions make it seem unlikely that it was really a regular wolf. Some have theorized that it was a species of prehistoric wolf (fossils of which have been found in China, Russia, Alaska, and California) forced to encounter humans, possibly due to a shrinking habitat. Had it actually been a *pack* of these giant wolves (some species were the size of small bears), it would explain why the beast seemed never to die even when mortally wounded. The beast that was shot when the killings ceased may have just been the last surviving member of his pack. Sadly, the hunt may mark the forced extinction of a giant wolf species.

Burgot and Verdun: Peasant Werewolves

On a dark and stormy night in 1502, French peasant Pierre Burgot was desperately trying to corral his loose sheep. They were frightened by the lightning and thunder, making Burgot's job even more difficult. Suddenly, Burgot looked up to see three dark figures on horseback, each cloaked in black. The lead horseman addressed Burgot and told him that he would be happy to offer the poor man a guarantee of future protection for his sheep. The man also offered Burgot a handful of shiny coins, a considerable sum at the time (especially to Burgot, a man of meager means).

Burgot asked what he must do in order to receive these gifts. The dark horseman said that, for the moment, all Burgot would be required to do was worship him as a god. Then the horseman explained that he would come to Burgot soon, and they would then discuss the rest of the deal. Soon the man came to Burgot as promised. He now explained that, in order to continue receiving these blessings of protection, Burgot would have to denounce all aspects of Christianity (basically, he would have to sacrifice his soul). Not the sharpest tool in the shed, Burgot happily agreed and immediately fulfilled these terms of the deal.

Months passed, and Burgot began to feel like he'd gotten a raw deal. After all, he'd given up his immortal soul. And for what? Some safe sheep and a handful of coins? Burgot began to consider going back to the church and forgetting about this deal altogether. Then a visitor came calling—Michel Verdun.

Verdun, a man from the same area, explained to Burgot that he was a servant of the dark master with whom Burgot had made his pact. He brought Burgot to the woods for a witch's Sabbath and told him to take off his clothes. Burgot did so, and Verdun applied a magic salve to his skin. As he did so, Burgot's shape changed into that of a wolf. He looked up to see that Verdun had also turned into a wolf. The pair then took a wild run through the woods and committed the most horrifying of crimes together.

When they came upon a boy of only seven, they fell upon the lad, tore him limb from limb, and devoured his flesh. They later did the same to a local woman. Another time, they snatched a four-year-old little boy and stole him away to the woods, where they strangled him and ate his flesh.

When Pierre Burgot was eventually caught and brought before the church court, he told them all of the aforementioned details. Michel Verdun was then arrested and convicted alongside Burgot. The two were sentenced to death and executed. After their executions, a reproduction was commissioned and hung on the wall of the local church as a warning to churchgoers of the evils that men do when they give in to the devil's charms.

Bark vs. Bite

Did the events that Pierre Burgot testified to actually occur? In a sense, they quite possibly could have. Some might theorize that, seeing as how Burgot was of a simple nature and appeared to be of below average intelligence, he may have been the subject of a practical joke that went too far. In fact, Michel Verdun and some friends were likely the "dark riders" Burgot first encountered. The salve could easily have been some form of hallucinogenic substance. Unable to reason through what he saw, Burgot may have believed that he'd really made a pact with the devil and become a wolf. Then again … maybe he did.

The Werewolf Tailor of Chalons

Most historians agree with the claim that this story is true. However, the many details of what occurred are hard to nail down. Little is known about the identity of the man now referred to as the "Demon Tailor of Chalons" or as the "Werewolf of Chalons." The details of his murders were so horribly gruesome that the presiding officials ordered all records of his crimes burnt to ashes. They wanted to make certain that no one would ever be able to reproduce his terrible deeds. This may have been for the best. However, the tale of his crimes lived on in the local lore, much of which was later written down.

This loup-garou was a tailor in the Chalons district of Paris, France. He had been brought to the court on December 14, 1598, after the skeletal remains of his many young victims were discovered in a number of barrels in the back room of his shop. The details of his crimes are forever lost to the fire. However, surviving accounts state that he would lure children into his shop. He would then torture them (often sexually) before slitting their throats. Once his victims were dead, he would then butcher their flesh as one would butcher an animal for meat. He then kept the flesh in freezers to cook and eat for his meals.

Unlike many who were tried for lycanthropy, the Demon Tailor never once confessed to anything. However, he never seemed disturbed or showed so much as a hint of sadness at his trial. Throughout the trial, most surviving accounts claim that his face remained a blank slate. However, some accounts also claim that he was prone to fits of rage that he would sometimes display even in the courtroom. It would seem that he refused to fear the courts, something that became even more evident during his execution.

On the day of the Demon Tailor's execution by fire, it is said that he screamed a flurry of perverse insults and blasphemies at the spectators until the flames finally claimed the last of his breath. Most accounts insist that this display of profanity was the final evidence that this monster of a man had entered into a pact with the devil and thereby become a loup-garou. The fires of Earth now sent him to face the fires of hell.

The Werewolf of Caude

In 1598, a group of hunters came upon what they first thought was an animal. Upon closer inspection, however, they were horrified to discover that it was in fact a man. The rambling man, who identified himself by the name Jacques Roulet, was half-naked and covered in blood. His hair was matted with dirt and leaves, and he held in his hand what appeared to be a large piece of raw meat. The meat was soon discovered to be the flesh of a 15-year-old boy whom Roulet had murdered and mostly devoured. The hunters were convinced that they had discovered a loup-garou, and they immediately dragged Roulet before the courts. News of the case spread, and Roulet was soon dubbed the "Werewolf of Caude."

Upon questioning, Roulet claimed that he'd been a traveling vagabond for years. However, he'd at some point in the past become obsessed with the idea of eating human flesh. He explained that his recent teenage victim was not his first, and he offered a number of gruesome details regarding many of the murders he'd committed in the past. Many of his victims had been state officials, and he seemed to have had a taste for lawyers and court bailiffs.

Based on his confession, Roulet was convicted of murder, lycanthropy, and cannibalism. Initially, he was sentenced to death (mostly likely an execution by burning). However, when a number of well-known scientific and medical authorities passionately testified that Roulet was not a werewolf but a madman (a condition they claimed to be able to cure), this sentence was changed. He was sentenced instead to rehabilitation at a sanitarium. After only two years of treatment, Jacques Roulet, the "Werewolf of Caude," was deemed cured of his insanity and released. What became of him after he left the sanitarium remains a mystery.

Bark vs. Bite

Roulet more than likely suffered from advanced schizophrenia or some similar brain disease that caused his odd and violent behavior. His case is unique among such werewolf trials, as he was at least identified as mentally ill. This small but important detail marks a significant turning point in accepted social perceptions of human actions.

Francois Bertrand, Werewolf of Paris

Francois Bertrand is referred to by some as the "Werewolf of Paris." The name is well deserved. During the mid-nineteenth century, Francois Bertrand had spent much of his adult life as a sergeant in the French military. He was first brought before the courts when he was caught vandalizing a number of tombs in a Paris cemetery. An examination of the scene led investigators to believe that it was not the tombs that Bertrand was after … but the dead bodies held inside.

The Savage Truth

The story of Francois Bertrand would later become the basis for legendary fantasy writer Guy Endore's widely popular horror novel *The Werewolf of Paris*. While the novel ignores many of the facts surrounding the real life of Bertrand, it takes advantage of the more fantastic elements of the case for the sake of interesting fiction. For more on Guy Endore's werewolf writings, see Chapter 10.

Under questioning by the courts, Bertrand explained that he had long harbored a compulsion to tear apart the corpses of dead women and young girls. He is said to have done so with nothing but his teeth and fingernails. Some of his experiences in doing these ghastly acts led to bouts of *necrophilia*. Other times, after tearing apart a corpse, he would devour some of its flesh.

Beastly Words

Necrophilia is a condition in which a person becomes unhealthily obsessed with corpses. This strange condition often leads to unusual behaviors such as stealing corpses and frequenting graveyards. It can also manifest in sexual ways.

Bertrand's actions caused him to be labeled by people as a loup-garou. His confession, however, led to his conviction. Unlike in many of the werewolf trials of past centuries, Bertrand was not burned or even executed. He wasn't even charged by the courts with being a werewolf (though the people of the area certainly considered him to be one). Instead of being executed, Bertrand was sentenced to a long prison sentence. He is believed to have died while incarcerated, though sources vary on this detail.

The Unique Lycanthropy Case of Jean Grenier

The record of Jean Grenier begins on a sunny afternoon in 1603 with a group of young girls watching over their family's herd of sheep. As the girls made small talk, some of the sheep suddenly became noticeably restless. A group of them had wandered into a nearby depression in the ground, only to come rushing back out to rejoin the main herd as if something had startled them. The girls, fearing that some predator might be lurking somewhere unseen, ventured over together to investigate what was scaring their flock. As the girls approached, huddled closely together, their trusty work dog sensed something was wrong and began growling and baring his fangs.

The girls reached the edge of the depression, expecting to see an animal. They were shocked to instead see a teenage boy sitting on a fallen log. The boy was 13-year-old Jean Grenier, and his unusual appearance frightened the girls. His dirty and matted red hair fell about his shoulders and face in long, wild, and unkempt clumps. He was wearing ragged clothes, and much of his body could be seen through the many tears and rips of his shirt and pants. He was very emaciated, as if from prolonged starvation. His skin was dark tan, and his eyes hollow. According to the record, his canine teeth were unusually long, and they often protruded from his mouth even when it was closed.

The girls said nothing to him at first, and for a few moments it seemed as if Grenier did not even notice their presence. The savage-looking boy just sat there stone-faced as the girls stood before him in a state of shocked bewilderment. They were finally pulled from this trance when Grenier turned his pale-blue eyes toward them and spoke with a beastly tone of voice. He asked the girls to decide which among them was the prettiest. The oldest girl demanded to know why Grenier wished them to decide such a thing. He replied that he was going to marry whichever girl proved to be the prettiest. They thought he was joking. After all, how could they marry someone they did not know?

The girls had never seen this strange boy before, and now demanded that he introduce himself. Grenier claimed to be the son of a priest. The truth of his answer seemed questionable to the girls, and they now asked him if the reason for him being so dirty-skinned and dressed in such tattered rags was because of the scandal regarding his conception (obviously, since priests were celibate and unmarried, this meant he was illegitimate).

The Curse

One might assume that, especially considering Grenier's shabby and dirty appearance, after running away from home the young boy was living and sleeping in the surrounding forests of Antoine de Pizon. Some speculate that, as a result of the horrors and hardships the young boy endured, the experience drove Grenier to the point of madness. Others point the blame at Grenier's father, and think that his behavior may have been caused by brain damage he suffered from being beaten by his father. In many modern cases of clinical lycanthropy (see Chapter 18), the condition has been linked to emotional trauma and brain damage.

Grenier told the girls that his skin was dark and dirty because he often wore a wolf-skin instead of clothes. When the girls asked where he got the wolf-skin, Grenier said it had been given to him by a man named Pierre Labourant. The girls had never heard of any man by that name living in the area. When they said this to Grenier, he let out a long and howling row of laughter that further added to the girls' fear of him. He stood and whirled around as if overcome with joy. The girls took a few steps back. Horrified, the oldest of them now began to suspect that this boy was either overcome by madness or possessed by demons.

Grenier suddenly stopped his fit of joy and explained to the girls that Pierre Labourant lived in chains, "in a place of gloom and fire." It did not take the girls long to figure out what he meant. Grenier was saying that Pierre Labourant, the man he claimed had given him a wolf-skin, was the devil. The girls were now petrified in terror.

The Curse

Grenier may have been having a little fun with the girls by using the name "Pierre Labourant." Literally translated, this would mean something like "stone laborer." His use of Pierre could also be seen as meaning "Mr. Laborer." Some have interpreted this as Grenier's way of saying that the life of a poor laborer (specifically, life in the social lower class in which he grew up) was a living hell.

Grenier then told the girls that when Pierre Labourant gave him the wolf-skin cape, he was transformed into a werewolf. He went on to explain that from dusk to dawn, every Monday, Friday, and Sunday, he would don his cape and again be transformed into a wolf. He claimed to have killed numerous dogs and drank their blood while in his wolf form. With malice in his eyes, he then told them that, more than the blood of dogs, he much preferred eating the tender flesh of young girls. He claimed to have eaten many young girls, and with a growling voice told them that, were the sun down, he would have eaten all of them. Grenier then burst into another joyous fit, this time frightening the girls so much that they ran from him in a screaming panic.

In truth, Jean Grenier was not the son of a priest as he had claimed. He was actually the son of a poor laborer (who is believed to have been an abusive father). Three months before the previously mentioned encounter, Grenier had run away from his home village (some believe he wished to escape brutal beatings from his father). It is unknown if he was living at any particular residence in the months that followed.

The Lost Boy and Marguerite

Facing starvation, and growing weary of living as a beggar, Grenier worked a number of jobs, mostly tending flocks for local farmers. Usually, he was soon fired for neglecting his duties. At the time, he had worked for several weeks at a rather low-paying job in the nearby village of Antoine de Pizon, where no one knew him. His job was to accompany the daughter of a livestock owner while she tended her father's flock of sheep. The girl's name was Marguerite Poirier, and she often complained to her father about Grenier's increasingly erratic and unusual behavior. She told her father that Grenier would often frighten her with horrifying stories, which the boy claimed were about his own savage acts and bloody crimes. Despite Marguerite's sincere complaints, her father thought nothing of the situation. He just assumed that she was exaggerating, or that Grenier was just having a bit of harmless fun (as boys tend to do) by telling scary stories.

One day, however, Marguerite returned home far earlier than normal. Quite out of character, she was in such a panic that she'd abandoned her father's flock of sheep. Her father finally took the matter seriously, and asked his daughter to tell him what had happened to make her come rushing home without the family's valuable flock.

Marguerite's Tale

Marguerite explained to her father how, on frequent occasions over the last few weeks, Grenier had told her a strange story of how he'd sold his soul to the devil in order to receive the power of a werewolf. He had also told her the same story he'd relayed to the other group of girls, that he'd killed dogs and eaten young girls. On one occasion, he told her in horrifying detail how he had killed a young girl and devoured every bit of her flesh because he was overcome by hunger.

On that particular day, however, Marguerite had led the sheep out to pasture as usual. This time, Grenier was nowhere to be seen. When she heard a commotion from some nearby bushes, she'd thought this was an attempt by Grenier to jump out and scare her. She made her way over to the bushes, planning to bring him out before he could cause any such mischief. Before she reached the bushes, however, she explained that a giant, hairy beast had pounced from the bush and knocked her down. It ripped at her clothing with its fangs and claws, and she showed her parents the tears in her clothes. Luckily, she had not lost her grip on her shepherd's staff.

Marguerite then fought for her life and succeeded in pushing the beast off of her. When it regained its footing and came at her a second time, she used the staff to beat at its head furiously until the beast suddenly retreated back. It then sat back on its haunches and, acting somewhat like a dog (though it is important to note that she never once said the beast *was* a dog), began to whine meekly. Marguerite said the creature had resembled a wolf in appearance, but was far more muscular and had a thicker neck and ribcage. Also, she reported that its head did not have as long a snout as a wolf's. Lastly, she explained that all of the beast's hair was red … and it was the same color of red, in fact, as Jean Grenier's.

Grenier's Confession

Soon, the local authorities decided they'd had just about enough with hearing complaints about Grenier's outlandish and brazen behavior. When the reports of the two preceding incidents reached the courts, they had Grenier taken into custody. They insisted that the boy explain his history, since nothing was known about who he was or where he'd come from. The story he told the court was quite different from the one he'd told others. This time, the court officials investigated every claim he made. As it turns out, they were able to confirm as true most (but not all) of the details from his official testimony.

Grenier testified to the court that, when he was 11 years old, he'd been taken into the forest by a close friend and introduced to a mysterious man with black skin. He claimed that the man's name had been Monsieur de la Forest. This strange gentleman, he explained, first signed his name into Grenier's palm with the tip of a nail. He then gave Grenier and his friend a magic salve and wolf-skin capes that allowed them to transform into werewolves.

The Curse

Once again, Grenier may have been having some fun with the courts by referring to the devilish figure by the name Monsieur de la Forest. This could be translated as either "Man of the Forest" or "Lord of the Forest." It is important to note that Grenier never once specifically refers to the man who gave him the wolf-skin cape as "the devil" or "Satan." He only alludes to the possibility that he'd made a pact with the devil, but never openly says so.

When questioned by the court about the detailed testimony of Marguerite Poirier, and about her claims that he'd attacked her in the form of the wolf, Grenier testified that she had been telling the truth. He admitted that he had attacked her in his werewolf form, but that she'd beaten him off with her staff (a detail that the court had not revealed to him). As for the rest of her testimony, he said there were some mistakes. He admitted that he had, as Marguerite claimed, once killed a white furred dog. Grenier denied, however, having drank its blood.

The court then questioned Grenier about the various reports that he'd openly admitted to others that he'd attacked, sometimes killed, and eaten the flesh of children. Grenier testified that he had certainly done so, but only on three specific occasions. He made an admission that he'd once come upon an empty house in a small village (but did not remember the name of it). He claimed to have snuck into the house in the form of a werewolf, and found an infant sleeping in a crib. He had snatched the child, dragged it away, and ate as much flesh as satisfied his hunger. He claimed to have given the remains to one of his normal wolf companions.

In the local area of Antoine de Pizon, Grenier testified, he had also attacked another little girl while she was tending her family's sheep herd. While he claimed that he did not know the girl's name, Grenier testified that she had been wearing a black frock. He explained that he had been so hungry on this particular occasion that, unlike the case of the infant, he had eaten most of the little girl's flesh to her bones.

Grenier then testified that he had attacked a third and final child only six weeks before, also in the region of Antoine de Pizon. He claimed to have come upon the child while crossing the parish's stone bridge. While he had taken a bite out of the child, he claimed that he'd been chased off by passersby who pelted him with rocks and beat at him with sticks.

Grenier had then traveled to the nearby village of Eparon, still in wolf form, where he attacked a hound on the estate of a Monsieur Millon. Before he could kill and devour the dog, however, he was again thwarted when Monsieur Millon emerged from the home and attacked the wolf/Grenier with his rapier (a thin but sharp sword used by nobles for dueling).

The court officials now inquired as to the nature and location of both the salve and wolf-skin cape that Grenier alleged to possess. Grenier explained that he kept them hidden in a large bush in a secret forest location, where he would also hide his clothes when in wolf form. He claimed that in order to make his transformation he would first cover his entire body with the salve before he donned the wolf-skin cape.

The Investigation Continues

When the court insisted to know where the wolf-skin cape was currently located, Grenier's testimony took a strange twist. He claimed that the wolf-skin cape was in the possession of his father, who had also sold his soul and often assisted him in his crimes. His father, he testified, was also a werewolf. In fact, he claimed that his stepmother had left his father after seeing him throw up the paws of a dog and fingers of a child that they'd killed and eaten.

As a result of Grenier's testimony, the court had Grenier's childhood friend, father, and stepmother taken into custody for questioning and examination. His parents both made testimonies that supported certain details of their son's claims. When Jean Grenier was brought into the room to again testify about his father's alleged role in the killings, he recanted his statements and said that he'd lied about that part. The court soon found Grenier's father and stepmother innocent of any wrongdoing (in their son's crimes, at least). However, further investigation proved that Grenier's other claims were mostly true.

Many of the details Grenier gave about his attacks on children were soon confirmed. Investigators tracked down and interviewed the parents of children who'd recently gone missing. Several reports coincided with the details of Grenier's testimony. For example, the detail of his report of attacking and eating a girl wearing a black frock was confirmed by her parents. She had last been seen leaving with the family's sheep flock, wearing a black frock.

One man who had rescued the child Grenier had attacked at the bridge was also located and came forward to testify about the event. The man turned out to have been the boy's uncle. Grenier had testified that one of the men had said "I'll have you presently." Without prompting, the uncle testified that he had shouted these exact same words when beating the wolf off of his nephew.

The court soon had all the evidence they needed to prove that Grenier had committed the crimes to which he'd already confessed. Normally, such a detailed confession would have been enough to convict a suspect in those times. However, his strange behavior led many to suspect that the boy was just a deranged liar. The only detail that the court was never able to confirm or dismiss was Grenier's claim that he could transform into a werewolf. The only evidence they had regarding this was the eyewitness testimony of Marguerite Poirier. Neither the magic salve nor the wolf-skin cape was ever found.

The Fate of Jean Grenier

A renowned French physician and scholar, the President of Assize, came before the court in order to testify about what he believed to be the true nature of Grenier's condition. In a long but well-presented speech, he addressed and proved false any claims that Jean Grenier was some dark agent of the devil or had become involved in witchcraft. He carefully demonstrated how this could be proven. He had examined the boy and showed how he had demonstrated an obvious lack of intelligence, maturity, and reasoning skills. Based on this, it was obvious that Grenier instead suffered from some form of mental derangement. He cited recent research supporting the idea that lycanthropy was nothing more than a delusional mental illness. He also asked that the court consider Grenier's young age, explaining that sending him to prison (at the time, teenage criminals were imprisoned right alongside adult criminals) would only serve to worsen his mental condition.

The court took the physician's testimony into account as they decided the fate of Jean Grenier. In the end, they concluded that prison was not the right place for the deranged boy. Instead, they sentenced Jean Grenier to a lifetime of imprisonment at the Bordeaux Monastery. The belief was that, at the monastery, Grenier would receive a proper education. He might also learn how to conduct himself appropriately in both social and spiritual matters. Additionally, and just in case Grenier really *was* an agent of the devil, the court probably figured that the righteous presence of the Bordeaux monks would be able to cleanse any such evil influences from his soul. There was, however, one strict condition to Grenier's lightened sentence—if he ever escaped, or even attempted to do so, then Grenier would immediately be removed from the monastery and publicly executed.

Grenier's arrival at the monastery was said to be rather disconcerting. Once he'd been released, he is written as having begun running around on his hands and feet, eyes wild. He ran from one end of the monastery to the other, howling loudly and growling like an animal. He soon came upon a pile of discarded, raw meat scraps and began to gobble down the bloody mess with enthusiastic voracity. He had completely eaten the entire pile in a matter of minutes.

Seven years into Grenier's sentence, investigators (both from the courts and medical community) came to the monastery to conduct a follow-up interview. The young man they found was little more than a shadow of his former, rebellious self. He spoke very little, and avoided making eye contact. Grenier's physical appearance had hardly improved. His eyes darted around wildly. His fingernails are said to have turned black, as if from bruising. Several of his blackened fingernails were also torn and broken, as if he had recently tried to claw his way through solid stone.

During the interview, Grenier was almost a vegetable. He rarely made verbal replies, and those he did make were short and/or incomprehensible. When presented with problems and questions that were designed to test him for any improvement in his intelligence, Grenier proved unable to provide answers for even the most simple of them.

Shortly after this follow-up interview, Jean Grenier died as a prisoner in Bordeaux Monastery. The cause of death remains unknown (though some speculate, based on his deteriorating intelligence, that he died from brain damage or some unidentified neurological disorder). At the time of his death, Jean Grenier was only 20 years old.

The Least You Need to Know

- The French word for werewolf is "loup-garou."

- The "Beast of Gevaudan" may have been some now-extinct species of giant wolf.

- While no one knows the true name of the monster dubbed the "Demon Tailor of Chalons," his crimes will live on in infamy.

- Sadly, Pierre Burgot may have been nothing more than the victim of a prank gone too far.

- Jacques Roulet, the convicted "Werewolf of Caude," was first sentenced to death but later deemed mentally ill and sent to an asylum.

- Jean Grenier was also deemed the victim of mental derangement, and was sentenced to life in a monastery.

Werewolf Chronicles

In This Chapter

- ◆ The Inquisition's dismemberment of the man known only as the "Werewolf of Padua"
- ◆ The she-wolf of Auvergne
- ◆ The wolf-girls of Orissa
- ◆ Vseslav Bryachislavich, the werewolf-sorcerer prince of Polotsk
- ◆ The modern case of Bill Ramsey

We have discussed the infamous werewolf trials, as well as the medieval church's resulting persecution of wolves and werewolves. We have also discussed the widespread werewolf obsession of medieval France. However, the story of werewolves in human history does not end with these. There still remain a multitude of historical accounts of lycanthropy that must be included in any comprehensive discussion of the subject. These are the werewolves who refused to fit into categories. These … are the werewolf chronicles.

The Werewolf of Padua

Job Fincel, in the second book of his manuscript *Wunderscheizen*, which roughly translates as "On Miracles," recorded the tale of one werewolf account in Italy. In 1541, in the Italian city of Padua (also spelled Padova), a nearby villager savagely attacked a large group of men when he came upon them in a rural field. The villager even succeeded in killing some of the men, using nothing more than his teeth and hands. After an extreme and violent struggle, the surviving members of the group managed to subdue him. They tied up the wild man and immediately dragged him to the local authorities of the Ecclesiastical Court of the Inquisition.

Upon questioning, the man insisted to the inquisitors that he was actually a wolf when he attacked. One of the inquisitors posed a question—if the man was indeed a wolf as he claimed, then where was his coat of fur? The man explained to the inquisitors that, unlike natural wolves, he wore his coat of fur in a concealed layer that was between his skin and his muscles.

The inquisitors decided that they would test the truth of his claim. If their test turned out to prove he was telling the truth, then he would be immediately executed as a werewolf. If he turned out to just be a madman, then they would set him free.

Unfortunately for the accused man, the inquisitors' so-called "test" was to chop off all of his arms and legs and then inspect the areas beneath his skin for any signs of fur. The man was tied down and dismembered. The inquisitors found no signs of the fur he had claimed to possess. As the man lay bleeding on the table (but still alive, apparently), the head inquisitor informed him that he had been found innocent of lycanthropy and would therefore be referred to their surgeons and released. The man, despite the surgeons' best efforts, died from blood loss only a few moments later.

She-Wolf of Auvergne

Auvergne is located just west of the city of Clermont-Ferrand, France. The account of the she-wolf of Auvergne rides the line between history and folklore, which is why it is included here instead of in Chapter 8.

Certain medieval sources do cite evidence for the story having been verified. However, such sources are not always entirely reliable. Once again, the choice of whether or not to believe the tale is left to you.

The story is believed to have been first told sometime around 1588. It says that, in the wooded regions of Auvergne, a large and savage she-wolf had for some time been making human prey out of the local hunters and woodsmen. One day, a local nobleman was inspecting his property when he came across a huntsman who was just about to embark into the woods. The nobleman admired the hunter's bravery, having heard the stories about the man-eating she-wolf that roamed those woods. The hunter explained that he was planning to hunt the she-wolf, as he'd heard that a bounty of 125 francs had been issued on the heads of all she-wolves in the region (likely in the hopes that one of them would be the man-eater).

Having become concerned for the safety of his wife, crops, and livestock (though not necessarily in that order), the nobleman asked the hunter if, after he'd finished the hunt, he would report back to him what, if anything, he had encountered. The hunter agreed to do so and continued to trek into the forest.

Later on, as the hunter stalked for game in the woods, he stumbled onto a giant she-wolf. The beast lunged at the hunter, not giving him time to release so much as an arrow. The man reached to his side and drew his knife. The man and beast struggled for their lives. Seizing hold of one of the beast's immense claws, the hunter stabbed and slashed at the attaching joint and succeeded in severing the appendage. The she-wolf, terribly wounded, fled into the woods and disappeared. The hunter tucked the severed paw away into his game pouch and made his way back to the nobleman's estate.

When the hunter arrived at the estate, he conveyed to the nobleman the story of his life-and-death struggle with the wolf. The nobleman asked if he might be allowed to see the giant claw that the hunter had kept as proof. The hunter reached into his pouch and removed ... a woman's left hand. For a moment, both men were dumbfounded by the sight. How, or even why, would the she-wolf's claw be transformed into the hand of a woman?

The hunter noticed something gleaming from beneath the blood and wiped one finger clean to reveal a shining gold ring with a number of encrusted jewels. The nobleman's eyes went wide. He had seen that ring before on his own wife's finger. This was her wedding ring. Doing his best to hide his reaction, he thanked the hunter for his time and sent the man away. Then he went through the estate, looking for his wife.

The nobleman found his beloved wife in the kitchen. She was wrapping a towel around what appeared to be an injury to her hand. He commanded her to remove the towel and show him what had happened. When she did not comply, he took it off himself. He was aghast to find that her entire left hand had been severed. Having seen the evidence, he interrogated her as to what she had done. His wife soon confessed that she was the same she-wolf that had been terrorizing the woods.

The nobleman immediately turned his wife over to the court authorities. She was tried and condemned shortly thereafter. Her sentence was execution by fire, which was carried out immediately.

The Orissa Wolf Children

This is another tale that rides the line between history and folklore. While it is certain that the accounts of this story are for the most part true, some of the details may have at some point been falsified. In recent years, some claims made by certain sources regarding this case have been proven false.

According to accounts, in the year 1920, two girls were discovered living in the woods near Godamuri, India. What was most astonishing, these accounts claim, is that it was found they were being cared for by a she-wolf. A hunter claimed to have rescued the girls from the animal, and they were soon brought to an orphanage in nearby Orissa (from which their nickname comes).

The oldest girl was thought to be eight years old and was given the name Kamala. The younger sister, thought to be around one-and-a-half years old, was given the name Amala. Accounts claim that the girls behaved like wild animals, preferring to walk around on all fours. In addition, they seemed to have developed nocturnal habits, sleeping during the days, waking around dusk, and becoming *very* active through the nighttime hours (much to the exhaustion of their caregivers).

The Savage Truth

Stories of wild children who were allegedly raised by wolves have sprung up multiple times in history. However, nearly all have been found to be cases of runaway or abandoned children who were neglected and/or abused to the point that they were not properly social-ized. This is what gives them the appearance of having animal behavior. To this day, not a single claim of children being nursed, raised, or even protected by predatory wild animals has ever been proven to be true. Is it impossible? No. But nearly all animal behavior experts agree that such a thing remains highly unlikely.

The accounts of the incident also claim that the girls preferred to eat little else but raw meat. At least one report claims that the girls could smell it from a distance and could use this ability to track it down. The girls were also said to have the eyesight and hearing of wolves and were faster, stronger, and more agile than the other children in the orphanage, many of whom they would often growl at when approached. If challenged, the girls were quick to use violent attacks. They were even said to have fought like animals, using only their teeth (fangs) and fingernails (claws).

Amala, the younger of the two girls, died after only a year inside the orphanage. (The cause of death often differs from one source to another.) She had never learned to speak so much as a word of lan-guage. Kamala, on the other hand, lived until the age of 17, when she died of an unspecified illness. Unlike her little sister, Kamala eventually learned to speak at least a handful of key phrases. For the most part, however, she continued to behave as she always had and, without her sister, lived a very solitary life until her death.

Prince Vseslav of Poland

Despite having a good amount of rather weird lore surrounding the details of his life, Prince Vseslav Bryachislavich of Polotsk doesn't appear to have been all that bad of a guy. He had a plethora of names, which included Vseslav of Polotsk, Vseslav the Seer, Vseslav the Sage, and Vseslav the Sorcerer. No matter what name you call him, this guy remains one of the most colorful (and perhaps most memorable) rulers in the land now called Belarus. Today, the country of Belarus is located on the southern borders of Lithuania/Lativa and the northern border of the Ukraine.

The weirdness surrounding Prince Vseslav seems to have originated on the day of his birth, which is believed to have been sometime between 1031 and 1039 C.E. (A number of sources vary on this detail.) Apparently, the word somehow got out that little baby Vseslav had emerged from his mother's womb with a *caul* (which simply means a part of the placenta membrane) wrapped around his noggin. At first glance, this would not seem like a big deal to most of us today. However, according to the longstanding local folklore of that time, such a birth was seen as irrefutable evidence that the child had been conceived through some enchantment or other form of sorcery. Many also believed that such a child would grow up to bear the Mark of the Beast, believed at the time to be a sign of a werewolf.

Beastly Words

A caul is a soft membrane that covers and protects the heads of embryos that are high vertebrates (such as primates and humans). This membrane is usually shed during delivery, slowly rubbed off and torn away as the infant travels down the tight birth canal. Many ancient and medieval cultures assigned certain omens (good and bad) to babies that were born with the caul still wrapped over their heads.

The sorcerers who were in the service of Prince Bryachislav Izyaslavich (Vseslav's father) at the time, however, insisted the caul was actually a positive omen, one that meant the boy's life was going to be blessed with good fortune. Apparently, Prince Izyaslavich liked their theory better and dismissed any talk that his son was born from any method of sorcery.

Bark vs. Bite

When one thinks about the situation, it is not a surprise that the sorcerers serving Vseslav's father did not want him to believe that his son's caul meant he was conceived by sorcery. Aside from the fact that this might have led him to suspect them of being involved, it could have potentially caused the ruler to believe that one of his sorcerers had coveted his princess ... which, you might imagine, could have cost all of them their lives.

When the reigning prince died in 1044, the young/possibly teenaged (depending on when he was actually born) Vseslav had to take the throne in order to secure his family's hold on the region of Polotsk. It would appear that many of those who had served Prince Bryachislav remained loyal to the throne and now devoted themselves to the service of their late lord's son. Despite being fairly young upon assuming his title of lordship, Vseslav grew up educated and proved to be a fairly competent ruler. He later commissioned the construction of a grand cathedral, dubbed the Cathedral of Holy Wisdom, which was finished in 1066. The structure stands in Polotsk to this very day, seen by many historians as a monument to Vseslav's reign, which would last until 1101 C.E.

The Savage Truth

His construction of the Cathedral of Holy Wisdom appears to have made Prince Vseslav a very popular figure, even to some of his neighboring rulers. Though it would only last for roughly a year, Vseslav was even given the title of "Grand Prince" over the neighboring Ukrainian region of Kiev.

Despite being a good ruler, the rumors surrounding Vseslav's involvement with sorcery seem never to have subsided among the people or his rivals. To the people of Polotsk, however, his rumored knowledge of sorcery doesn't seem to have been that big an issue (probably because he was a fair and just ruler). Many of the neighboring Russian rulers, on the other hand, often tried to use it against him. Some feared him because of it, while others just considered such practices blasphemy.

The werewolf association with Vseslav reached a peak when he became father to his seventh and final son. (As you might remember, many cultures considered seventh sons to be werewolves.) Were he not a sorcerer and a werewolf, many of his rivals argued, then why would he allow himself to conceive no more or less than seven sons? Of course, these rivals often failed to mention that he also had a daughter somewhere in there. This detail would have meant Vseslav's last son was actually his eighth child (which meant he had not chosen to have only seven).

No matter what rumors were spread about Prince Vseslav of Polotsk, they appear to have been impotent in shaking him. Many of his descendents would perform great works for the empire. For her compassion and service to the church, one of Vseslav's granddaughters would even be deemed the patron saint of Polotsk.

The Reformed Werewolf of Southend

The official police case regarding Bill Ramsey began on July 22, 1987, though his experiences with werewolflike behavior are thought to have begun long before this initial incident. Ramsey had for many years worked as a carpenter in the Southend area of London, England. It is important to note that, before this incident, the 40-something Ramsey was considered a respectable member of his community, with no history of violence or even a criminal record to speak of. But on one eventful July evening, something wild was unleashed from inside Bill Ramsey.

That evening, Ramsey presented himself to the Southend police station. Once there, he encountered some officers in the parking lot. When they asked Ramsey why he was there, he told them he could not remember but that he thought he really needed to be locked up. While speaking to the officers, who at first thought the man was just having a laugh, Ramsey suddenly went on a rampage.

First Ramsey began to growl and bare his teeth at the officers. Then he attacked. According to reports, the nearly middle-aged man lifted one officer (who was said to have been much larger than Ramsey) over his head and tossed him to the tarmac. The officer received serious injuries as a result. Soon other officers saw the commotion and came to assist in subduing the snarling man. When all was said and done, it took about six officers to hold Ramsey down and restrain him in both wrist and leg irons.

The officers dragged Ramsey into a holding cell, which did little to calm him down. Reports claim that he began trying to shove himself through the cell's dinner tray slot. He managed to succeed in getting one arm and his head through the slot before becoming trapped. Not phased a bit by this, Ramsey continued to snarl and growl and would claw and bite at anyone who tried to come near.

The officers, fearing that Ramsey would further harm himself if left stuck in the tray slot as he was, decided to call in the local fire department to find a way to free him. One look at the enraged Ramsey, however, and the firemen refused to go anywhere near him. A local doctor was then called to sedate Ramsey with drugs. It took another group of policemen to hold the wild man's arm still long enough for the doctor to inject the sedative. The reports indicate that it took more than triple the average dose for the sedative to have an effect on him.

The following day, when Ramsey recovered from the sedative, he claimed to have no memory of the event. He was referred to a mental health facility for evaluation. At first the doctors diagnosed the man with clinical lycanthropy (see Chapter 18) and placed him on a treatment of antipsychotic drugs. However, unlike in other cases of the condition, the drugs seemed to have no effect on Ramsey's bouts of wolflike behavior.

Some years later, news of Bill Ramsey's case came to the attention of the demonology/paranormal research team of Ed Warren and wife/partner Lorraine Warren. The Warrens had made a name for themselves with their involvement in the well-known 1977 haunting case referred to as the "Amityville Horror." The pair traveled to London and, after a few dead ends and being laughed out of a few police stations, managed to track down the Southend detective in charge of the initial case, who arranged for them to meet with Bill Ramsey. The detective himself was convinced that, whatever was wrong with the man, it was something beyond the scope of the many doctors who'd attempted to treat him. Ever since, when Ramsey would come to the police station on occasion, the officers would immediately lock him up in a confinement cell. Some of the residents had come to call Ramsey (much to the man's humiliation) the "Werewolf of Southend" or the "Werewolf of London." The detective hoped that perhaps the Warrens could do something.

The Warrens conducted an initial interview with Ramsey, who informed them that he'd had bouts of wolf behavior since his childhood but until recently had not feared that he might try to harm anyone.

Ramsey conveyed to the Warrens the tale of a childhood experience that he believed was the origin of his condition, and which he'd tried to keep a secret for most of his life. Ramsey told the Warrens that one Saturday afternoon when he was 10 years old he was playing in his backyard after helping his mother with chores. Earlier that day, his parents had taken him to see a movie about fighter pilots in World War II. Still electrified by the film, he ran around the backyard and imagined that he was a fighter pilot.

Suddenly, the young Ramsey was struck by a surge of cold all over his body. However, the day had been warm and the sun had not yet gone down. His skin felt frozen, he felt immobilized, and his every muscle shook in fear. He then smelled a strange and terrible odor, and felt as if he might throw up. Suddenly, the mysterious stench and cold sensation faded. The boy had no idea what had just happened, but Ramsey reported that he never felt the same again. He said that this experience was the last time in his life that he would feel like a little boy. He couldn't even play make believe anymore, which had long been his favorite playtime activity.

As days passed, Ramsey reported that his mind was frequently bombarded with images and thoughts about him becoming a wolf. One day, as he tried to play in the backyard, his mind was saturated by such thoughts and images. When his mother called the boy to come inside for the night, Ramsey suddenly felt overcome by a severe and uncontrollable rage. He turned at his mother and growled. He reached for a nearby fencepost and tore it right out of the ground. His mother was terrified and screamed for her husband. Ramsey's father came out and saw his enraged son swinging the enormous fencepost and howling loudly.

As his father tried to talk some sense into Bill, the boy yanked a string of metal fencing wire into his mouth and bit down on it. He launched away the heavy post and crouched, still chewing on the wire. To his parents' horror, he even managed to rip the strong wire with his teeth. Bill's father tried to get the boy to his feet, but found that his son's physical strength was now incredibly greater than his own. He later tried to pull a fencepost as his son had, and could not. He eventually discovered that what his little boy had done with such apparent ease was actually extremely difficult, even when he had two other grown men helping him.

Bill's mother began to cry, and he said that this was what brought him out of his fit. Hearing her sobs made him realize the pain and fear he was causing. The young boy felt the rage fade from him, and ran to his frightened parents for comfort. For a moment, they barred the door. Realizing that their boy had now returned to normal, however, they let him inside. The three of them cried and embraced each other. They never again spoke of the incident.

In the years that followed, Ramsey did his best to control the beastly urges that tried to overtake him. For decades, he had succeeded. However, by the time of his incident at the Southend police station, Bill felt that he was beginning to lose the battle.

After their interview, the Warrens came to the conclusion that Bill Ramsey suffered not from clinical lycanthropy or any other mental disorder, but from a form of demonic possession by some kind of malevolent wolf-spirit. They arranged for an exorcism to be conducted on Bill Ramsey, with the assistance of a local bishop.

Regardless of what the truth of Ramsey's condition was, one cannot argue with results of the Warrens' exorcism. After the ceremony was performed, Bill Ramsey ceased to experience any further bouts of this uncontrollable werewolf behavior. Most of his fellow inhabitants from Southend have even learned to let bygones be bygones, and few refer to him as a werewolf any longer. In fact, it would seem that most of his neighbors, while cautious of him, felt sympathy for this man. Aside from his bouts of werewolf behavior, all accounts of Bill Ramsey have portrayed him as a kind and generous man.

Why Are Werewolves in History?

When one compares werewolves to any other monster in human folklore, it is interesting to note that there are far more *historically* documented encounters with werewolves than with any other mythical creature. While this book offers but a sampling of these historical accounts, dozens more exist. Some sources claim that, if one were to tally up every single historical mention of werewolves, the total amount would well exceed 200 incidents. Why is this so? Why do historically documented encounters not occur with such frequency when it comes to similar beings such as vampires or zombies?

There could be any number of possible answers to this mystery. Some have argued that werewolves were for a long time used as scapegoats, for one of two reasons. In some cases, when killings were being committed by a wild animal and the animal could not be caught, it is possible that authorities would use the werewolf legend to fabricate charges against various "undesirables." In some cases, it is undoubtedly true that the belief in the werewolf legend was used to account for how a human being was capable of committing the most inhuman of crimes. Basically, when it was impossible for the people to fathom how any person could be so diabolical, it became easier to believe that the person was a werewolf.

So … which answer is right? They all could be right answers. Then again, maybe many of these accounts of werewolf encounters actually are real. They could all be wrong answers as well. The rebellious werewolf, even in this case, seems to refuse both categorization and classification. As usual, werewolf lore seems to insist that we decide on the truth for ourselves.

The Least You Need to Know

- The "Werewolf of Padua," after insisting he had wolf fur between his skin and muscles, was dismembered by inquisitors to decide his guilt.

- Though many sources from the time claim the she-wolf of Auvergne actually existed, modern historians view it as a folktale.

- While Prince Vseslav of Polotsk was often called a sorcerer and werewolf by some of his rivals, it would seem that his wisdom as a ruler outweighed such accusations.

- The case of Bill Ramsey is thought of by some as an occurrence of clinical lycanthropy, while others deem it a case of demonic possession.

Part 3

The Modern Werewolf

Werewolves are no longer depicted in an exclusively negative or evil light. In fact, modern pop culture has embraced the werewolf as a rebellious antihero. Similar to modern-day motorcycle gangs, they move and hunt and live and die as a pack, and they live outside society's rules. Pack law is the only law. In the last century, werewolves have been embraced by every medium of pop culture. They've become major figures in literature, films, art, comic books, and even video games. In America, urban legends about werewolves have sprung up with increasing frequency over the last 50 years.

Chapter 10

Werewolves in Literature

In This Chapter

- ◆ Marie de France's *Bisclavret* and its relationship with Arthurian legends
- ◆ The devilish story of *Wagner the Werewolf*
- ◆ Rudyard Kipling's short story *The Mark of the Beast*
- ◆ Guy Endore's *Werewolf of Paris*
- ◆ The werewolf stories of legendary author Jack Williamson
- ◆ The "new-school" werewolves of Stephenie Meyer's *Twilight* series
- ◆ Remus Lupin from J. K. Rowling's popular *Harry Potter* series

Unlike the history of lycanthropy, the medium of literature has grown increasingly kinder in its treatment of werewolves over the last thousand years. The role of werewolves in literature has evolved to include a diverse cast of potential character types. Some are tragic fools, while others are rather admirable antiheroes. From the twelfth century to now, what follows is a collection of primary works that makes up the canon of werewolf literature.

Marie de France's *Bisclavret*

Written in the twelfth century by Marie de France as one volume in a series of twelve *lais*, *Bisclavret* was the first published werewolf story to be written by a female author. Marie's story is full of the romantic elements of unjust misfortune, forbidden love affairs, and marital betrayal. This same plot, however, can also be found in other stories, including one Arthurian legend from the period as well (see Chapter 3).

Beastly Words

Lais (spelled *lays* in English) were once a very common form of romance poetry, used especially in medieval England and France. One relatively well known lai is "The Franklin's Tale," from Geoffrey Chaucer's fourteenth-century work *The Canterbury Tales*.

The title of the story comes from the name of its main character, Bisclavret, who was a British baron. Ever since his marriage, Bisclavret's wife noticed that her new husband disappeared every week for a span of exactly three days. Believing that he was having an affair or was up to some other type of foul mischief, she demanded that he tell her the truth about his weekly three-day excursions. After much begging, and under threat of scandal, he agreed to reveal his secret. His answer, however, was far more unusual than anything she had imagined.

The Curse

It is not uncommon for characters in medieval texts, especially knights going on religious quests, to travel or perform some special action (such as a battle) over three-day periods/intervals. This is usually a metaphorical reference to the three days between Christ's crucifixion/death and resurrection in the Christian New Testament.

Bisclavret revealed to his wife that he was a werewolf, though only by power of a special enchantment. He went on to tell her that when he entered wolf form he concealed his clothing in a secure hiding spot because, without it, he could not return to human form. She asked him where such a hiding spot could be, and (for whatever insane reason) he told her that he hid his clothes in a large hollowed out boulder. The wife, out of either malice or disbelief, formulated a plot of betrayal.

The next time Bisclavret went off on one of his wolf excursions, his wife approached one of her husband's knights. She had long known that this particular knight was in love with her and used this to her advantage. She convinced the lovesick knight to retrieve her husband's clothing from the hollow stone. He went out to find the rock and soon returned with his lord's clothes. Three days came and went, followed by several more, and Bisclavret did not return to his estate.

Well aware of his regular excursions into the woods, everyone in the castle assumed that Bisclavret had fallen into the jaws of some beast. No one suspected his wife of any foul play, even when she quickly remarried the knight who helped her. Meanwhile, Bisclavret remained in the woods, unable to return to his estate because he was now trapped in his wolf form.

One year after Bisclavret's disappearance, the king that he once served as a baron was in the woods hunting with his hounds. They soon encountered Bisclavret in his wolf form, and the hounds began to pursue him. Recognizing the hunter as his liege, Bisclavret rushed to the king's stirrup/foot and began to show signs of canine affection, licking his leg. The king was so astounded by this that he had his hounds restrained by his squires. He came down from his horse and petted Bisclavret. All who were present stood awestruck by the gentle nature of this wolf. The king decided to bring Bisclavret to stay with him in his castle. For some weeks, Bisclavret resided with the king and proved to be an obedient and gentle creature.

One day, however, the knight who married Bisclavret's deceitful wife came to visit the king. Knowing full well what this man had done, Bisclavret attacked the knight. Bisclavret was subdued, and the knight concluded his business and returned home. The wise king, having not once seen Bisclavret show so much of a hint of aggression, came to the conclusion that this knight had committed some transgression against the animal. He decided to learn the truth of this matter and soon went to visit the knight at Bisclavret's former estate … and he decided to bring the wolf and his most wise of advisors with him.

While at the estate, the knight had his servants escort the king and wolf into the sitting chamber. Not wanting to be attacked again, he sent his wife in to greet them. When Bisclavret saw the face of the woman who betrayed him so terribly, he went into a rage and attacked her. Before anyone could intervene, Bisclavret ripped her nose right off of her face.

The Curse

There are some who claim that Marie de France took the plot of *Bisclavret* from a similar story in Arthurian legend. On the other hand, there are some who claim that later writers of these Arthurian stories stole the plot from Marie de France and inserted it into the mix. The truth of where this story originated is still debated. In all honesty, it probably began as a folk legend, which means it belongs to humanity and cannot be credited to any single writer.

The king's advisor, well familiar with the always gentle nature of the wolf, pointed out that the animal had never attacked anyone. He then went on to point out that this woman was once the wife of Bisclavret, who had vanished one year before. The king considered this and decided to "question" the wife (which means he has her tortured). Almost immediately, the woman admitted to her crimes. She confessed to the plot and to convincing the knight to help her and revealed where she had been hiding the clothing Bisclavret needed to return to human form.

The king retrieved the clothing and brought it before the wolf, who turned away from it. The king was puzzled until his wise advisor suggested that they take the clothes and wolf into his chambers so he could change in privacy. The king gave this a try, and a few moments later, the newly restored Baron Bisclavret emerged from the room.

The king returned to Bisclavret all that had been taken from him. The knight and Bisclavret's now noseless ex-wife were permanently exiled from the land under the penalty of death. According to the story, the female descendants of Bisclavret's ex-wife were from that day on born without noses.

Wagner the Werewolf (1847)

George W. M. Reynolds's *Wagner the Werewolf* (originally published with the spelling *Wagner the Wehr-wolf*) was published in 1847 as a *penny dreadful*. The story was one of the first English stories to offer a depiction of the fictional werewolf figure. It is a story of one man's tragic struggle to redeem the lost glory of his wasted youth.

Beastly Words

The **penny dreadful** was a popular nineteenth century form of fiction known for its lurid and sensational content. The name comes from the fact that these were cheap (usually costing only a penny), relatively short, paperback-bound stories that usually involved "dreadful" plots of crime, murder, and a fair amount of sexual content. As one might imagine, these books were primarily sold to the younger male members of England's vast working class. George W. M. Reynolds is often referred to as "Master of the Penny Dreadful."

The main character of the story is Fernand Wagner, who found himself alone in the latter years of his life. He was soon approached by a dark figure by the name of John Faust, who made Wagner an offer he couldn't refuse. If Wagner would serve him during what should be the final year of Faust's life, then he would reward Wagner with youth, power, riches, and beauty. There was, however, a far more terrible price for these rewards than just his year of servitude to Faust. Wagner would also have to endure the life of a werewolf for the rest of his days. On the day that marked the end of Wagner's year of servitude, Faust died and left everything promised to Wagner. However, you know what they say … be careful what you wish for … you just might get it.

The Curse

The name of John Faust comes from a well-known figure of fiction and theater named Faust. Faust was a sorcerer who spent his life pursuing the study and practice of the mystical arts. Wishing to benefit from this, he eventually succeeded in summoning a demon by the name of Mephistopheles, who offered to fulfill all of Faust's desires in exchange for the man's soul. Faust agreed, but his rewards never lived up to his expectations. The name of John Faust in *Wagner the Werewolf* suggests a similar fate will befall Fernand Wagner.

Wagner soon fell in love with a cold yet beautiful woman named Nisida, who came from a familial lineage that carried with it some (originally unspecified) dark and mysterious secret. Nisida and Wagner both lived in constant fear of being discovered, which formed a strong bond between them. They knew they couldn't remain in the Italian city of Florence for long. The pair planned to book passage to an island in the Mediterranean, where both of them could live out their lives with their secrets intact. However, Wagner's life was soon plagued by misfortune. Only days before Wagner would again transform into a werewolf, he was arrested and taken into the custody of Inquisition authorities. Nisida, out of fear that her lover was now lost to the gallows, left without him on a ship out of Florence.

Wagner learned that he was standing trial under the suspicion of being Faust's murderer, and some of the judges even thought him to be a werewolf. The court found him guilty and tossed him into the Florence prison called *Palazzo del Podesto*. The lead judge, wanting to put an end to all talk of him being a werewolf, scheduled Wagner's execution for the very night that he was to transform. As he was rolled before the gallows in a wagon-cell, however, Wagner transformed and broke out, shattering his iron and wood cage to pieces. Now free and under the savage influence of his wolf form, he went on a bloody nocturnal rampage through the city.

Wagner managed to get onto a ship out of the city and began searching for the vessel that Nisida left on in the hopes of finding her. In his travels, he encountered some members of the mystic *Rosicrucian Order*. They explained to Wagner that only death could release him from his werewolf curse, but that (since werewolves are immortal and invulnerable) death would only come for him if he saw the bleached skeletons of two innocents that were hung from the same beam. He eventually reunited with Nisida.

> **Beastly Words**
>
> The **Rosicrucian Order** was a seventeenth century group of scholars, philosophers, and aesthetics who studied and collectively shared knowledge related to the secret arts of mysticism, metaphysics, and alchemy.

Later, Wagner and Nisida were forced to journey to the land of her family when Ottoman soldiers took them prisoner. There they were brought to the house of Nisida's brother, Francisco, where they were released. Francisco had sent the soldiers to retrieve Nisida so as to ensure that his sister would be present for his wedding (to a woman Nisida hated). Family law required that all siblings be present on that day so that a certain manuscript could be removed from its secret chamber and read aloud in order to reveal to all present the truth of that family's dark secret.

When they all entered the secret chamber, however, on the wall were two bleached skeletons hung from the same beam. Apparently, the bones once belonged to innocents because Wagner immediately recoiled and fell to the floor in convulsions. His darling Nisida rushed to him, and moments later he died in her arms.

The Mark of the Beast (1890)

Most people are more familiar with Rudyard Kipling from his 1894 work *The Jungle Book*, which was set in the jungles of India. Previously, however, Kipling published another story that was also set in India but involved one man's curse of lycanthropy. Kipling titled the story *The Mark of the Beast*, and it was first published in a periodical called *The Pioneer* in July 1890. At the same time, it also received publication in *The New York Journal*.

The Mark of the Beast tells the story of a westerner named Fleete Strickland, who came to India with a high level of ignorance regarding the customs, dialects, and people. Shortly after arriving, Fleete celebrated New Year's Eve at a nearby western-styled nightspot called "The Club" and had a few too many drinks. As Fleete stumbled home in a drunken stupor, he came across a shrine to the revered Hindu Monkey God, Hanuman. Seeing that his cigar has burned down too far, he extinguished it on the Hanuman's statue. A nearby Hindu holy man, who was also a leper, witnessed Fleete's act of shrine desecration and lunged at him. During the struggle, the enraged holy man bit Fleete on the chest. Fleete broke free and began to run home. As the westerner disappeared down the road, another priest arrived and commented that Hanuman had not yet even begun to punish him for what he'd done.

Soon enough, Fleete started to feel the effects of the holy man's curse. He was overcome by strange and powerful urges. He had an uncontrollable craving for raw meat. At times, he found himself walking in his garden on all fours and howling into the night sky. When Fleete sought out a medical diagnosis, the doctor told him that he was suffering from rabies. Fleete, however, believed that he had been cursed.

Fleete and another man eventually tracked down the leprous Hindu sage who initially gave him the bite that was causing Fleete's strange behavior. They then tortured the ailing holy man until he agreed to remove Fleete's lycanthropic curse, the "Mark of the Beast." The holy man lifted the curse, and Fleete was able to return to his normal human self.

The Savage Truth

The "Mark of the Beast" that Kipling refers to in this story's title is not a part of the Hindu mythology of India. In fact, the concept comes from western lore. It would appear that, in this story, Kipling attempted to fuse western werewolf lore with an eastern setting.

The Werewolf of Paris (1933)

The Werewolf of Paris was written by New York author Samuel Guy Endore (also known as Guy Endore) and was published in 1933. The story was inspired when Endore learned of the details surrounding the case of Francois Bertrand, a corpse-obsessed maniac who was dubbed by some as the "Werewolf of Paris."

The Werewolf of Paris tells the story of Bertrand Caillet, who was born on the most auspicious day of Christmas Eve. His mother was a servant girl who was raped by a rogue priest. As a result of the scandal surrounding the child's conception, his mother brought him to the home of his step-uncle, Aymar Gaillez, in order to raise him.

From a very young age, Bertrand experienced unusual desires. These desires, many of which were somewhat sexually sadistic, remained only in his dreams for much of his life. However, Bertrand later discovered that many of these disturbing nocturnal visions were not dreams at all but memories of his experiences as a werewolf.

Soon enough, his uncle Aymar discovered that Bertrand was a werewolf. After Bertrand committed a number of crimes—attacking a prostitute, murdering a local villager, and raping his own mother—he had no choice but to leave the village. Bertrand went to start a new life in Paris, where again he resumed his savagely sadistic crimes of rape and murder.

Uncle Aymar, however, went to Paris, attempting to track down his werewolf nephew. He began to look into the details of the most heinous violent crimes in Paris and by doing so determined that Bertrand was responsible for a great many of them. While in Paris, Bertrand had raped and killed prostitutes, murdered a number of other people, and desecrated freshly buried corpses.

Bertrand soon realized that he must earn a living somehow and so joined the Parisian Guard to serve in the Franco-Prussian War. However, he did very little time in actual combat. One day, Bertrand fell head over heels in love with a local barmaid named Sophie. He truly cared for the girl and did not wish to harm her. Sophie tried to suppress her lover's werewolf transformations by cutting open her own flesh so that Bertrand could suck out some of her blood. For a brief time, this satiated Bertrand's werewolf tendencies. However, with each occurrence, Bertrand became more aware that Sophie's blood would not do the trick forever. Of course, Uncle Aymar was still on the trail of Bertrand and soon located him. However, when Aymar saw how Bertrand was so gentle with Sophie, he decided not to kill his nephew. At first glance, Aymar was convinced that his nephew's lycanthropy had somehow been cured by the power of his love for Sophie.

Bertrand felt the change coming upon him once more and knew that Sophie's blood would not stop it this time. Not wanting to bring any harm to his beloved Sophie, Bertrand ran out into the city and assumed his werewolf state. He soon found a worthy enough victim, whom he immediately attacked with the intent of devouring the man. This time, however, Bertrand was caught in the act (and in the state of transform-ing into wolf form) and was thrown in jail. Uncle Aymar heard of this and cursed himself a fool for believing that Bertrand had changed.

Aymar went to the court and implored the judges to burn his nephew at the stake and bring an end to his foul curse. The courts, however, did not believe that Bertrand was a werewolf. They decided that Bertrand must suffer from a type of madness and therefore sentenced him to treatment in an insane asylum.

In the asylum, Bertrand was kept constantly sedated. He was kept in a cell that was so cramped that he couldn't stand or stretch in it. One day, Bertrand saw an opportunity to flee and got loose from his cell. Not knowing where to run, and being disoriented form the drugs, he ended up on the roof of the building gripping the wrist of a girl he thought was Sophie. Bertrand rushed over the edge of the roof, dragging the poor girl with him. Both were killed. Unbeknownst to Bertrand, months before Sophie had been overwhelmed by her heartache from losing her beloved. He killed himself without knowing that the real Sophie had already taken her own life.

The Werewolf Stories of Jack Williamson

Today, Jack Williamson is considered one of the greatest *pulp fiction* writers of all time. He published a multitude of short stories in such classic pulp magazines as *Weird Tales, Astounding Stories, Thrilling Mystery,* and *Amazing Stories.* The stories about him almost read like folklore themselves. It is said that Williamson primarily educated himself, using nothing but his local public library.

Williamson was one of the most prolific story writers of his time. Out of his plethora of work, however, a dozen have been preserved as his greatest masterpieces. At least two of the most renowned of Williamson's stories consist of werewolf themes—*Wolves of Darkness* (published in 1936) and *Darker Than You Think* (published in 1938). While the academic world has never acknowledged the value of Williamson's stories, it cannot be denied that they were among the best-selling and most widely read works in the year of their publication.

Beastly Words

The term **pulp fiction** refers to inexpensive magazines or novels written for a mass market audience. Such works often contained violent or sexual material. The moods of such stories were generally melodramatic in dialogue and sensational in tone.

Williamson's *Wolves of Darkness*

Wolves of Darkness is the story of a man named Clovis McLaurin, who received an urgent and odd letter from his father. Clovis's father was a scientist named Dr. Ford McLaurin, and in the letter he begged his son to return to the family ranch as soon as possible, as strange things were afoot. Despite it being the middle of winter, Clovis made the harsh journey to his father's ranch estate.

When Clovis arrived at the nearby town, he discovered that the people had long been under siege by a pack of man-eating wolves. Their situation was growing increasingly desperate. For some months, he learned, not a single day had passed without someone being killed by the murderous beasts. Knowing the nature of his father's experiments, Clovis knew that he needed to hurry home.

Clovis continued on to his father's ranch and on the way was attacked by a group of wolves. He managed to escape, but from the attack he discovered a terrible truth. Running with the wolf pack was a young woman whom Clovis recognized as Stella Jetton, the daughter of his father's lab assistant. He saw her running through the icy snow alongside the wolves, wearing nothing more than a skimpy silk slip. Her mouth was stained with the blood of their kills. Even though he escaped the attack, the experience jarred him considerably. Long ago, Clovis had been deeply in love with Stella.

When he reached the ranch, Clovis learned that his father's experiments had unlocked the secrets behind the unimaginable powers of wolves. Stella, he discovered, was no longer the girl he once loved. Her eyes were those of a wolf. If Clovis wished to save Stella from her fate, he would have no choice but to confront the frightening power that she now wielded. In the end, he found a way to reverse the process and rescue the girl he loved.

It's *Darker Than You Think*

The opening pages of Williamson's novel, *Darker Than You Think*, offer the reader an announcement from a fictional ethnological expedition to Mongolia. The announcement claims that human beings have recently been discovered who possess the ability to shapeshift into animals. The reader then joins the expedition, whose leader has recently been killed.

One member of the expedition was Will Barbee, a journalist and friend of the dead expedition leader. He suspected foul play and believed that another anthropologist on the expedition, the beautiful and intelligent April Bell, was responsible for his friend's death.

As Barbee continued on the expedition, still suspicious of April, the two discovered a terrifying lost truth. Barbee uncovered ancient artifacts that told of an ancient war between humans and werewolves. In the end, humans had won the war. The few werewolves that survived learned to live in secret among their human enemies. However, they did not plan to stay that way.

The artifacts also told of a werewolf prophecy of the coming of the Son of Night. This apocalyptic figure, once arisen, would lead the werewolves in a war against the humans once more. The prophecy also said that, this time, the humans would lose. Barbee must stop this werewolf apocalypse as well as solve the mystery of his friend's murder … all without being killed.

The *Twilight* Wolf Pack

In recent years, the werewolf characters of Stephenie Meyer's best-selling *Twilight* series have spawned a renewed interest in werewolf lore. Her werewolves deviate from the traditional depiction in literature of cursed beings that kill mercilessly and cannot control their shapeshifting abilities. In fact, Meyer's depiction of werewolves is quite the opposite of those from the western tradition.

Compared with the popular werewolves of modern cinema and literature, which are commonly depicted as giant, furry, bipedal monsters, Meyer's werewolves are certainly in a league of their own. Her werewolf characters are members of the Quileute tribe, which is a real Native American tribe of the Pacific Northwest (see Chapter 2). Meyer's werewolves are not monsters, but men who, through secret tribal rites of lycanthropy, have gained the ability to transform themselves into actual wolves. They also appear to retain a great amount of mental control, even in their wolf forms. In comparison to most modern fictional werewolves, Meyer's characters are unique.

The main werewolf character in Meyer's series is named Jacob Black, a male teenager and member of the Quileute tribe. He is part of a love triangle that exists between him, Isabella "Bella" Swan (a human girl Jacob has known since childhood), and Edward Cullen (a vampire who has sworn off feeding on humans).

The Savage Truth

Stephenie Meyer's *Twilight* series has recently been adapted into a series of full-length motion pictures. The first film, *Twilight*, was a huge box office success, grossing over $382 million in worldwide theater sales. The DVD release of the first film has grossed over $146 million in sales. The box office release of the film adaptation of the second book, *New Moon*, is expected to fair just as well.

The Native American werewolves of Meyer's books are the natural and sworn enemies of all vampires. However, long ago the tribe made a pact with the Cullen family, a group of peaceful vampires to which Edward belongs. The Cullens agreed not to trespass on Quileute land, and in return the Quileute werewolves agreed to let them live in peace by not revealing what they were to the white human settlers.

The relationship between Jacob, Bella, and Edward is a complicated one. Bella's heart belongs to the vampire Edward. However, Edward views himself as a threat to Bella's safety and often retreats from her. When he does, Jacob is often there to seize the opportunity. For a time, Bella entertains the notion of allowing herself to love Jacob. However, she cannot let go of her deep feeling for Edward.

In the end, Bella must make a choice between her two immortal suitors. Will she pick the vampire or the werewolf? For the sake of not spoiling the story, the answer to this question will not be included here. If you want to find out, you will have to read Stephenie Meyer's *Twilight* series.

The Curse of Remus Lupin

The *Harry Potter* series of author J. K. Rowling is one of the most well-known works of literature in recent years. Rowling's storyline follows the adventures, trials, and tragedies that occur in the life of a young man (Harry Potter) as he attends a magical boarding school, Hogwarts School of Witchcraft and Wizardry. Beginning in the third book of the series, *Harry Potter and the Prisoner of Azkaban*, readers are introduced to an interesting new character called Remus Lupin.

Professor Lupin initially comes to Hogwarts as the new Defense Against the Dark Arts instructor (throughout the series, a new professor is appointed to this position every year). As the story progresses, however, it becomes clear that there is more to the new professor than meets the eye. He is often gone for days at a time, returning with scratches and bite marks on his body. Eventually, Harry Potter and his friends learn the truth about the condition that is afflicting their beloved professor.

Remus, once a close friend of Harry's deceased parents, was infected with lycanthropy as a child. He was bitten by a werewolf named Fenrir Greyback as payback for insults by Remus's father. Later, when admitted to attend Hogwarts, the school's headmaster, Albus Dumbledore, had a shack built on the outskirts of the nearby town of Hogsmeade. The large shack was constructed without any passable external entrances. Every month, on the nights of his transformations, Remus would enter the shack through a tunnel that ran under a large enchanted tree (the Whomping Willow) on the edge of the Hogwarts grounds.

The Savage Truth

The character of Remus Lupin appears in four installments of the *Harry Potter* series. In addition to his first appearance in *Harry Potter and the Prisoner of Azkaban*, Remus shows up again in the final three novels, *Harry Potter and the Order of the Phoenix*, *Harry Potter and the Half-Blood Prince*, and *Harry Potter and the Deathly Hallows*.

Without any humans to attack when in his violent werewolf state, however, Remus's bloodlust would always overtake him. This caused the poor young man to bite and scratch himself, resulting in terribly painful wounds. Remus's screams of pain and anguish were so loud that they reached the ears of nearby Hogsmeade residents, who soon came to the conclusion that the place was haunted by violent spirits. The shack was eventually dubbed the "Shrieking Shack," and people kept their distance (which was probably a good thing, since the screams were coming from a blood-mad werewolf).

Eventually, however, Remus's close friends James Potter (Harry's father), Sirius Black, and Peter Pettigrew discovered the truth about his condition. They could not stand the idea of their friend being alone during such a horrible ordeal. In order to join him, they learned to transform into animals (according to Rowling's story, werewolves only bite humans). James could become a stag, Sirius a black dog, and Peter a rat. The four young men became the best of friends, and their bond helped Remus to cope with his difficult condition.

The Least You Need to Know

◆ Marie de France's *Bisclavret* is considered the first werewolf-themed story in English literature.

◆ The werewolf was long a favorite in popular literary genres of the past, such as pulp fiction and the penny dreadful.

◆ The majority of literary werewolves are portrayed as cursed or tormented figures.

◆ The most recent manifestation of werewolves in literature comes from the *Twilight* series by Stephenie Meyer, whose werewolves are based on the secret lycanthropic practices of the Quileute tribe of the Pacific Northwest.

◆ Professor Remus Lupin is the main werewolf character of J. K. Rowling's popular *Harry Potter* series.

Chapter 11

Werewolves in Film

In This Chapter

◆ The roles of werewolves in the history of cinema

◆ A discussion of the first werewolf movie, the 1925 silent film *Wolf Blood*

◆ Werewolf films of the early twentieth century

◆ Werewolves in the movies of the 1960s

◆ The werewolf paradigm shift of the 1980s

◆ New portrayals of cinematic werewolves over the last two decades

The werewolf is undoubtedly one of the most popular monsters in the history of cinema. From the horror genre to comedy, werewolves have captivated filmmakers for decades. There exists a multitude of werewolf films. Some are classics … others successes … while a good many have also turned out to be total flops. To discuss every werewolf movie ever made would probably require a book itself. What follows is a sampling of the many portrayals of werewolves in cinema.

Wolf Blood (1925)

Released in December 1925, *Wolf Blood* was one of the first werewolf films in the history of cinema. Released as a silent film, it was written by Cliff Hill. The movie was directed by George Chesebro, who also starred in the tragic lead role of the lumberjack-turned-werewolf, Dick Bannister.

The movie began at a Canadian logging camp being overseen by boss Dick Bannister. Bannister's logging enterprise had recently entered into a small but violent conflict with a rival logging company. Things grew more complicated when Bannister's chief investor, a wealthy woman, came to visit and inspect the camp with her soon-to-be husband, a young and rather brilliant practicing surgeon.

One night, Bannister was attacked by loggers from the rival camp. They beat him severely and left him for dead. The badly bloodied Bannister was discovered and rushed back to the logging camp. The visiting young surgeon realized that Bannister had lost far too much blood and asked for volunteers to begin a transfusion. The superstitious loggers, however, all refused to take part.

Having no other option, the surgeon used the blood of a wolf to do the transfusion. By doing so, he managed to save Bannister's life. The logging boss's problems, however, were far from over. Bannister began having strange dreams in which he was running through the forest with a pack of ghostly wolves. In one dream, he and the pack slaughtered the men from the rival logging camp.

It was soon discovered that the men from the rival camp appeared to have been attacked and killed by a number of wild animals. The other lumberjacks also learned about Bannister's violent and similar wolf dreams. A large majority of the loggers decided that Bannister was a werewolf and organized a lynch mob to destroy him.

Werewolf of London (1935)

Based on a story by Robert Harris and adapted for the screen by John Colton, *Werewolf of London* was one of the first talking pictures to deal with the subject of lycanthropy. The film was directed by Stuart

Walker and starred Henry Hull as Dr. Wilfred Glendon, a brilliant young botanist whose studies led him on an expedition to Tibet.

While traveling through Tibet in search of rare and exotic plant life, Dr. Wilfred Glendon sought out and found the amazing mariphasa plant, the flowers of which only bloom under the light of the moon. During the expedition, however, he was attacked and bitten by what he believed to be a wild animal. In truth, it was a werewolf. After performing some initial lab tests, Dr. Glendon hypothesized that the flower bore a number of special properties that could benefit the medical and scientific communities. Ignoring the warnings of his local guide about the bite he had received (namely that werewolves seek to destroy the thing they love most—in this case, Glendon's wife), the young botanist returned to London with the rare flower for further experimentation.

On the next full moon, Dr. Glendon transformed into a werewolf. Horrified by what he had done, he sought to find a cure through his experiments with the mariphasa flower. At first he was able to create a temporary antidote from the flower's extract. Dr. Glendon's experiments with the flower came to the attention of a strange Tibetan physician by the name of Dr. Yogami. It later turned out that Yogami was the werewolf who bit him back in Tibet.

Police later came to Dr. Glendon's home while he was fighting Yogami (with both men in their werewolf states), and the officers opened fire on both of them. Yogami and Glendon were both killed and returned to their human forms. The police came to the conclusion that Yogami was responsible for the recent slew of murders committed by Glendon while under the influence of his werewolf state. The authorities deemed Dr. Glendon's death to be an unfortunate case of mistaken identity and believed that he was fighting with a murderer to protect his family.

The Wolf Man (1941)

The Wolf Man was one of the first widely popular werewolf films. Released in 1941, the movie was directed by George Waggner and the screenplay written by Curt Siodmak. *The Wolf Man* starred Claude Rains as Sir John Talbot and Lon Chaney Jr. as the tragic lead character, Lawrence "Larry" Talbot. The film also starred horror movie icon Bela Lugosi as Bela, a gypsy cursed with lycanthropy.

For 18 years, the very level-headed Larry Talbot had lived in America. When his older brother was killed in a hunting accident, however, Larry returned home to his family's estate in England. When he arrived, he was met by his grief stricken father, Sir John Talbot, who begged Larry to forgive him for always neglecting him and lavishing attention on his brother. Father and son made amends, but all did not remain peaceful. That night, while looking through his father's telescope, Larry set eyes on the beautiful Gwen Conliffe, the daughter of a store owner in town.

The next day, Larry went into town and visited the store of Gwen's father. While there, he purchased an unusual cane, the silver head decorated with the head of a wolf and a pentagram. Gwen even told Larry that the pentagram was a sign of the werewolf, but he laughed this off as superstition and bought it anyway. He also learned, with some disappointment, that Gwen was engaged to Frank Andrews, the game keeper for his father's estate. Nonetheless, Gwen invited Larry to join her later that evening, along with her friend Jenny, to visit a local gypsy camp to have their fortunes read by a man named Bela.

That night they went to the camp, and Bela the gypsy, upon seeing Jenny's hand, said that she bore the werewolf's mark on her palm. As the group walked away, disconcerted by his behavior, they soon heard howling coming from the woods. Jenny was suddenly attacked by a large wolf. Larry did his best to fend off the beast by beating it with his wolf-head cane, and he received a bite during the struggle that caused him to drop it. In the end, however, Larry was unable to save Jenny's life. He and Gwen fled from the scene.

Larry escorted Gwen home and then returned to Talbot Castle. He was greeted there by the local magistrate, Colonel Paul Montford, who was also an old childhood friend of his. Colonel Montford explained that he had recently come from the gypsy camp, where Jenny's mauled remains were found. He also explained that a man named Bela was found beaten to death nearby. Next to the man's body, he explained, Larry's wolf-head cane had been found. Larry tried to explain that they were not attacked by a man but by a wolf. He then held out his hand to show Colonel Montford the bite, which had mysteriously disappeared.

That night, Larry went back to the gypsy camp with Gwen and her fiancé, Frank, at his side. There they met Bela's mother, a gypsy matriarch named Maleva. She asked Larry if he had been bitten. When he told her he had, she explained that her son Bela was cursed with lycanthropy. She also told Larry that anyone who is bitten by a werewolf and lives will also bear the curse of lycanthropy. Larry did his best to dismiss what she told him as the ravings of a superstitious old woman. Regardless, the encounter shook him up a bit.

That night, Larry watched his mirrored reflection in horror as he transformed into a werewolf. Under the influence of his wolf-state, he ran howling into the night. He came upon a local grave digger named Richardson and killed the man. Later, the scene was inspected by Colonel Montford and a local physician, Dr. Lloyd. They discovered wolf tracks leading away from Richardson's corpse.

In the morning, Larry woke up and discovered a trail of wolf tracks that lead from the window to his bedside. Larry went down for breakfast with his father and asked him about the werewolf legend. Sir Talbot told his son that the werewolf legend is a metaphor for the inner struggle between good and evil within a man's own soul.

In the meantime, Colonel Montford and Frank Andrews spent the day setting traps for what they believed was a man-eating wolf. That night, when Larry transformed into his wolf-state and ran wild, he was caught in one of the traps. Maleva found him and, once he returned to his human form, freed him from the trap. Larry couldn't remember how he got there and was extremely disturbed.

Larry rushed back to town to find Gwen and tell her that he must leave immediately. She confessed her feelings for him and offered to run away with him. When Larry caught a glimpse of her palm, unfortunately he saw the mark of the werewolf on it. He told her that she couldn't join him and returned to Talbot Castle. He tried to confess what had happened to his father, who concluded that his son had gone insane. Just in case, however, he tied Larry to a chair. He then locked his son in his room. Larry told his father to find the silver wolf-head cane and keep it with him. Believing it best to humor his deranged son, Sir Talbot took the cane.

Sir Talbot arrived at the outskirts of town and discovered that all the hunters in the area had gathered to bring down the man-eating wolf they believed killed Richardson. He encountered Maleva, who told him that his son was indeed a werewolf but that as long as he possessed the silver cane he would be protected. While all this was going on, Larry transformed, broke free of his bonds, and took off into the woods. Sir Talbot went into the woods ahead of the hunting party, leaving Maleva behind. Gwen then showed up looking for Larry and followed Sir Talbot, despite Maleva's warnings that to do so would end her life. Maleva then went into the woods as well.

In the woods, Gwen was attacked by the werewolf. Sir Talbot came running, wielding his silver cane, and began trying to beat the beast off of her. Sir Talbot killed the beast, saving Gwen but taking the life of his own son. The werewolf transformed back into Larry's human form just as the hunting party arrived with Colonel Montford. The magistrate concluded that a normal wolf had attacked Gwen and that Larry, judging from his torn clothes, must have been killed trying to save her. Overcome by the truth, Gwen fainted and was caught by the arms of Frank.

The Curse of the Werewolf (1961)

The Curse of the Werewolf was released in 1961, written by Guy Endore (see Chapter 10) and Anthony Hinds. The film was set in eighteenth century Spain and starred Oliver Reed as the lead character, Leon Corledo. It remains the only werewolf movie ever to be made by the legendary horror film company, Hammer Studios.

Leon Corledo, the film's main character, was born on Christmas Day in Spain to a mute servant girl (the jailer's daughter) who was raped by a wandering vagabond who had been put in jail. The woman died giving birth to Leon, who was adopted by the nobleman she had served, Don Alfredo. As Leon grew, however, it became painfully clear to him that he was a werewolf.

Don Alfredo took the young Leon on his first hunting trip, and the boy transformed into a werewolf shortly after they returned. Leon did his best to control his savage urges, but ultimately failed to contain the beast within him. When Leon grew up, he took a job at a wine cellar and fell in love with the owner's daughter. Unfortunately, his love for her couldn't stifle the beast inside him, and Leon again transformed into a werewolf. He went on a wild rampage through the town until he was ultimately brought down.

The Savage Truth

The Curse of the Werewolf screenplay was heavily based on elements from Guy Endore's werewolf story *The Werewolf of Paris*. For example, both characters were the product of rape. Both characters were also born around Christmas, though Caillet on Christmas Eve and Corledo on Christmas Day.

The Howling (1981)

Director Joe Dante's *The Howling* was one of the first werewolf films in modern cinema. Very much done in homage to the werewolf films of the past, this new treatment made use of new technologies in special effects. For example, this film was the first to use animatronics and full-body costumes in order to create a more realistic-looking werewolf. The film starred Dee Wallace as Karen White and Patrick Macnee as New Age therapist Dr. George Waggner.

The movie is mainly about the female journalist Karen White's journey into lycanthropy. At first, Karen was contacted by a serial killer who refused to communicate with anyone but her. When she tried to assist the police in catching the killer (referred to as Eddie) by meeting him at a local video store, he attacked her and was shot down by police. The experience traumatized Karen, and she sought psychiatric care from an unorthodox therapist named Dr. George Waggner. Dr. Waggner suggested that Karen and her husband, Bill, spend some time at his private retreat called The Colony.

The Savage Truth

The name of the character Dr. George Waggner was chosen in order to pay homage to the real-life George Waggner, who was the director of the 1941 film *The Wolf Man*.

The Savage Truth

After the success of *The Howling,* a number of attempts were made to produce sequels. They were box office flops. After the terrible failures of the second and third films, the rest have been horribly done B-movies, created solely as straight-to-video releases.

The night after Karen and Bill came to The Colony, they began to hear loud and unusual howling coming from the woods around their cabin. While they were there, a couple of Karen's fellow journalists, named Chris and Terry, began a background investigation on Eddie's life and turned up nothing. They went to the medical examiner and learned that Eddie's body had disappeared from the morgue. They went through Eddie's personal effects and found a number of strange drawings that depicted creatures resembling werewolves. The pair then went to a local occult store to study up on werewolf lore. The store's owner had long had a set of custom-made silver bullets, made for a customer who never returned to pay for them. He sold the bullets to Chris and Terry.

Back at The Colony, Bill decided to join the other men in the group for a hunting trip. Dr. Waggner organized the hunt when several of his livestock were found mauled to death, and Karen told him about the nightly howling. All they killed, however, was a rabbit that Bill shot. He took the rabbit to fellow Colony-member Marsha, a nymphomaniac. She came on to Bill, but he refused and headed back to his cabin. On the way, Bill was attacked and bitten by what he convinced himself was a giant wolf.

That night, Bill couldn't sleep and wandered out into the moonlight. He discovered Marsha, and the two had sex as they both transformed into werewolves. As days passed, Karen began to suspect something changed in her husband and felt that her life was in danger. At the same time, Chris and Terry realized the truth about Eddie. He was alive … and he wasn't human. Unfortunately, they didn't figure this out in time to keep Terry from being killed. Chris rushed from the scene and headed for The Colony to meet up with Karen and tell her what had happened.

When Chris arrived, he found Karen and they tried to leave. Their path, however, was cut off by all the inhabitants of The Colony. As it turned out, they were a pack of werewolves led by an alpha male ... Dr. Waggner. Chris was killed, and Karen was bitten and forced to become a werewolf.

An American Werewolf in London (1981)

An American Werewolf in London, written and directed by John Landis, is considered by many to be a modern werewolf cinema classic. The movie, released in 1981 (the same year as *The Howling*), also capitalized on new advancements in special effects. The film starred David Naughton as college student David Kessler.

American college students David Kessler and Jack Goodman were hiking their way across England in order to tour the countryside. One night, however, the pair was attacked by a werewolf. Jack was killed, but David survived with only a bite. The townspeople arrived and killed the beast, which returned to human form, allowing them to deny that it had been a werewolf.

The Savage Truth

In 1997, a similarly styled film, *An American Werewolf in Paris,* was released. In many ways, this film pays homage to the original. With only a few differences in setting and plot, however, many consider these two movies to be identical.

David soon began to experience nightmares about hunting and killing in the form of a wolf. Soon, however, the ghosts of his dead friend Jack and others began appearing to him. In what became a darkly comedic twist, the ghosts insisted that David find a way to kill himself in order to release them from their cursed spectral forms. Because they were killed by an unnatural creature, they explained, their souls would remain trapped between worlds until the line of werewolves that killed them died out. David was now the last of that line. Since this film is a classic and was made in the last 30 years, the ending will be left out here in order to avoid spoiling the movie.

Silver Bullet (1985)

The 1985 werewolf film *Silver Bullet* was written by legendary horror author Stephen King and directed by Daniel Attias. The movie starred a very young Corey Haim as a paralyzed boy named Marty Coslaw, and Gary Busey was the boy's guardian, Uncle Red. Everett McGill played the creepy Reverend Lowe, a clergyman-turned-howling-creature-of-the-night.

Marty lived with his sister, Jane, and Uncle Red in the quiet rural town of Tarker's Mill. What he loved more than anything was the souped-up custom wheelchair that his Uncle Red modified for him, making Marty the fastest thing on two wheels. Everything seemed great in the town until people started turning up dead. At first everyone believed that there must be some insane killer on the loose, and lynch mobs formed in order to hunt the murderer down. Marty, however, after a brief encounter with the beast, believed that the killings are being done by a werewolf.

Recruiting the assistance of his sister, Jane, Marty went on the hunt to discover the human identity of the werewolf. What they discovered, however, was far more terrifying than anything they could have imagined. Once again, you probably don't want the ending spoiled for you on this one, so let's just leave it at that.

Teen Wolf (1985)

Teen Wolf was a hit when it was released in 1985. The film starred Michael J. Fox as Scott Howard. It was directed by Rob Daniel and written collaboratively by Joseph "Jeph" Loeb and Matthew Weisman. Unlike the more frightening and bloody werewolf films of its time, *Teen Wolf* was meant to offer a lighter, more comedic treatment of lycanthropy.

Scott Howard was an awkward and fairly unpopular teenager at his high school. As he reached the end stages of puberty, however, he began to undergo some unexpected changes (like his eyes glowing red, growing fangs, and growling). When his secret became common knowledge, however, Scott went from outcast to the most popular guy in school. His powers made him the star of the basketball team, which made him the new desire of the hottest girl in school. In the end, however, Scott had to make a choice between being the werewolf that everyone adored … or being the nice guy that his friends and family had always loved.

Werewolf, the TV Series (1987)

In 1987, Fox ran a short-lived TV series under the simple title *Werewolf.* Though the show only had a 29-episode run, it has grown to be considered a cult classic of the werewolf genre. In recent years, fans of the show have demanded that it be released on DVD since the only available copies have long been nothing more than poor-quality bootlegs.

Graduate student Eric Cord (played by John J. York) didn't believe it when his roommate claimed that he was a werewolf. However, when the guy transformed and attacked Eric, it made him a believer. During the struggle, Eric killed his roommate. Unfortunately, he still got bitten.

The show followed Eric's long journey to rid himself of the werewolf curse. In order to do so, however, he had to track down and kill the source of his bloodline, whom he believed to be a sadistic figure by the name of Captain Janos Skorzeny (played by Chuck Connors). Unfortunately, Eric's first transformation left a trail of bodies in its wake, which made him the target of a bounty hunter named "Alamo" Joe Rogan (played by Lance LeGault). Eric hunted Skorzeny and was hunted by Rogan. Could he free himself of this cursed lycanthropy before the bounty hunter catches up to him?

The Savage Truth

Much to the joy of fans of the *Werewolf* series, the entire collection was released onto DVD by Shout! Factory in September of 2009. For more information on the show or to purchase the DVD, you can go to www.shoutfactory.com or www.werewolftv.com.

The Monster Squad (1987)

The Monster Squad was a film released in 1987 as part of the popular "kid-venture" genre of the 1980s.

When the diary of legendary vampire hunter Abraham Van Helsing was discovered in a spooky house on Shadowbrook Road, it ended up as part of a garage sale and was sold to a woman who gave it to her monster-obsessed son, Shawn, as a present. Shawn (played by Andre Gower) was thrilled by the gift but was disappointed to discover that it was written entirely in German. He showed the diary to his friends, who together were members of a "Monster Club." When strange things started happening in his town, which Shawn learned by eavesdropping on his father (a police detective), he concluded that monsters were responsible and dubbed the group "The Monster Squad."

They took the diary to the neighborhood "scary German guy," who translated it for them. They learned that on the next night, at the stroke of midnight, Dracula and his monstrous companions would open a hole in limbo and destroy the world. Among these monsters was, of course, a werewolf. Unlike the other monsters, however, the werewolf was an involuntary pawn being controlled by Dracula's wolf-headed silver cane.

The primary reason that this movie is mentioned here is because it spawned one of the most highly quoted movie lines regarding werewolves. The boys had a long-standing debate as to whether or not werewolves had "nards." When confronted by the werewolf in Dracula's mansion, Shawn commanded his friend, "Kick him in the nards!" To which his friend replied, "He doesn't have nards!" "Do it! Do it!" The young man kicked the werewolf in the groin, and the creature doubled over in pain. The awestruck kid stood there for a moment and quietly commented, "Wolf-man's got nards." A classic line ... no question about it.

Dog Soldiers (2002)

The 2002 British film *Dog Soldiers* was written and directed by Neil Marshall. It starred Sean Pertwee as the rough and tumble Sgt. Harry G. Wells, along with a very large cast of actors from the United

Kingdom. This movie is probably the most well-known werewolf film to be produced by British cinema.

The movie is about a squad of British soldiers who were in the wilderness of the Scottish highlands on a routine training exercise. The first night, however, they heard something moving in the woods. Suddenly, a dead rabbit was thrown into their campsite. It gave the men a scare, but they dismissed it ... until the next day when they found an entire unit of Royal Special Forces soldiers torn to pieces. They inspected the weapons of the dead to find that they were carrying live rounds. Knowing something wasn't right, they armed up and prepared to get the heck out of dodge. They discovered one survivor, a man that one member of the squad recognized as a British black ops agent. They questioned the man, who only rambled on that, "There was only supposed to be one of them." They were ambushed by werewolves, and several squad members were ripped apart.

The Savage Truth

Dog Soldiers, many fans agree, contains one of the greatest fights of all time. One soldier, Cooper, went wild and tangled with a number of werewolves one-on-one ... first with a sword ... then a kitchen knife ... then even with his bare fists. Any person who watches the movie cannot help but stand in awe at how bravely and savagely Private Cooper went down fighting.

Eventually, the soldiers were rescued by a mysterious woman with a truck. She took them to an abandoned cabin, where they tried to radio for help. The radio, however, was hit by a round during the battle and was now useless. The men fortified the house and successfully fended off wave after wave of werewolves. With a dead radio and a destroyed truck, however, all avenues for an escape were soon totally cut off. For how much longer would the soldiers be able to survive? What happened to the Special Forces unit? And exactly what was this woman doing in a cabin out in the middle of nowhere?

Underworld Series (2003)

The first part of the *Underworld* film series was released in 2002. Written and directed by Len Wiseman, this film series is among the most popular werewolf films of recent years. What's more, it has provided moviegoers with an entirely new portrayal of werewolves.

The Savage Truth

There are two further installments that make up the rest of the *Underworld* movie trilogy. The second film is *Underworld: Evolution*, which was released in 2006 and explains the origins of werewolves and vampires (according to the mythology of the film) as well as the fate of Selene and Michael. The third and final movie of the series, *Underworld: Rise of the Lycans*, is a prequel that tells the story of just how the long war between werewolves and vampires began.

The *Underworld* series involves a centuries-old war that has raged between werewolves (called "lycans" in the films) and vampires. In the first movie, it was learned that the vampires had nearly won, and that only a handful of the most powerful werewolves now survived. Among the vampires, a group of warriors, called "death-dealers," was responsible for hunting down and eradicating the few remaining lycans on Earth. When a female death-dealer named Selene discovered that the lycans were tracking a specific human named Michael Corvin, she investigated further and learned that his blood was the key to creating a powerful hybrid that was both werewolf and vampire. She soon developed feelings for Michael Corvin, who she learned was the last descendent of the first immortal being who a forgotten legend said spawned both of the immortal races—a man named Corvinis. Eventually, Selene had to choose between her allegiance to her own kind and her love for Michael.

Blood and Chocolate (2007)

The interesting Romeo-and-Juliet-like film, *Blood and Chocolate*, was released in 2007. The film was directed by Katja von Garnier and was based on the screenplay by Ehren Kruger and Christopher Landon.

Set in Bucharest, Romania, *Blood and Chocolate* follows an American comic artist named Aiden who came to do research on a graphic novel he was creating about werewolves. While there, he met a girl named Vivian and was rather taken with her. Little did Aiden know, however, that Vivian was descended from an ancient werewolf bloodline.

The Curse

When compared to the werewolves of other modern films, those of *Blood and Chocolate* are unique. Whereas most films of today portray werewolves that are giant and humanoid in appearance (walking on two legs, etc.), the werewolves of *Blood and Chocolate* are humans that turn into actual, normal looking wolves.

Vivian was an orphan, her parents killed by human hunters in the Colorado Rocky Mountains. As a result, she was sent to Romania to be raised by her aunt. Vivian was betrothed to the pack's alpha male, Gabriel. So when she developed feelings for Aiden, it threw a wrench into things. Gabriel, enraged with jealousy, brought the two lovers before the other werewolves on the night of the full moon to face the justice of the hunt. Would the two star-crossed lovers be able to survive?

The Least You Need to Know

- The first known werewolf movie was a silent film called *Wolf Blood*, released in 1925.

- The first "talking pictures" werewolf movie was *Werewolf of London*, released in 1935.

- *The Howling* and *An American Werewolf in London* are considered the first modern werewolf films, which is marked by their uses of advanced special effects.

- *Teen Wolf* offered a unique portrayal of werewolves that was funny and lighthearted.

- Much of the modern perception of werewolves comes from the *Underworld* film series.

- Unlike in most modern films, the werewolves of *Blood and Chocolate* were depicted as humans who transformed into normal wolves.

Chapter 12

Werewolves in Art and Comics

In This Chapter

- A look at anthropomorphism in the religious art of the ancient world
- A discussion of anthropomorphism in art and its relationship to lycanthropy
- The multitude of werewolf characters in comic books and graphic novels
- Werewolves in the Japanese comic media of manga and anime
- The relationship of the popular manga/anime series *Wolf's Rain* to the Shinto myths of the O-kami
- The werewolf characters of Marvel Comics

The visual arts have long attempted to create portrayals of werewolves to suit their fantastic images within human imaginations. Even in the ancient past, humans imagined such figures and fashioned images that displayed spectacular integrations of human and animal traits. In recent decades, lycanthropy's appeal to the imagination has led to the widespread inclusion of werewolf-themed characters in the pop culture realms of cartoon art, animation, comic books, and graphic novels.

Anthropomorphism in Ancient Art

In the ancient world, the most common use of *anthropomorphism* was in the depictions of divine and supernatural beings such as gods or spirits. Artifacts displaying such depictions are especially common from ancient cultures that practiced polytheistic nature religions, where gods were often associated with animals and forces of nature.

> **Beastly Words**
>
> **Anthropomorphism** refers to figures that embody both human and nonhuman traits. The word comes from the combination of the Greek *anthropos*, meaning "man/human," and *morph*, meaning "shape/form."

Werewolves often fall under the category of anthropomorphic figures, especially when depicted in their most popular hybrid/humanoid forms. Werewolves were by no means, however, the first anthropomorphic figures to be depicted in the assorted media of human art. In fact, some of the oldest known anthropomorphic depictions come from ancient Mesopotamia, commonly known as the "cradle of civilization."

The oldest known anthropomorphic depictions in the ancient world date back to nearly 4000 B.C.E. and are representations of the gods and nature spirits of the Sumerian, Assyrian, and Babylonian civilizations of Mesopotamia. The majority of these have been found on small stone engravings called cylinder seals, which when rolled over wet clay tablets create panoramic-style pictures. The cylinder seals were often used to quickly create religious charms meant to invoke certain beneficial gods or to ward off any number of malevolent deities/spirits, which were in those times thought to be the bringers of famines, disease, and natural catastrophes. For example, the ancient figure known as Lilith (associated with the conflicting elements of childbirth/death, creation/disease, and agriculture/storms) was often depicted in cylinder seals and relief carvings as a beautiful, winged female with the talons of a raptor for her feet.

When it comes to the anthropomorphic integration of human and canine features, werewolves are still not the oldest of the bunch. The dark ancient Egyptian god of death, Anubis, was depicted in drawings, carvings, and statues as having a human body and the black head of a canine (which many people would describe as resembling the head of a Doberman Pincer).

The Book of Jack

The Book of Jack is based on the original French story *Le Livre de Jack* written by Denis Pierre Filippi. The *graphic novel* was translated into English by Piche and Kelly and then released in America in July 2002 by Humanoids Publishing. The graphic novel's artwork was done by Olivier G. Boiscommun.

The story begins with a young man named Jack trying to gain acceptance into a local gang of boys. As part of his initiation into the group, Jack must go into an old abandoned house that is supposedly haunted. Not wanting to be seen as a coward by the others, Jack accepts the challenge and ventures with them, crossing the threshold of the strange house.

Beastly Words

A **graphic novel** is a comic-style book that typically has a more complex, full-length story than is usually found in comic books. It usually is created for a more mature reading audience.

Once inside the house, Jack stumbles upon an odd and dusty book. He opens it but cannot read. Sam, the only female member of the gang as well as the only one who can read, informs Jack, much to his astonishment, that the book appears to be telling the story of his life. When they reach the final pages, which are blank, words magically begin to appear that tell the story of Jack's present actions. He decides to take the book with him when he leaves, and as a joke he has someone write in the book that he becomes a werewolf. The next morning, Jack thinks twice and decides that perhaps he should return the book to the house. Unfortunately for him, it has now mysteriously disappeared.

As days pass, the book remains missing, and Jack soon discovers that he is transforming into a werewolf … just as he'd had it written. In the hopes of finding a way to break the curse of his new lycanthropy, Jack must go on a strange quest to find the lost book and return it from whence it came. Sam stays with Jack and helps him despite his monstrous transformation. They manage to find the man Jack had write in the book and by doing so are able to return Jack to normal. The story ends with Sam and Jack returning the book to the house.

The *Crescent Moon* Series

Crescent Moon is the English title of a Japanese *manga* series called *Mikan no Tsuki*, which basically translates as "The Incomplete Moon." Both the story and the art of the *Crescent Moon* series were created by Haruko Iida. It was originally released in Japan by publisher Kadokawa Shoten. It was later translated into English and released to American audiences by the corporation TokyoPop.

Beastly Words

Manga is a Japanese term that literally translates as "involuntary sketches." However, manga is now used in reference to a popular genre of book-length, black-and-white Japanese comics. The term is believed to have first been coined in 1814, when a Japanese artist named Hokusai created a book of impromptu black-and-white sketches, many of which had elements of storytelling, which he called manga.

The story of *Crescent Moon* follows the unusual adventures of a young girl named Mahiru Shiraishi. Mahiru was born with a gift that allows her to bestow good fortune upon people simply by touching them. She cannot apply her gift of good fortune, however, to her own life. Sadly, because it is her own good fortune that she gives to other people, she has very little of it left for herself.

At one point, Mahiru begins to experience a series of reoccurring dreams involving strange beings. These dreams later cause her to encounter a group called the "Lunar Bandits," all of whom are part of a race of special mythical beings referred to as "The Lunar Ones." The name of this race of mythical creatures comes from the fact that their powers are dependent upon the phases of the lunar cycle.

Mahiru meets a number of these "Lunar Ones," among them a vampire, a *kitsune* ("demon fox"), and a *tengu* (a winged and beak-faced mountain spirit). The youngest member of the "Lunar Bandits" is a 16-year-old, rather carefree werewolf by the name of Akira Yamabuki. Akira later develops a crush on one of Mahiru's classmates, a girl named Keiko.

Beastly Words

In Japanese, the word **kitsune** can be used to refer to a normal fox. However, in Shinto, it is often used to refer to a mischievous "fox spirit." In Shinto, the **tengu** is a clever, mischievous, and sometimes destructive nature spirit, usually found in the mountains and described as having wings and a beaked face.

The "Lunar Bandits" tell Mahiru that she is the descendent of the "Moon Princess" and that they need her in order to find and take back the stolen source of their powers, called the "Lunar Teardrops." In addition to helping the "Lunar Bandits" recover the powers that are rightfully theirs, Mahiru must also try to mend the fear and hostility that has grown in humans toward these forgotten creatures of the moon.

Wolf's Rain

Wolf's Rain is the English title of the *anime* and manga series *Urufuzu-Rein*. The series was created by Keiko Nobumoto and animated by Toshihiro Kawamoto. The anime was directed by Tensai Okamura and was originally released in 2003 by BONES Studios. The series was later adapted into a two-volume manga series.

Wolf's Rain follows the harsh journey of four wolves who are seeking a lost paradise of legend. They have learned to make themselves appear like normal people to the eyes of humans. In this postapocalyptic world, few wolves still survive. After nearly being completely wiped out

Beastly Words

The Japanese word **anime** means "animation" and generally refers to cartoon series that are most frequently adapted from previously well-received manga.

almost 200 years ago, the wolves learned to conceal their existence from humans, and they have long lived among them in secret. The four main characters of the series have names that are related to wolves and are as follows:

- *Tsume:* His name means "claw," and he is a grey- and black-furred wolf that bears a giant scar on his chest. In human form the scar remains visible, but he looks like a tall, thin, and muscular younger man, with silver-grey hair and black clothes. In the story, he has long lived as a leader of a gang of human thieves. He later abandons this life in order to join the others in their pursuit of the wolf paradise.

- *Kiba:* His name means "fang," and he is a white wolf. As a human, he appears as a dark-haired young man in blue jeans, a t-shirt, and a jacket. Kiba's pack was wiped out by humans when he was a cub, so he's spent his life away from them in the wild (though as a cub he was nursed back to health by American Indians friendly to wolves). Kiba comes to the city following the scent of the lunar flower, which he thinks is the key to paradise. At first, he is repulsed by the idea of trying to look like a human, but he eventually comes to see the wisdom in it.

- *Hige:* His name means "whiskers," and his fur is tan. Hige is young and carefree, and as a human he looks like a teenager in a yellow jacket. He is the only wolf of the group to wear a collar. He doesn't know where he got it, and the purpose of it isn't unveiled until later on in the story. Hige mainly cares about only two things—food and finding himself a female mate. Hige also has a keen sense of smell.

- *Toboe:* His name means "howling," and his fur is brown. He is the youngest and most naïve/innocent of the group. The others consider him to be a "puppy" because, for most of his life, he was raised by an old woman who found him as an abandoned wolf cub. Unlike the others, Toboe is usually friendly to humans because of this experience. Regardless of what the others think of him, he has the best ears in the group.

The Curse

Usually, manga that are successful are later turned into anime. In the unusual case of *Wolf's Rain*, however, the opposite occurred. It was first an anime series and later was adapted into a two-volume manga. While the two versions are certainly similar, there are a number of key differences between them. For example, many characters from the anime version are not included in the manga. Also, the ending of the manga is markedly more positive then the one from the original anime version.

These four wolves all realize that they have come to Freeze City because they caught the scent of a lunar flower, a special flower that only blooms under the light of the moon. At first, Kiba is the only one who believes in the wolf paradise. Eventually, however, all four wish to find it. When they find the source of the flower's scent, they realize it is coming from a strange girl named Cheza who is being held in stasis by the nobles who own the city. Kiba realizes that she must be the "Flower Maiden" from legends who will lead the wolves to paradise.

According to the mythology of the story, the O-kami, or "wolves," will return when the end of the world is at hand, and they will be the only ones who know the way to paradise. Few of the people in the story's postapocalyptic world believe this to be anything more than an old fairy tale, but there are some who know better—the nobles who own the cities. They want the wolves' paradise for their own and plan to escape the planet by going to it using the lost and advanced arts of alchemy. These nobles believe they can use Cheza's body to force open the gate to the wolves' paradise.

The wolves free Cheza from the nobles and begin following her to paradise. The powerful armies of the nobles, however, pursue them every step of the way (when they aren't fighting with each other, of course). As if traveling through a barren wasteland wasn't bad enough, the nobles' forces are not the only ones chasing them.

A former sheriff and extreme alcoholic from a town called Kyrios (a Japanese transliteration of the English word "curious"), named Quent Yaiden, has dedicated the rest of his life to the extermination of all wolves. One day, long ago, his home was burned and his young son was killed. Quent looked at the burning scene and saw a wolf standing over his son's body. Because of this, he believes that wolves were responsible and now hunts them with the aid of his half-wolf dog, named *Boo-roo/* "Blue" (a black-furred dog with blue eyes). When Blue learns that she is part wolf and discovers she is able to assume human appearance and communication, she has no choice but to run away from her former master because she believes he will kill her.

In the end, all of these characters assemble for a final confrontation with the last paradise-obsessed nobleman. Who will be the ones to lay claim to paradise, the noble or the wolves? Better yet, will there be a paradise for any of them? Since this is a relatively new series, you will have to see *Wolf's Rain* for yourself if you wish to know the answers to these questions.

"Werewolf by Night" and the Braineaters

The "Werewolf by Night" character Jack Russell remains the oldest werewolf character still in print (though somewhat sporadically) in American comics. The cursed werewolf character Jack Russell first appeared in Marvel Comics in the second issue of *Marvel Spotlight* in February of 1972. Jack Russell was born in Romania under the name Jacob Russoff to parents Gregor and Laura Russoff. When he was only a baby, Jack's father Gregor was found out to be a werewolf and was shot down by villagers with a silver bullet. His mother soon remarried to his father's brother, Philip, and they all immigrated to America, where they were given the anglicized last name "Russell" and Jacob's name was changed to "Jack." Jack grew up not knowing the truth about his real father.

On the night before Jack's eighteenth birthday, a full moon, he was first transformed into a werewolf. The next day, during his birthday party, Jack felt himself transforming again and had to run away from the festivities to hide his secret. While he was away, his mother was killed in a tragic car accident. He later learned this was not an accident and that the brakes to his mother's car had been cut when his step-father had refused to pay a blackmailer who knew about the curse of lycanthropy that had plagued Jack's father.

Jack Russell's life would soon become one of tragedy and lonely wandering, as he did his best to control the beast within him. Later, he learned to control his abilities and, for a time, embraced his werewolf side and even created his own pack of werewolves, who dubbed themselves the "Braineaters."

Eventually, the exploits of Jack Russell and his Braineaters would become popular enough to warrant a comic book title of their very own. The series was entitled *Werewolf by Night*, but it ran for only 43 issues from 1972 to 1973. A second series of the *Werewolf by Night* story again had a brief run during the 1990s. In 2007, a single-issue comic involving the Jack Russell character was published by Marvel under the title *Legion of Monsters: Werewolf by Night*. In January 2009, the character of Jack Russell was once again reinvented for a brand new audience, released as a four-part miniseries under the title *Dead of Night*.

Nick Fury's Howling Commandos

The Howling Commandos were originally a hero team concept from Marvel Comics, who were led by the character Nick Fury and fought as a special commando team in World War II. This original form was a part of the popular war genre of comics. The series was not exclusively restricted to the stage of World War II; Nick Fury and his Howling Commandos also completed missions in the Korean War and Vietnam. However, while the original team members were indeed special, they were not supernatural.

In December 2005, Marvel released a totally new version of *Nick Fury's Howling Commandos*. The new story had a six issue run until it's cancellation in May of 2006. While still under the supervision of the older Nick Fury, now chief of the American elite military organization called S.H.I.E.L.D. (Strategic Hazard Intervention, Espionage, and Logistics Directorate), the new team consisted of supernatural creatures, and was designed to deal with paranormal missions. Aside from its six issue run, the Howling Commandos only ever appeared in one other comic, in the third issue of the recently resurrected vampire hunter series *Blade*.

In the field, the Howling Commandos were now lead by a character named Warwolf, whose real name is Vince Marcus. He has the power to transform into a werewolf at will, as long as the planet Mars is in the night sky.

The Creature Commandos

The original Creature Commandos first appeared in November 1980, in issue 93 of the DC Comics series *Weird War Tales*. The original story concept was created by Pat Broderick and J.M. DeMatteis. The Creature Commandos were an elite military unit made up of soldiers who had been given supernatural powers through an experimental project codenamed "Project M."

The original Creature Commandos led by a human officer, Lieutenant Matthew Shrieve, were meant to serve as an elite team in the fight against the Nazis in World War II. The members consisted of a vampire (Sergeant Vincent Velcoro), a gorgon (Dr. Myrra Rhodes), a clone of Frankenstein's monster (Private "Lucky" Taylor), and a werewolf (Warren Griffith). Later in the series, the team was joined by an android soldier, J.A.K.E., codenamed the "G.I. Robot." The series ended with the team, once the war had ended, being forced inside a rocket aimed at Berlin. The rocket, however, veered off course and shot into deep space.

The Savage Truth

War comics were a popular genre of American comic books for about 60 years. The genre first took off in the late 1930s, and even before the United States became involved in World War II, several war genre comics (such as the famous *Captain America*) depicted heroes fighting Hitler's Nazi regime. The war comic genre hit its peak after the close of World War II, but began to die out during the mid- to late 1990s.

In 2005, the *Creature Commandos* series was resurrected under the storyline that the rocket had somehow found its way back to Earth. Significantly aged, the team finds its way back to Project M. They receive modifications that significantly extend their lives. However, they are so extremely altered that they are no longer able to assume human forms. The series ran until 2006, when the mini-series of which it was a part finally reached the end of its run.

Only the End of the World Again

Only the End of the World Again was the creation of legendary comic writer Neil Gaiman (most well known for writing the popular *Sandman* series) and artist Troy Nixey. Released in 2000 by Oni Press (who bought the original serialized story), *Only the End of the World Again* was an immediate hit with hardcore fans of Gaiman's work.

The main character of the story is Neil Talbot, a Brtish businessman who comes to the strange town of Innsmouth to work as an adjuster. Soon after his arrival, a fat local man begins screaming out that the world is ending. What's more, the man claims that the world will be destroyed because of a werewolf. Soon, Talbot begins to experience a number of strange and mysterious occurrences, launching him into several odd adventures. These adventures soon lead Talbot to suspect that he is the werewolf foretold of by the town's overweight doomsdayer.

The Least You Need to Know

- Anthropomorphism has existed in human art since ancient times.

- Usually, ancient depictions of anthropomorphic figures portrayed the gods and nature spirits of ancient polytheistic religions.

- The Japanese anime series *Wolf's Rain* is not technically about humans who turn into wolves, but wolves that can make themselves look like humans.

- The longest running werewolf character in American comic books is the Marvel character known as Jack Russell.

Chapter **13**

Werewolves in Gaming

In This Chapter

◆ An explanation of the "Werewolf" party/card game tradition

◆ The werewolf hero of the 1988 arcade class *Altered Beast*

◆ The "old-school" *Werewolves of London* game for the now-antique Commodore 64 computer

◆ The rather funny elements of the Japanese-designed post-apocalyptic video game, *Werewolf: The Last Warrior*

◆ *The Beast Within*, part of the short-lived "point-and-click" interactive genre of PC gaming

The powerful image of the werewolf is a longstanding character icon of the gaming world. From party games to role-playing and video games, werewolves can be found in nearly every gaming outlet imaginable. Since it is unlikely that any of us will get to experience the reality of being a werewolf, games offer us the next best thing by providing an imaginative outlet where our minds can briefly allow the beasts within us to be unleashed in a safe and fun way.

"Werewolf" (Card Game and Party Game)

The "Werewolf" game is easy to set up, and just about anyone can learn how to play relatively quickly. This game can be played with five or more people, a pen, and a few evenly sized squares of paper. The first thing you will need to do in order to play "Werewolf" is make a set of the following cards:

♦ One card that says "Game Master" or "Moderator"

♦ One card that says "Seer"

♦ Two cards that say "Werewolf"

♦ Enough cards that say "Villager" for the remaining people playing

These cards represent each person's role in the game. After you've made them, they need to be well shuffled and handed out to the players. Remember, the number of cards must match the number of players exactly. Otherwise, the key cards (Game Master, Seer, and Werewolf) might not be put into play, and without them the game would get confusing. Once the cards have been handed out (one card per player), all players should quickly glance at their card but keep their role to themselves. Only the Game Master should reveal his role to the group, or he can be chosen by the group ahead of time and just given the card.

Two players are now werewolves, and it is their goal to kill all of the villagers (in the game, of course) without being discovered. There is one player, the Seer, who has certain privileges that allow her to detect which two players are Werewolves. All the other players are now Villagers (potential werewolf victims).

The Savage Truth

The "Werewolf" game is thought by most to have originally been based on a preexisting, similarly constructed kind of party game called "Mafia."

The game is played in two alternating phases—night and day. The opening phase of the game should always be night. When it is night, the Game Master will instruct all players to close their eyes. Then he will say, "Werewolves, open your eyes." At this point, whichever two players hold the Werewolf cards should open their eyes and take notice of each other. Then the Game Master should instruct the Werewolves to pick someone in the group to kill. The Werewolves must then agree (quickly and without speaking, of course) on which Villager they want to kill by pointing that player out or using some other silent signal. It is very important that all players be spaced out well enough so as not to detect movement. The Werewolves should also try not to make too much noise. Once the victim has been chosen, the Game Master will say "Werewolves, close your eyes."

The Game Master now says, "Seer, open your eyes." Whichever player drew the Seer card should now open her eyes. The Seer will now choose one player to point to in an attempt to uncover which two are the Werewolves. The Game Master will confirm or deny the choice, usually by giving a thumb's up/down or by nodding/shaking the head. A "yes" answer means the person *is* a Werewolf, and a "no" answer means the person is *not* a Werewolf but a Villager. The Seer must also be careful not to make noise because, if the Werewolves discover who she is, they will want to knock her out of the game as fast as possible. Once the Seer's choice has been acknowledged, the Game Master will say, "Seer, close your eyes."

The Game Master now says, "All players open your eyes. It is now day." Once everyone's eyes are opened, the Game Master will point to the person chosen by the Werewolves and say, "You have been ripped to pieces by werewolves." This player is now out of the game and should reveal his card to the others and set it down, facing up. Once a player is dead, he *cannot speak*. The player can go do something else if he wants, but he can't talk to any of the remaining players. Any arguments must be made *before* the votes are cast. Also, only dead players may show their cards to anyone.

Now the real fun of the day phase begins. All players must get together (including the unknown Werewolves) and choose someone to lynch. In this phase of the game, anything goes. There are no restrictions on what can or cannot be said. Players can completely deny anything they want, just as long as they don't show anyone their card. If the Seer knows who a Werewolf is, she must do her best to draw the group's attention to that player without letting it out that she is the Seer (because there is still another Werewolf, who would then kill the Seer on the next night). The Werewolves can lie, deceive, and misdirect the other players as they please in order to avoid being lynched. Werewolves can even turn on each other to throw off suspicion.

All players must now vote on which of them is going to be lynched as a suspected Werewolf, and the majority vote always wins (which means it is usually easier when you have an odd number of villagers because a tie doesn't count). Once this has been done, the Game Master points to the lynched player and says, "You have been lynched and are now dead." This player now reveals her card. Needless to say, the Villagers do not want to lynch the Seer.

When this has been done, the Game Master says, "All players close your eyes. It is now night," and the cycle begins again. The game will end in one of two ways. If the Werewolves manage to kill enough Villagers that they outnumber them, then the Werewolves win. If the Villagers succeed in lynching both of the Werewolves, then the Villagers win.

The Birth of the Arcade Werewolf

One of the first werewolf-themed video games to hit arcades was Sega's 1988 hit *Altered Beast*. The game was originally released in Japan under the title *Juoki*, or "The Beast Lord." *Altered Beast* was later adapted into versions for the Sega home game system, other home game systems, and personal computers (though many of these were unable to offer the same level of game play, with the available computers of the time). In most of these different versions, *Altered Beast* was designed to be a one-player game. The game was part of what has come to be called the "beat-'em-up" genre of scrolling games, in which the character walks from one side of the screen to the other and employs combinations of basic moves in order to defeat enemies.

The Curse

Though *Altered Beast* was based on certain characters from Greek mythology, no such story exists where Athena is kidnapped by Hades. There *is* a story in which Persephone, the daughter of the earth goddess Demeter, is kidnapped by him. However, Zeus did not send a resurrected warrior with werewolf powers to save her.

The game is set in ancient Greece and begins with the goddess Athena being kidnapped by Hades, god of the underworld. Zeus searches for a hero to save her and decides to resurrect a fallen warrior. Zeus then grants this warrior the ability to shapeshift into a powerful beast so that he will be able to do battle with the many terrible creatures of the underworld.

The warrior leaves on his quest and encounters legions of monsters that he must defeat in order to continue on. When certain monsters are defeated (usually the ones that are flashing), orbs are released. As the warrior collects these orbs, he begins to transform. Once three orbs have been absorbed, the warrior assumes his full "altered beast" form, making him stronger, faster, and (for whatever reason) allowing him to throw fireballs. After he defeats the boss at the end of every stage, however, the warrior returns to his human form.

Werewolves of London

The game *Werewolves of London* was created by Viz Design, with versions to fit home computers of the time like the now-obsolete Commodore 64. The 8-bit game (which is a laughably low graphic quality in modern times) was originally scheduled for production and subsequent release by Ariolasoft in 1985, but the company went bankrupt before beginning production on the game. Two years later, the game was finally picked up for production by Mastertronic and released.

The Savage Truth

One special version of *Werewolves of London* was stored on a special tape medium called a "Flippy," which could be used with both the ZX Spectrum and Amstrad CPC home computers. This allowed purchasers to simply "flip" the data cassette to either side, depending on which of the two computers they owned. Basically, these tapes allowed for dual compatibility at a time when software was still being designed to work only for specific computers.

Werewolves of London is, as one might expect, set in London. The goal of the game is for the player, as a werewolf, to kill eight particular people. The targets were each members of an aristocratic family that cursed the player character with lycanthropy. However, the resulting transformations occur nightly instead of just during the full moon.

Werewolves of London offered players an interesting mix of action, role-playing, and strategy game elements. The game was even designed to adapt to the individual player's reactions to certain situations. One could not simply go on a rampage and hope to win the game, for example. One element of the game was to avoid being found out by Scotland Yard, and more unnecessary murders would lead to increased police activity.

If the player, while in werewolf form, is touched by a police officer holding handcuffs, then the character is held in prison until the following day (when, in a situation only possible in the gaming world, the character is inexplicably freed from the cell and returned to human form). However, there is also a window of opportunity for the player to escape from the jail if a crowbar and torch can be found. These items allow the player to break out of the cell and escape via the prison's underground sewers.

Beastly Words

NPC stands for "Non-Playable Character," and refers to characters in a video game that cannot be controlled by the player. Such characters include assistance characters and opponents/"Bad Guys."

Another interesting element of the game is that health is awarded for every person the player eats (whether it is one of the eight target characters or just some random *NPC*). When the character gets shot, the health meter begins a slow but steady decline, represented by an icon that is supposed to be a bag full of blood (but it's hard to tell that's what it is supposed to be, especially if you don't already know). Finding and using certain items in the game, such as bandages, can slow this down (but not stop it). Once the player's "blood bag" is empty, the character dies and the game is over ... then it's back to square one.

Werewolf: The Last Warrior

Werewolf: The Last Warrior was developed and released by the Data East Corporation in 1990. Originally released in Japan under the title *Choujinrou Senki Warwolf,* this game was designed for use with the Nintendo Entertainment System, which was the most popular home gaming system of the time.

In the game, the player assumes control of a character simply named, somewhat amusingly, "Werewolf." This Werewolf guy has his hands full with saving a postapocalyptic wasteland from the clutches of his evil nemesis, a most atypical mad scientist named Dr. Faryan. Apparently, Dr. Faryan has nothing better to do with his time than to create monstrous, man-eating mutants in order to make the situation even worse (after all, the game is supposed to take place in a *post*apocalyptic world). Using his mutant-monster minions, the game explains that Dr. Faryan has managed to imprison every person on the planet (except you, of course).

To make the situation even more hilarious, the player's character starts out the game as nothing but a normal dude just walking around the wastelands without a shirt on (and, due to the old graphics, he looks a lot like a hunchback). But have no fear because, once the player leads the character into contact with a big "W" (which, for reasons that are left fairly unexplained, is just sitting out in the middle of nowhere), he transforms into a werewolf. Even after a random homeless guy explains to the player what has happened, it still doesn't really make sense how touching a big letter gives the character lycanthropy. Regardless, Werewolf now heads off to save the imprisoned inhabitants of the world and spends pretty much every second of the game kicking the snot out of some serious mutant-monster-minion booty.

Perhaps the most hilarious bad guy character rears his ugly head now and again throughout the game. He is a big bald guy, also with no shirt on (apparently, shirts were mostly optional after the apocalypse), whom the game dubs the "Giant Head." This is funny because his head isn't any more giantlike than it should be for his size. In fact, it's pretty proportional. This character, many players have commented, is perhaps the easiest one to kill in the whole game. Every time the Giant Head is defeated, the player's werewolf powers are given another boost ... which also occurs for unexplained reasons.

In the end, Werewolf comes face-to-face with the evil Dr. Faryan, who immediately drinks some crazy concoction of werewolf juice that he whipped up in the lab. Of course, now he turns into a werewolf, too ... only he has giant blades for arms (unlike you) ... because he's a *mutant* werewolf ... that makes sense, right? *Werewolf: The Last Warrior* may not go down in history as one of the greatest games ever to bless the many consoles of the Nintendo Entertainment System, but it is certainly good for a laugh or two.

Wolfchild

The game *Wolfchild* was developed and released by Core Design Ltd. in 1992. Several console-compatible versions were created for a plethora of systems such as the Sega Genesis, Super NES, and Atari ST, to name just a few. *Wolfchild*, like many werewolf games of its kind, is of the side-scrolling, "beat-'em-up" style.

The story of the game follows the adventures of Saul Morrow to rescue his kidnapped father, Dr. Kal Morrow, who is a genetic scientist specializing in human-animal hybrids (because, apparently, you are supposed to believe that such a field of science exists). Saul's entire family was murdered during the kidnapping, which was carried out by a terrorist group called CHIMERA, leaving him as the sole survivor.

Using his father's experiment notes, Saul manages to find a way to transform himself into a wolf-man hybrid (though apparently only in certain circumstances because he only changes when a certain number of the right enemies have been defeated). With his new powers, Saul Morrow heads out on a mission to save his father and take his revenge on CHIMERA for murdering his family.

Wolfsbane

The PC game *Wolfsbane* was developed by Moonlight Games and released by Merit Studios Inc. in 1995. The game was meant for DOS-prompt computers, a now-defunct operating system that required the user to type in routing and execution in order to open and operate its programs or software. While the game had a "point-and-click" style of play, the computers it was designed for certainly did not.

In *Wolfsbane*, players assume the role of a traveling merchant who is attacked and bitten one night by a werewolf. He survives but now has the curse of lycanthropy. The goal of the game is for the player to follow clues and solve puzzles in order to discover a cure for the merchant's werewolf curse before a set time limit expires.

The Beast Within

In the 1990s, third-person interactive games were considered a breakthrough in gaming. Unfortunately, however, the "interactive" part was usually limited to pointing and clicking on one choice from a list of options. While this allowed the game to have several possible outcomes, the player could not directly influence or take part in the resulting action sequences after each choice. These games used combinations of preshot video clips of live actors that linked together like a movie that could have a number of different plot twists and, sometimes at least, different final outcomes.

One such game was called *The Beast Within*, which was the second installment of a series called *Gabriel Knight Mystery*. The game was developed and released by Sierra On-Line, Inc. in 1995. The main character of the game, Gabriel Knight, looks and acts sort of like a mix between the detective Sherlock Holmes and a younger Abraham Van Helsing. The plot explains that Knight is descended from an ancient bloodline of "shadow-hunters," men who are destined to battle the forces of evil.

After the first game, Gabriel Knight moves to his family's castle in Bavaria. Shortly after settling in, a group of local villagers come to him and beg his help. They explain that a little girl from the village was mauled to death by a wolf, and they believe the wolf is actually a werewolf. Knowing that Gabriel Knight is a shadow-hunter, they ask him to destroy the creature. His investigation leads him into a shaky alliance with an ancient Bavarian group of monster hunters, aptly named the Hunter Society.

Underworld: The Eternal War

Based on the *Underworld* movie franchise, *Underworld: The Eternal War* was developed by Lucky Chicken Games and released by Play It Ltd. in January of 2004, soon after the successful run of the first film of the series. The game is designed in the now rather popular "third-person shooter" format. This means that the player controls the firing and other actions of the played character from an elevated view.

Underworld: The Eternal War offers the player a choice between the two sides of the war between vampires and werewolves, on which the movie plots are based. On one hand, the player can choose to be the werewolf-killing vampire Selene. On the other hand, the player may choose to be the powerful werewolf named Raze. As far as game play goes, this one is very much a "shoot-'em-up" but with three dimensions of movement thanks to the wonders of modern gaming technology.

White Wolf's Werewolf RPG Series

Probably the most popular werewolf-based role-playing game in history began with *Werewolf: The Forsaken* from White Wolf Publishing. The developers of this game went all out in order to create a new and unique depiction of werewolves. The game offers a number of different werewolf types and tribes in order to suit the tastes of just about any lycanthropy enthusiast.

In the game, the werewolves refer to themselves as the "Garou," which was taken from the obscure Frankish term that is the latter root for the French word for werewolf, *loup-garou*. These werewolves, much like the werewolves of *Twilight* and *Underworld*, consider themselves to be natural and sworn enemies of vampires. The player creates his or her own Garou character, using any combination of elements that ultimately make up the said character's conception, origins, background story, and tribal affiliation.

The Savage Truth

In recent years, White Wolf has phased out the original *Werewolf* game guides and replaced them with a new, more universal system called GURPS: Shapeshifters. GURPS stands for Generic Universal Role-Playing System. Since the new game system allows players to choose from a vast array of shapeshifters, *Werewolf* was slowly pushed out. These days, old copies of the original *Werewolf: The Forsaken* and *Werewolf: The Apocalypse* guidebooks can sometimes be found in certain bookstores, comic stores, or online.

The game first offers gamers a choice of three possible origins (or "breeds") for their werewolf characters, which are as follows:

- ◆ **Homid:** This title refers to werewolves who were raised in human society, totally unaware of their lycanthropy until they experienced their initial transformation. This is the most commonly found breed of the Garou.

- ◆ **Lupus:** These are werewolves raised almost like natural wolves, mostly in the wild and away from people. They don't fit in very well among humans, often sticking out like sore thumbs. Many werewolves of this breed do not even speak a human language, and usually they are hostile toward humans, believing that most of the world's ailments are caused by them.

- ◆ **Metis:** This title refers to the sadly deformed and sterile offspring that often result from a mating between two werewolves. They are not as civilized as the Homids but not nearly as wild as the Lupus. Unlike the other two breeds, however, their wolf-human forms are permanent, and they are incapable of shapeshifting.

Once the player has chosen his character's origin, it is time to choose a tribe. The Garou are divided into 13 primary tribes, thus allowing the player an even larger field from which to choose a group that suits his personality, beliefs, or tendencies. The tribes of the Garou are as follows:

- **Black Furies:** An almost completely female tribe of tough warriors, they only allow males among them if they are of the sterile Metis breed.

- **Bone Gnawers:** Basically, werewolves that live and act like homeless people.

- **Children of Gaia:** A peaceful tribe that seeks to secure a unity between all the Garou, regardless of breed or tribe. However, if forced to fight they do so with all the fervor of religious fanatics … because that's what they are.

- **Fianna:** This is a tribe of werewolves from the Celtic regions, most well known for being partiers, storytellers, and *very* heavy drinkers. However, they are also the keepers of much of the Garou's lost or forgotten myths.

- **The Get of Fenris:** Basically, think werewolves mixed with Germanic Vikings. Some members of this tribe hold to the German fascist beliefs of the recent past.

- **Glass Walkers:** This tribe of werewolves behaves more like a corporation. Glass Walkers really dig technology, and as a result they have very strong connections with the human world … from corporations to organized crime.

- **Red Talons:** This tribe is militantly antihuman, so it does not allow Homid-bred members. They believe that the only way to heal Gaia (what we would call "Mother Earth") is to wipe humans off the face of the planet.

- **Shadow Lords:** This tribe seeks to assume leadership of the Garou and hates the Silver Fangs who continue to claim that the old traditions of birth give them the right to assume that role no matter how poorly they execute it.

- **Silent Striders:** Werewolf gypsies … enough said.

◆ **Silver Fangs:** In the past, this tribe led the Garou. According to tradition, they still do. However, inbreeding with too much human nobility has led their later generations to be fairly incompetent.

◆ **Stargazers:** A rather small tribe that consists primarily of converts from other tribes. Think werewolf hippies and you get the idea. However, they are not bad fighters since they are the only remaining keepers of the Garou's lost tradition of martial arts.

◆ **Uktena:** This tribe was originally Native American, but it has long had an open policy for taking in members from immigrant minorities who came to the New World. They are thought of by the other Garou tribes as dangerous mystics who too often mess with things they shouldn't.

◆ **Wendigo:** This tribe is purely Native American, and they hold a longstanding grudge against European werewolves for taking part in the confiscation of their lands. They tolerate the Uktena tribe and Silent Striders, but werewolves from any of the other tribes are met with violent hostility. They have a special dislike for the Get of Fenris, Shadow Lords, and Silver Fangs.

BiteFight.org

At the free online community game site BiteFight.org, players can join the ages old war between werewolves and vampires. With nothing more than a computer and e-mail address, anyone can join the *BiteFight* network. BiteFight.org was developed and continues to be hosted by the German gaming-technology company Game Forge AG.

After joining, players can choose to fight as either werewolves or vampires. Both character types come with their own set of skills, strengths, and specific weaknesses. *BiteFight* players must learn how to effectively capitalize on their own strengths, as well as to take advantage of their enemy's weaknesses, in order to succeed in the online world of the game.

Once their character types have been chosen, players must decide whether to play independently or to create or join werewolf/vampire clans of their own. One of the primary aims of the *BiteFight* game is to become a part of a powerful clan, either by gaining membership or by creating and recruiting other players. The more players, and more powerful players, a clan has, the more powerful it becomes and the higher it is ranked on the network.

Wolf Team

In June 2009, the game development company Softnyx released their online werewolf-based game, *Wolf Team*. The *Wolf Team* game, once it has been bought and downloaded, allows players to assume the roles of French werewolf mercenaries on the run from the French military. Players must gauge between fighting in their well-armed human or strong but savage werewolf forms, using their judgment to decide when and if they should use their more powerful werewolf forms.

The *Wolf Team* story explains how a pharmaceutical company, while researching the development of a new antibiotic, stumbled upon a serum that could allow a certain amount of the world's population, those with a specific genetic makeup, to transform into werewolves. The French government took possession of the serum and recruited skilled soldiers with the right genetic makeup from all over the world, using them to create a team of werewolf super-soldiers, which they dubbed "The Second Foreign Legion."

The French government, however, soon found that they could not maintain enough control over these new werewolf soldiers. The men often went on violent rampages while on missions, going berserk and destroying anything and anyone who got in their way. Sometimes, they would even fight amongst themselves. Plans began to be put in place to eliminate the werewolf soldiers.

Before the plans could be executed, the werewolf soldiers were sent on a final mission. Soon, reports came in that seven of the soldiers had been killed when the team members began to fight with each other in their werewolf forms. The government sent human soldiers and a team of scientists to investigate. They never returned alive, each of them killed.

Knowing that the government would never allow them to live, the werewolf soldiers went rogue. They went into hiding and used their elite military training to drop off the grid. They now work all over the world as independent mercenaries, completing missions for the highest bidders, while also doing their best to avoid being detected and captured by the same French military authorities who originally turned them into the creatures they have become.

The Least You Need to Know

◆ The "Werewolf" party game is the easiest to play because all you need are enough people and a pen and paper to make up cards.

◆ While *Werewolf: The Last Warrior* is good for laughs, it is not one of the better werewolf games out there.

◆ *Underworld: The Eternal War* is based on the plot of the centuries old wolf-vampire war of the *Underworld* movie franchise.

◆ The most interesting contribution of the *White Wolf* role-playing series was the creation of new breeds and tribes that paved the way for a modern mythos regarding werewolves.

Chapter 14

Werewolves and Urban Legends

In This Chapter

- ◆ The many sightings of the creature known as the Beast of Bray Road
- ◆ A look at the legend of the Michigan Dog-Man
- ◆ The unusual (as well as somewhat hilarious) case of the 1972 incident in Ohio referred to as the "Werewolf of Defiance"
- ◆ The many British legends of ominous deaths following unusual encounters with ghostly black hounds

Urban legends and local folklore exist in every society. Sometimes it is but a single misunderstood incident that leads to such tales, which often spread and influence the perceptions of others. In other situations, it may one day prove true that all legends begin with an original historic truth. What follows is a collection of such legends, some of which are believed (by some people, at least) to be true historic accounts of encounters with werewolves over the last few centuries. One of the most enjoyable things about investigating urban legends is that usually one can discover the actual historic events that sparked them. What can be even more entertaining is investigating further and discovering how the word-of-mouth stories that are inevitably created following these actual events continue to grow until they become, metaphorically speaking, "beasts that cannot be fed."

The Beast of Bray Road

Local folklore about this Wisconsin creature has been around for nearly a century, though the name "Beast of Bray Road" is a fairly new title. This name comes from the location of the first sighting of the beast where the witness went public with what she'd seen. There is an unusual level of consistency in nearly all accounts of past and present encounters with the creature, which is usually described as a large, seemingly intelligent beast. Some insist that this creature is a Sasquatch, commonly known as Bigfoot. Others believe that this may be some nearly extinct species of North American gorilla or some other large primate that has learned to remain far from humans in order to survive. There are many, however, who hold to the belief that it is a different creature entirely … one that far more resembles the common mental image of a werewolf. Most concede that this animal is likely not a shapeshifter, but they still insist that it may be responsible for the werewolf legends.

The so-called Beast of Bray Road is usually said to walk in a bipedal fashion and is described as standing at roughly 7 feet tall. Encounters with this beast when assuming a four-legged stance commonly describe it at an average of over 3 feet high. Size estimates vary greatly, ranging anywhere from 250 to 700 pounds. However, some argue that this may be because it is not one creature but a pack. Some theorize it is a pack of giant prehistoric wolves that are thought to be extinct. Others, however, call the beast the

The Savage Truth

Bray Road is a rural road in southeastern Wisconsin that runs in a fairly east-west direction between the cities of Elkhorn and Bowers and bypasses the busier roadways of Interstate 43 and State Road 11.

"Werewolf of Wisconsin," and believe that these people have come face to face with a lycanthrope.

One Scary Halloween on Bray Road

The first sighting to bring nationwide attention to the Beast of Bray Road occurred on Halloween in 1999. Eighteen-year-old Doristine Gipson was driving east along Bray Road, having just left her hometown of Elkhorn, Wisconsin. While slowing down as she approached an intersection, Doristine reached down to adjust the station on her radio. Suddenly, the front right corner of her car jerked up. Believing she had hit something, the girl pulled over. She got out so she could see what she hit. However, she couldn't see anything in the road to explain what made the car jump. It was dark and cloudy, and the visibility was not ideal.

Suddenly, Doristine saw the outline of a hulking figure in the darkness, no more than 50 feet away, but she could not readily identify it. Then the creature charged at her without warning. She heard the heavy pounding of its rushing feet against the surface of the road, and the animal's hard, heavy breathing. In a panic, she immediately raced back into her car and locked the doors. She felt the entire car shift suddenly as the enormous creature pounced onto the rear hood of the vehicle. She started the engine and began to drive away. The beast held on for a brief moment but soon slid off of the car's slippery wet surface and onto the road. Shaken but unharmed, Doristine continued on with her plans to take a younger girl out for some trick-or-treating. She tried to tell herself that it must have been a bear that probably grew enraged because she'd hit it with the car. However, Doristine's encounters with this beast were not yet over.

Later that night, Doristine was driving back along Bray Road. The girl she'd promised to take trick-or-treating was in the passenger seat. When she reached the same intersection where she believed she'd hit a bear, she pulled over. This time, however, she stayed in the car (as most thinking people probably would at that point). Soon a tall, massive, and hairy figure stepped out from the side of the road. Seeing this, Dorsitine immediately told the other girl to lock her door. When the beast again began moving toward them, Doristine burned rubber out of there.

The next day, Doristine realized that there was some disturbing damage to her vehicle. Unsure what to do, she decided to confide in another woman, her friend and neighbor. She told the woman what had happened and showed her the damage to the vehicle, mainly consisting of deep scratches (as if from claws) in the paint and some wide but shallow dents on the trunk. Both women decided to let fellow locals know what had happened, just in case they encountered the animal (because it appeared to be violent). Talk of the incident was soon all over the area, and Doristine would learn that she was not alone. Several people in the area came forward with their own accounts of close encounters with a large beast (many while driving along Bray Road). Like Doristine, many had just convinced themselves that it had been a bear. Others feared that people would think they were crazy and so kept it to themselves. Doristine realized she was definitely not the first person to encounter this animal ... and she certainly would not be the last.

So a Werewolf Walks Into a Bartender ...

Later that same fall, 24-year-old Lorianne Endrizzi, the manager of a local watering hole, was driving west along Bray Road on her way home to Elkhorn. At a spot less than a half-mile from the site of Doristine Gipson's encounter, she saw what at first looked to her like a person hunched over. Thinking that perhaps it was an injured person or a bar patron who had just had a few too many, she slowed the vehicle down to a crawl. She approached cautiously.

The dark, kneeling figure less than 6 feet from the passenger side of her vehicle, which she now saw was eating something out of its palms, lifted its head and looked her dead in the eyes. Lorianne did not stop the car. Though she passed by the creature relatively slowly (likely from the shock), the smart young woman just kept right on driving (once she felt out of the beast's reach, of course, she sped up considerably).

Lorianne estimated that she had her eyes locked on the beast for roughly three-quarters of a minute. In her eyewitness account, she described the creature she saw as very large and muscular, with gray-brown fur, pointy ears, eyes that reflected yellow against her headlights, and a long wolflike snout, from which protruded a set of fangs. She also added that she'd caught sight of its hands, which she claimed were certainly not claws but long, fur-coated fingers similar to a human's.

Lorianne, when asked what the animal was, could not come up with an answer. She had never seen anything like it. Some time later, however, while flipping through a book, she came upon an illustration of a werewolf. Thereafter, she claimed that this illustration was the only thing she'd seen that had a close resemblance to the creature she saw. This added the element of lycanthropy to the creature.

Bark vs. Bite

Did Lorianne really come face to face with a werewolf (or something close to one)? This is certainly possible. However, there may be another explanation. Considering that word of Doristine Gipson's encounter had recently spread through the area, it's not unlikely that news reached the ears of some prankster(s). Choosing a spot not too far from where it was said Gipson saw the creature, some joker could've donned a furry disguise (a padded gorilla suit or werewolf costume) and waited to see headlights. He might've then crouched on the roadside until Lorianne's car passed by. Though she claims its eyes reflected her headlights like an animal's, custom glass animal eyes from a quality mask could possibly have achieved this effect.

The Michigan Dog-Man

Among experts who study such cases, there are those who believe that the two creatures, referred to by residents as the "Michigan Dog-Man" and the "Werewolf of Wisconsin/Beast of Bray Road," are not actually separate entities but one and the same beast. It is undeniable that the majority of eyewitness descriptions of the Michigan Dog-Man are nearly identical to those from encounters with the Beast of Bray Road.

However, there is one issue with the theory that this is the same creature. In order for the animal to be in even half of the primary sighting areas, it would have to travel the roughly 350-mile-long trek (mostly along the southern coast of Lake Michigan) between the Bray Road area of Wisconsin and the most common Michigan sighting locations and do so rather frequently. Not to mention, it would have to do so without being seen since it has never been spotted *between* the two locations. However, it is entirely possible that these are two (or possibly far more) creatures that are simply of the same or similar species.

Bark vs. Bite

The majority of Michigan Dog-Man sightings have occurred around Manistee County, home to the Manistee National Forest wildlife preserve. This preserve is home to a fair population of both black bears and coyotes. It is entirely possible that many Dog-Man sightings are from people who simply experienced frightening or unexpected close encounters with these animals. Having heard the local legends, their panicked minds may have concluded that the creature they saw was the Dog-Man. Then again … maybe it really was.

The 1967 Manistee Sighting

In 1967, two fishermen were returning their rowboat to the south shore of Manistee County's Claybake Lake after a day of catching little to nothing in the way of fish. As they got closer to shore, one man noticed some kind of animal was swimming right for their boat. At first, they thought it must be a deer. But why would a deer, a naturally wary animal, be moving toward them?

By the time the creature was upon them, they were certain that this was no deer. They saw a hairy, humanoid figure with a doglike snout and pawed hands and feet. They stood there, awestruck, as the creature suddenly slammed into the boat. It placed its front paws over the side of the boat and began to pull itself on board. The two men finally got their nerves back together. They took up oars and began to beat the creature back before it could get onto their boat. Eventually, the creature let go and the two men rowed for the shore. Once safely on land, they scanned the area. The creature was by then nowhere to be seen.

The 1987 Luther Sighting

In July of 1987, an animal attack call came into the Lake County Sheriff's Office. Apparently, a large animal had tried to force its way into a small cabin in the area, doing some damage in the process. The sheriff headed to the scene, but only after contacting a forestry ranger and asking him to come along. The two men even made jokes about the Dog-Man during their telephone conversation.

When they arrived on the scene, however, their laughter turned to shock. Wood planks on the cabin's exterior had been shredded in certain places, and deep gouges in the wood appeared to have been made by massive claws (some were as deep as 2 inches). The outer screens to nearly every window of the cabin had been torn to pieces. The sheriff commented that it must have been a bear. The cabin owner, however, insisted that it had definitely *not* been a bear. The cabin owner also pointed out unusual tracks in the dirt, which could not have come from a bear. In fact, they resembled a dog's paw prints ... only *much* bigger. The sheriff and ranger filed the case as an attack by an "unidentified animal." Apparently, neither public servant was willing to submit the incident as a "Dog-Man attack."

The 1993 Reed City Sighting

In the late winter months of 1993, a teenage girl named Courtney (who reported the event a decade later) encountered a Dog-Man near her parents' rural home near Lake Todd in Reed City, Michigan. The sighting occurred as Courtney was sneaking a cigarette behind the house. At the time, around dusk, she reported that she had been facing a dilapidated barn on the neighboring property.

A piece of farm machinery near the barn seemed to move, and Courtney thought it might be a deer. Suddenly, however, trees nearby the barn began shaking and she heard the sound of branches snapping. Suddenly, a very large animal emerged from the woods, apparently standing on two legs. She claimed that it also had a canine snout and pointed ears. The sun had set by now, and the darkness impeded her vision. Courtney dropped her smoke and dashed indoors for a flashlight. By the time she came back outside, however, the creature had disappeared.

The 2009 Temple Sighting

In early 2009, two teenage girls were babysitting for a neighbor in Temple, Michigan. After nightfall, they put the children to bed and sat together in the living room to watch television. Suddenly, they saw a hulking shadow pass across the window. They were both terrified, believing that a potential intruder might be lurking outside.

In order to help them see outside, and to prevent the person outside from seeing in, they immediately shut off every light in the house. Soon after, they heard a loud rustle that seemed to be coming from the property's nearby barn. The girls headed for a window on that side of the house, now believing that this might be a bear after the owner's chickens. Just in case, one girl grabbed her digital camera from her purse.

They got up the nerve to step out onto the porch together. As soon as the girls emerged, they described what they saw as a "giant dog" coming out from around the barn. It looked at them briefly before taking off into the woods. One girl managed to snap off a picture with the camera just in time. The picture is now considered an impressive piece of evidence that supports the Dog-Man's existence. In truth, the figure in this photo does seem to look very "werewolflike." Copies of the photograph are available all over the Internet.

When the owners returned, the girls told them what had happened. The man of the house went out to the barn to investigate. He claimed to have found a number of rather large paw prints in the snow around the barn. Unfortunately, they were destroyed by new snowfall before they could be cast or documented.

Bark vs. Bite

Many skeptics have pointed out one hole in the validity of this sighting. The girls had a digital camera at the time the owner found the paw prints. This means that he could have at least photographed the prints. Why did he not use the camera to take pictures of the prints, instead of waiting until he could cast them later?

Defiance, Ohio: A Werewolf in Blue Jeans

From the last week of July into the early weeks of August in 1972, some "thing" was lurking in darkness around the area of the Norfolk-Western railroad tracks, located on the outskirts of the small town of Defiance, Ohio.

The first encounter was on the Saturday night of July 25, 1972, when railroad employee Ted Davis found himself confronted by a 6-foot-tall, hairy ... thing. Thinking this must be a practical joke, Mr. Davis started to say something. The thing, however, ran off into the nearby woods before he could say a word. The next night, he and another co-worker saw it again, this time at a distance. Both men decided they should let authorities know about it. Their descriptions were fairly similar (for example, both men said it had been wearing blue jeans ... something werewolves are known to do ... right?) except when it came to height. Mr. Davis told officers that it was about 6 feet tall. His co-worker, however, claimed that it was more like 8 feet tall. Authorities decided to investigate but chose not to disclose the report to the local townspeople. After all, this was probably just some bored local kids messing around.

In the days that followed, witnesses began coming into the Defiance police station with similar, but mostly vague and unusual, descriptions of nocturnal attacks. They insisted that their assailant was tall (between 7 and 9 feet, according to many eyewitness statements to police), covered with fur, with fangs and the head of an animal ... basically explaining that it/he looked a *lot* like a werewolf. Within a little more than one week, at least three people had reported being violently accosted by the same furry perpetrator.

The Savage Truth

The small town of Defiance is located in northern Ohio and is less than an hour's drive from the southern border of Michigan. This has led a few beast investigators to theorize that these, too, were encounters with a beast of the same species as the Beast of Bray Road and the Michigan Dog-Man. Unlike sightings of those creatures, however, sightings of the Defiance werewolf have not occurred since the late summer/ early fall of 1972.

One detail, however, soon blew most of the air out of the initial theories that these attacks were being carried out by a werewolf. In the second week, another man was attacked by something tall and hairy. This time, however, the thing smacked him over the head, "pro wrestler style," with a wood two-by-four. Though dazed, the man managed to escape.

The night just after this, a group of three unidentified locals entered the Defiance Police Station in a state of absolute panic. They begged the officers to protect them. When asked what they needed protection from, the only answer they could provide was that they were being chased by a "thing." Apparently, they'd heard this "thing" but never actually laid eyes on it. Sometime shortly after this, it would seem almost the whole town of Defiance, Ohio, went temporarily insane. Chaos (and some hilarity) soon ensued.

That same night, just after one in the morning, a panicked local man came to the police station to report that something had begun following him near the tracks earlier the previous evening. He'd run to a local hotel to take shelter in the lobby, where he appears to have been for most of the night before going to the police.

Only 10 minutes later, a local woman called the station, telling officers that a friend had come by her house in a state of absolute hysteria. She'd only just heard the story about this "thing" and had gone frantic because for the last few weeks, at two o'clock every morning, someone (or perhaps some "thing") had been rattling the knob of her front door. Hearing about the "thing" and realizing how close to two o'clock it was, the woman had immediately fled her own house (probably still wearing her nightgown). She sought refuge at the nearby home of a friend, who then called the police.

Sightings continued on for a couple of weeks, mostly coming in from railroad employees and motorists. However, the attacks seem to have stopped. Perhaps the so-called "Werewolf of Defiance," who was almost certainly some idiot in a mask, decided that he liked being a local legend much better than consistently sucking at being a mugger.

Bark vs. Bite _____

You probably don't need to be told that the Defiance werewolf likely wasn't a werewolf at all. Exhibit A … it didn't kill anyone. Exhibit B … werewolves are not known to use two-by-fours to take someone down (and if they did, it would probably be fatal). More than likely, this was some drug addict or homeless person who, needing money and having no other disguise than a rubber werewolf mask, put the thing over his head and started attacking people in attempts to rob them. FYI, he was never reported to have successfully done so (which, ironically, was probably due to the mask he was wearing).

The Black Hounds of Britain

In towns and shires all across the United Kingdom, one can find a multitude of local legends regarding unusual occurrences related to encounters with ghostly black dog figures. The ill fates that are often said to have befallen those who have seen these dogs have led many to label them with the title of *hellhounds*.

Beastly Words _____

Hellhounds are exactly what their title suggests—hounds that come from hell. This idea likely originated from an ancient myth, such as that of the giant, three-headed dog named Cerberus that guards the gates of the underworld (the domain of the death god Hades) in Greek mythology. These dogs are often described as black, sometimes resembling shadows, with glowing red eyes.

The exact origins of these stories are unknown. Some say they are literally true, while others view them as mythic metaphors associated with the fear of death and/or misfortune. Many black dog legends claim that the number of times one saw a hellhound dictated what would happen. Most commonly, one time means joy, two times means ill fortune, and a third time is a sign of an untimely death (of the person or someone close to him or her).

The significance of three suggests an origin from ancient mythology, when monstrous canines were often said to guard the threshold to certain realms of the dead. For example, Norse myth has the figure of Fenrir, a gigantic wolf that is bound until the arrival of Ragnarok (the Norse version of the apocalypse). Most westerners are more familiar with the Greek myth of Cerberus. Cerberus was a terribly strong and enormous dog, said to have three heads, that guarded the gate to the underworld. This likely led to an anglicized version of the legend that seeing a black dog three times is an omen of death.

The Curse

In the popular television series *Supernatural,* hell-hounds are demonic beasts that collect the souls of those who have made deals with a "crossroads demon."

How'd That Dog Get in Here?

One story from the latter half of the sixteenth century tells of one such black dog encounter that befell a church in Suffolk. A terrible thunderstorm rattled the structure of the church during a regular sermon. Suddenly a snarling, pitch black dog appeared near the pulpit before the entire congregation. The dog's presence inside of the church was especially odd because all windows and doors had already been secured to keep out the storm.

The dog stepped forward as the congregation watched in stunned silence.

The shadowy animal brushed against one churchgoer, who was probably paralyzed with fear. The man immediately fell stone dead to the floor. The man's wife reached for him and also brushed against the black fur of this hellish creature. As a result, she too was struck dead, following her husband into the afterlife. A third man boldly took hold of the creature to remove it from the church. His fate was even worse. The story goes that he shrieked feebly as his entire body shriveled like a prune, as if his very life-force was being drained from his body. He soon fell to the floor, looking much like a mummy.

There's That Dog Again!

According to the legend, this same black hound also appeared before a congregation at a church in Blythburg almost immediately after the incident at the Suffolk church. This was thought unusual because the churches sat roughly 7 to 8 miles away from one another.

The outcome of the black hound's appearance at the Blythburg church would be no less tragic than at Suffolk. Again, the hound took the lives of three church members. The head clergyman stepped forward, leading a group of fellow priests and invoking the name of God in an attempt to restrain the dark beast. The entire group, however, was blown clear across the church by some unseen force. Today, many landmark buildings in Blythburg can be seen with dog-shaped weather-vanes, said to represent this black hound of death, as a grim memorial of the incident.

The Savage Truth

In the *Harry Potter* series by J. K. Rowling, a character by the name of Sirius Black assumes the form of a black hound. This causes Harry and his friends to mistakenly believe that Harry has fallen under the shadow of an evil omen called "The Grim." J. K. Rowling's use of this idea was likely inspired by the British lore about ominous black hounds.

He Don't Brake for Hellhounds

Another British hellhound story dates from the late nineteenth century and allegedly occurred in or around Norfolk. The story usually goes that, on that particular day, two farmers were in a hurry, running late with their goods, which they were to sell at the town market (most versions claim the market was in Norfolk). They whipped their horses, forcing them to pull the heavily packed wagon as fast as possible—without throwing their precious cargo, of course.

A black dog with blazing red eyes stepped into the wagon's path, though it was still a good ways ahead. The farmer who was driving the wagon, not wanting to risk being slowed down or having his wagon tipped by attempting to avoid the animal, is said to have driven right over the shadowy beast without so much as slowing down. This would certainly have been considered a rather disrespectful (not to mention stupid) transgression against an obvious messenger of death. Suddenly both men began to notice the heavy odors of sulfur and smoke. They soon came to the realization that, much to their horror, the entire wagon (which, as one might expect, was made entirely of wood) was now completely engulfed in flames. The hound, it seemed, had disappeared into a raging ball of fire.

The men now had no other choice but to leap from the wagon, both barely escaping with their lives. Sadly, however, they lost all of their sale goods, not to mention their wagon and both of the horses. Some versions of the story say the two horses ran straight through the market of Norfolk, dragging behind them the ball of fire that had once been a wagon full of valuable goods. Spurred on by the flames (which to them probably seemed to be pursuing close behind), the horses eventually ran themselves to death.

As for the driver who so hastily drove over the fiery beast? Well, most versions of the legend tell that the wagon driver was dead before the next morning (though some versions claim he died at sundown, at the moment when the last rays of the sun disappeared over the horizon). Some stories say the other farmer escaped with only some form of permanent injury or maiming, while others say that he, too, was soon dead. However, the details regarding when the second farmer died are rather vague. It would be obvious to anyone that the man died eventually, but many such versions of this legend fail to elaborate as to whether he died *much* later or just by a matter of days. One version claims that the wagon-driving farmer died at sunset (which is, incidentally, when the moon became fully visible) and the other farmer met his end upon the following sunrise (when the moon disappeared).

The Least You Need to Know

- ◆ While some insist that the Beast of Bray Road is a Sasquatch, most locals insist that it looks like a werewolf.

- ◆ Some beast investigators theorize that the Michigan Dog-Man and the "Werewolf of Wisconsin" are actually the same creature or at least animals of the same species.

◆ The incidents surrounding the so-called "Werewolf of Defiance" would probably be more appropriately referred to as "The Heyday of Some Moron in a Wolf Mask."

◆ The United Kingdom has a multitude of local folklore, much of which includes stories about terrible occurrences caused by encounters with shadowy canine figures.

Part 4

Of Wolf and Man

How do we as individuals address the bestial side of our natures? What should one expect to experience (hypothetically) if bitten by a werewolf or otherwise somehow afflicted with it? What should one do if confronted by a werewolf (aside from run screaming, of course)? What are the potential rational explanations for lycanthropy? What do werewolves represent to the psyche? The answers to these questions and more are conveniently at your fingertips.

Chapter 15

Once Bitten ... Then What?

In This Chapter

- How to know if you or someone you know has been infected with lycanthropy
- A close examination of each of the three degrees of lycanthropic infection
- What every newly infected werewolf needs to know about his or her first transformation
- Just how much you may or may not need to concern yourself with the moon
- A look at some of the potential cures for those infected with lycanthropy

So you've been bitten by a werewolf, have you? This probably means that any number of possibilities has occurred. Perhaps you failed to heed the warnings provided in Chapter 1 and decided that you would just go looking for a lycanthrope on your own. Then again, you may have gotten hasty and decided you would try to hunt down a werewolf before you finished reading (or even bothered looking at) Chapter 16 on how to properly deal with one. Of course, there is also the possibility that you had a run-in with a werewolf long before you ever got your hands on this book. The matter of how you came to be in this precarious situation is, quite honestly, no longer of any real consequence. What's done is done … right?

If you have been bitten by a werewolf, or just suspect you have, then at the present moment there is probably only one question going through your mind. What in the world are you supposed to do now? Well, sometimes the best medicine is to be as well informed as possible. The following pages can at least help you in that regard … but unfortunately, that is about all it *can* do for you. Best of luck, my future furry friend! Please keep in mind, most of the information in this chapter addresses cursed lycanthropy. Clinical, psychological, and enchanted forms do not always correspond to these symptoms or methods. Remember, there are many different types of lycanthropes.

The Primary Symptoms

Let's not panic just yet. It's quite possible that you were just bitten by some stray dog, rabid coyote, or some other breed of undomesticated canine. In any case, you should probably bandage the bite and just take this book with you to the emergency room so you can get yourself checked out. You can always read this over while you wait to be seen. Don't worry about "wolfing out" at the hospital. Most available accounts support the idea that you've still got enough time left to see a doctor before you start randomly attacking, biting, or eating people. Of course, knowing this may not be all that comforting.

There are a number of primary symptoms for which you should be on the lookout. The initial symptoms of lycanthropy infection are commonly thought to include combinations of the following:

- A sudden change in skin tone (usually the skin pales).

- Sporadic trouble controlling or focusing your eyesight.

- Temporary episodes during which you're *extremely* sensitive to certain sounds (especially if high pitched).

- Tear duct malfunctions, leading to shifting extremes of eye dryness and overflowing tears.

- You always feel thirsty, but water doesn't seem to help quench your thirst.

- A sudden development of *hydrophobia*, or "fear of water." (This doesn't count if you had hydrophobia to begin with.)

Beastly Words

Hydrophobia (hydro = water, phobia = fear) is an irrational and debilitating fear of all water. Many pieces of werewolf lore state that lycanthropes have an unnatural aversion to water.

- The Mark of the Beast appears on your body, usually described as a pentagram, circle of seven stars, or triangle. (On some occasions, it is wise to call your buddies to make sure you didn't just get a bad tattoo the previous night.)

Physical Symptoms

After the primary symptoms have set in, you will (or, hopefully, will not) begin to exhibit the more extreme and noticeable physical symptoms of lycanthropy. Unlike the primary symptoms, these physical symptoms are a bit harder to deny or explain away. The most extreme physical symptoms of lycanthropy are as follows:

- Constant body aches, yet at times you feel more energized than ever before in your life.

- Skin irritation, rashes, or constant itching.

- Increased body hair growth and thickness. (Sometimes this includes hairy palms.)

- Canine teeth begin to protrude and/or increase slightly in mass. (This change is usually minor until the first transformation.)

- Third and middle fingers begin to increase in length (as well as those same toes).

- Increased body mass, both skeletal and muscular.

Psychological Symptoms

The mind and body are undoubtedly linked. Therefore, it shouldn't come as a surprise that the onset of lycanthropy includes a number of psychological symptoms. At first, these will usually manifest as out-of-character behaviors or sudden changes in personality. For example, if you are the type of person who avoids confrontation, you may suddenly find yourself itching for a fight. If you are the type of person who is timid by nature, you may begin staring other people down to assert dominance. These manifestations are caused by the interaction between your preexisting human nature and the foreign invasion of the wolf nature brought on by lycanthropy.

The most common psychological symptoms of lycanthropy include the following:

♦ A strong, almost constant craving for red meat

♦ Unnecessary or uncharacteristically antisocial behavior

♦ Antiauthoritarian behavior

♦ Unprovoked acts of rebellion

♦ An uncontrollable urge to act out wolflike behaviors such as growling, howling, etc.

♦ Sudden and extreme increase in your *libido*/sex drive

Beastly Words

The **libido** is a Freudian term for the human sex drive. Newly infected lycanthropes are often said to experience a sudden and extreme increase in sexual appetite and endurance.

Degrees of Infection

For the sake of this book, the various levels of lycanthropic infection have been broken up into three main stages—first-, second-, and third-degree lycanthropy. To summarize, the basic criteria for each degree may be thought of as follows:

♦ First degree: Bitten/infected but has not yet undergone the first transformation

♦ Second degree: Has experienced first transformation but is still adapting to the new state of lycanthropy

◆ Third degree: Oldest and most powerful; can change shape at will and is believed to retain a high level of mental control in wolf form

If you've been bitten by a lycanthrope or in any way infected with lycanthropy, then you are experiencing first-degree lycanthropy. For the most part, you will continue to be in the first degree until the first transformation. This is commonly believed to occur roughly 30 days after the initial infection. In this stage, it is important to watch out for widespread combinations of the aforementioned physical and psychological symptoms. If you are uncertain as to whether or not you are infected with lycanthropy, your best bet is to isolate yourself as much as possible and wait 30 days. If you really have been infected, then it should become painfully obvious by then.

Second-degree lycanthropy infection begins at the moment of your first transformation into wolf form. At this stage, you will likely be unable to control your abilities. It is also unlikely that you will be able to change at will. Second-degree lycanthropy is usually the longest in duration since it is in this stage that your mind and body must adapt to its new forms and abilities.

Third-degree lycanthropes are the most dangerous. They are the oldest, strongest, and most skilled among werewolves. It would seem that few lycanthropes survive long enough to make it to this stage. A third-degree lycanthrope can shapeshift from human to wolf form and back at will. (However, some lore states that even third-degree lycanthropes are forced to change during the night of a full moon.)

The First Transformation

If you were thinking that your first transformation was going to be a blissful communion with nature, think again! Nearly every resource makes the same assertion. Your first lycanthropic transformation is going to hurt like hell. After all, your body is being forcefully transformed on both cellular and genetic levels. Does that sound pleasant to you? Of course, these rules may not apply to enchanted lycanthropes that use magical means to attain their forms.

There are a handful of sources that offer a couple of mildly comforting ideas. Some sources argue that it is only the initial transformation that is painful, and they claim that lycanthropes in the mid to latter stages of the second degree no longer experience pain when they transform. Others claim that the transformation itself is so severe in its impact on the human mind that the infected person does not even remember it once back in human form. So yes, there is no doubt that your first lycanthropic transformation is going to hurt and that it's going to hurt *a lot*. However, the good news is that there exists a very slim chance you won't even be able to remember the experience when you regain consciousness the next morning, back in your human form … stark raving naked … in the middle of the woods … with a dead rabbit in your mouth. There, now … don't you feel better?

The Full Moon

There is a bit of controversy in modern werewolf lore as to the role of the moon when it comes to its influence on lycanthropic transformations. The oldest lore states that a lycanthrope enters the werewolf state *only* on the night of a full moon. Later werewolf lore, however, as well as the majority of modern lore, insists that this is a misconception.

According to most current beliefs, a "young" werewolf (meaning one who still exhibits the early stages of second-degree lycanthropy) can't control his or her transformations. Therefore, the moon is at first the primary trigger for a "young" werewolf's transformations. However, it is thought that, somewhere in the middle stages of second-degree lycanthropy, extreme emotions such as anger or sexual arousal become secondary triggers for the change.

What about the full moon, however? Well, some modern lore claims that *all* lycanthropes involuntarily transform into either the werewolf or the full wolf state on the night of a full moon. Some believe that older werewolves (those who are well into the stages of third-degree lycanthropy) are able to resist the full moon's influence. Among some, there exists the belief that the whole idea that the moon influences lycanthropic transformations is nothing more than an old story and that it has no real merit. You may be wondering which of these is correct. As with much of the conflicting pages of werewolf lore … you'll just have to decide for yourself.

A Cure for Lycanthropy?

Unfortunately, there is no certain cure for an infection of actual lycanthropy (this does not include clinical lycanthropy, also known as psychological lycanthropy, which will be discussed in Chapter 18) unless one considers death a valid cure. However, in older werewolf lore, there were a number of methods believed to be effective in reversing the curse of lycanthropy. However, one must remember that most of these methods were written during or shortly after the Dark Ages, back when lycanthropy was considered a supernatural occurrence.

The known cures for lycanthropy, according to the old lore, are as follows:

- Exorcism
- Iron bars
- Charms or magic potions
- Calling the lycanthrope by his or her human name
- Simply telling the lycanthrope that he or she *is* a werewolf

The Demons Within

Lycanthropy, in much of the early church's lore on the subject, was caused either by making a pact with the devil or demonic possession. Therefore, it was believed that performing a rite of exorcism on the afflicted individual would cure him or her of lycanthropy.

The Savage Truth

The only officially sanctioned Roman Catholic rite of exorcism, which includes both written invocations and detailed physical instructions, may be found in any copy of the text referred to as the *Rituale Romanum*. This text is rather difficult to find in English translation. Unfortunately for the layman, the entire text is written in Latin. Therefore, it may be a little difficult to follow without the aid of either a priest or at least someone who has a working understanding of Latin.

The belief that lycanthropy was the result of demonic influences was probably spread throughout Europe during or shortly after the influx of Catholicism into the region. Many of the old religions, traditions, and beliefs were labeled as *pagan*. Before Christianity, this word was used to refer to country people who were considered "uncivilized." The Roman Church later adopted the word to refer to those who still practiced the "old ways," or pre-Christian religions.

Beastly Words

The term **pagan** originally comes from the Latin word *paganus*, which means "rustic" or "country person." During the rise of Christianity in the Roman Empire, the word came to refer to the "uncivilized" people who continued to practice polytheistic or pre-Christian religions. The word later took on a negative connotation and came to be associated with dark arts, devil worship, evil, etc. In recent years, the term has begun to shed this negative connotation as more people have begun to practice these old religions openly, now that they can do so without fear of harm.

Eventually, the Roman Church denounced nearly all pagan practices as witchcraft or in some way related to demonic rites or devil worship. As a result, it was most likely reasoned by the church that lycanthropy (a concept which, like other pagan beliefs, predated the arrival of Christianity in Europe) was also a product of interactions with the devil. This would explain how exorcism came to be seen as a potential cure for lycanthropy. However, the level of success (or failure) for this method is unclear or at least undocumented.

Got Iron? Or Potions?

The good news is that throwing or waving an iron bar, knife, or any other iron artifact over a werewolf will return it to human form. The bad news is that this method appears only to work against enchanted or magical lycanthropes. There are no recorded cases of this method being used against cursed lycanthropes. Though this would appear discouraging, the upside is that no one can say that it definitely *won't* work. I mean, considering the alternative, you'd probably want to exhaust all potential options.

Iron was considered a strong element for protection against magic/ curses or in the negation of spells. Similar methods were believed to be effective against witches. The belief was that, by doing this, one could temporarily render impotent any magical power. Therefore, it makes sense that this was believed to work in returning magical or enchanted lycanthropes to their human forms. In lore, these kinds of werewolves were often said to gain their abilities to assume the wolf state from a belt or shawl (usually constructed from wolf's skin).

As for potions, there were a few that claimed to cure lycanthropy. Unfortunately, after looking at the ingredients, one would likely come to the conclusion that these potions were written by people who considered death to be a valid cure. Nearly all of these potions contain at least one (usually more) highly poisonous or toxic ingredient that is more likely to *kill* anyone who drinks them than they are to cure anything. As a result, the details of these potions will not be provided in this text for the sake of safety.

Say My Name!

Could curing lycanthropy really be this simple? Well, according to some lore ... yes! According to a number of stories and myths, curing lycanthropy can be as simple as calling the werewolf by his or her human name. Unfortunately, the details about doing this are a little sketchy. For example, they don't explain whether or not just saying the afflicted individual's first name alone will do the trick. It is entirely possible that the person's last name will be needed as well. Perhaps the person's full given name is necessary. The stories are also unclear as to whether or not the name must be said while the person is still in wolf form (though one would imagine it would since it would stand to reason that many people would refer to the person by a human name when he or she is in human form). In using this method, it would be best to err on the side of caution.

What Am I?

Some lore explains that, similar to the "name" method, lycanthropy may be cured by simply informing afflicted people that they are a werewolf (because apparently they aren't already aware of it?). There is one story of such an occurrence that is told (in various but fairly similar versions) throughout regions of northern Europe.

There was once a man who had been afflicted with lycanthropy his entire life. However, he seemed to have learned to live with it fairly well since he managed to acquire a wife and home in his lifetime. One evening, however, he found himself still on the road home (driving a wagon with his wife sitting right beside him no less) as the full moon began to reveal itself in the darkening sky. He halted the wagon and handed the reins to his wife. The man got down and explained to his increasingly disconcerted wife that she was to wait with the wagon until he returned. He instructed her that, if any animal were to approach, she was to snap at it with her apron … and nothing more. Having given her these directions, the man disappeared into the woods.

Shortly after, the wife heard howling. Suddenly a werewolf (or, in some versions of the tale, just a wolf) charged from the woods and attacked her. She did as her husband had instructed and began to snap the werewolf's snout with her apron. Though the werewolf tore a chunk of the apron with its sharp fangs, the woman continued to fight. These strikes eventually seemed to bring the werewolf (her husband) back to his senses somewhat. Remembering himself, the werewolf ran back into the woods and again disappeared.

Moments passed before the woman's husband again emerged from the woods. He was completely disheveled, his clothes torn and hair a mess. From his mouth dangled the torn piece of fabric from his wife's apron. Seeing this, the wife cried out, "My husband! By God, you are a werewolf!" To which he replied "Thank you, my dear wife. I am finally free." From that day forward, it is said that the man never again experienced transformations of lycanthropy. Luckily, it would appear that his wife was willing to let "dead dogs lie," so to speak.

The Least You Need to Know

- If you have been bitten by a wolf or wild dog, the best thing to do is get to a hospital immediately. (A rabies infection is not fun.)

- Most lore supports that a newly infected lycanthrope will not transform until either 30 days passed or the next full moon after the initial bite.

- There are three degrees of lycanthropy, and one who has recently been bitten is only experiencing the first degree.

- Most lore supports the belief that all werewolves involuntarily transform on the night of a full moon.

- While there are a number of theoretical cures for lycanthropy, none of them is known for certain to be effective.

Chapter 16

How to Kill a Werewolf

In This Chapter

- ◆ Weapons that are believed to be effective against lycanthropes ... and some that are *not*
- ◆ A closer look at wolf's bane, also known as "werewolf repellent"
- ◆ Magic vs. lycanthropy
- ◆ The proper disposal of a downed werewolf

There is a long-held belief in western pop culture that there exists but one way to kill a werewolf. However, this is not the case. In fact, depending on which parts of werewolf lore you believe (or perhaps it would be better to say, that you believe enough to bet your life on), there are a number of ways for dispatching a troublesome lycanthrope. Of course, in the rare case that you find yourself in the presence of a werewolf while equipped with the proper tools to fight it, your chances of surviving the ordeal uninfected are still slim to none. To be honest, if you ever do find yourself being stalked or chased by a werewolf, your best chance for survival is to run ... and run fast.

Remember, you don't have to be the fastest runner in your group (unless you were crazy enough to come alone). You just can't be the slowest.

Silver: Old Faithful

For those who are uneducated in such matters, the silver bullet has long been considered the sole method for killing a werewolf. Of course, most of us have probably wondered the same thing at least once—if this is true, then how did people kill werewolves before the invention of firearms? The truth is that any weapon, such as a sword, stake, or dagger, made from pure silver should be effective against a werewolf. According to most legends, only by using pure silver will your weapons have the proper effect. A blade that is only partially made from silver may not be as effective (and is not really the kind of thing one would want to gamble on). The older werewolf lore claims that silver is magical, symbolic of purity, or a blessed/sacred element. Most modern lore suggests that silver, for whatever reason, prevents the werewolf's wounds from regenerating until the weapons are removed. So take a mental note. If you are lucky enough to put down a werewolf, don't pull the blades out (at the very least, don't do so until you have properly disposed of it). One of lycanthropy's strongest gifts is the ability to regenerate *very* quickly. If a weapon is removed from a wound prematurely, then (depending on the severity of the wound) the werewolf could recover in a matter of seconds.

The Savage Truth

The most recent manifestation of silver's role in werewolf lore is believed to have originated with the "lycans" from the *Underworld* films. In these films, lycans who have been too mortally wounded by silver weapons cannot regenerate until the weapons are removed. If they are not removed in time, the lycan dies. The werewolf-slaying "death-dealers" from the same films create bullets of "liquid silver" that enter the target's bloodstream, making them especially fatal to lycans. In these films, this specially designed ammunition prevents the lycans from being able to remove the projectiles in order to regenerate.

Of course, you may not be too keen on the idea of going toe-to-toe with a beast that is so very significantly larger, stronger, and faster than you. If so, then you might want to invest in some silver bullets. Unless you already own a specific firearm in which you plan to use them, it would be prudent to have several different types of silver rounds made in the most commonly used calibers—.38, 9mm, and .45 calibers, for example. This way, you are more likely to have rounds that will fire from whatever assorted firearm that "just so happens" to come into your possession.

The Savage Truth

The use of a silver bullet as a weapon against werewolves first appeared in the 1760s, with the lore surrounding the well-documented case of the Beast of Gevaudan. One story claims that a local clergyman eventually killed the beast with a silver bullet. Another version claims that a specially made silver bullet was blessed, by either a priest or a sorcerer, and given to a skilled hunter who took the beast down. For more details on this case, see Chapter 8.

Though its use has never been mentioned in werewolf lore, it would stand to reason that silver buckshot fired from a heavy-gauge shotgun would also be effective. Since shotguns spray a multitude of shot pellets at your target, less experience, training, and accuracy is required. Shotguns are "point-and-click" weapons, so to speak.

Despite silver's effectiveness in antiwerewolf ammunition, it is important to take note of something. In film, silver bullets are often portrayed as a "one hit = kill" weapon. Most accepted werewolf lore does not support this idea. Just hitting the werewolf with a silver bullet will not do the trick. A vital organ must be damaged enough in order for the werewolf's other body functions to shut down. The heart and the head would be the best targets for this. Hitting a werewolf in a nonlethal area such as the leg might be enough to slow the beast down, but it's unlikely to kill it.

The Quicksilver Dilemma

Nearly all of werewolf lore is in agreement that silver is effective for antiwerewolf weaponry. When it comes to mercury, however, this is not the case. This point of conflict seems to stem from an uncertainty as to how this idea originated. You see, in centuries past, mercury was referred to as "quicksilver" and was considered to be the same as silver, only in a liquid form. Since silver was effective, this may have led to the mistaken conclusion that mercury would be as well. Since there has never been a single documented case (in werewolf lore or otherwise) of mercury being successfully used to combat werewolves, you might not want to rely on this one.

Mercury isn't exactly the best material for weaponization. Of course, it can be combined with silver. However, since most information supports the idea that *pure* silver should be used, it might not be a good idea to rely on a weapon made from a combination of it and mercury.

On the flip side of this debate, some argue that it could be that quicksilver/mercury was actually used first. Since it was thought to be a liquid form of silver, this school of thought reasons, it was assumed that silver was also effective. However, this idea seems far less likely.

Aren't Wooden Stakes for Vampires?

Most people are familiar with the belief that a stake through the heart is the best way to kill a vampire. According to some lore, however, this can also be an effective weapon against werewolves. In contrast to the vampire method, however, very specific wood types are supposed to be used. Most lore seems to agree on wood from only three tree types—ash, cinder, and (of course) silver trees.

Unlike with silver weapons, the wooden stake method requires that the werewolf's heart be thoroughly pierced. Similar to methods involving silver weapons, the stake should not be removed ... *ever.* As with mercury, not everyone agrees that this method would work. In all honesty, it's not your best bet for survival. Piercing a werewolf through the heart with a wooden stake would require the wielder to be way too close to the werewolf. In such a close-quarters scenario, it is far more likely that you would be mauled, killed, or worse ... infected with lycanthropy.

Nature's Werewolf Repellent—Wolf's Bane

There is one thing you need to be perfectly clear on when it comes to the use of this poisonous herb. Wolf's bane does *not* kill werewolves. However, it is known to be lethal if ingested by regular wolves. If anything, the lore surrounding the use of wolf's bane states that it only works as a deterrent. Think of it as a kind of "werewolf repellent." If you have to get close to the beast, having some of this on your person might be a good idea. Having wolf's bane on a necklace, for example, might keep you from being bitten long enough to deal the werewolf a debilitating blow.

Once again, not all werewolf lore agrees on the effectiveness of wolf's bane, even as a deterrent. So as usual, you might bring it, but you probably shouldn't rely on it too heavily for protection. Remember, most of this stuff about what works against a werewolf is hypothetical.

Keep Growling and I'll Chop It Off!

There are many who agree that werewolves can be taken down by conventional means. However, because of their amazingly fast regenerative powers, such means require quite a bit more work. According to this method, either the werewolf's heart or brain (or both, if possible) must be removed from the body or destroyed. Missing one or both of these organs, it is believed that the lycanthrope's legendary power to regenerate will be shut down. The werewolf's regeneration, it is believed, requires at least a minimal function of the brain or heart (or both) in order to remain active. Though there exists some older werewolf lore claiming that, even without a brain or heart, almost any dead werewolf will regenerate if left under the light of a full moon. Though this sounds rather unlikely, it's up to you whether you feel like gambling on it.

The simplest method for cutting off the werewolf's brain from its body is decapitation. It is almost universally agreed upon that a werewolf does not have the ability to regenerate a severed head. Even if you have incapacitated the werewolf by other means, most lore strongly suggests that you immediately chop off the head and cut out the heart as a precautionary measure against possible regeneration.

There are some other body parts that are said to bring down a werewolf if severed, though one should note that most of these are somewhat less likely or credible. For example, one myth states that chopping off a werewolf's penis will destroy it (which once again proves that the wolf-man does, in fact, have nards). Most men would probably agree that this would bring down anyone. However, this method might leave one wondering what one should do if the werewolf is female?

Magical Antilycanthropy Weapons

In times past, there were several "magical" methods for combating and/ or detaining a werewolf. These methods may sound rather difficult to believe. However, you should consider whether these claims are any more or less believable than the idea of a human being transforming into a gigantic wolf-creature.

Possible magical or alchemical methods against werewolves include the following:

- Rubbing opium into the nostrils (must be done before it trans-forms, according to most instructions).

- Forcing the werewolf to drink a mixture of whey and milk for three days (good luck with that!).

- According to some, werewolves won't come near ash, cinder, silver, or mistletoe—climbing up any of these trees will offer (temporary) protection.

- Forcing the werewolf to drink saltwater (once again, good luck and Godspeed if you are going to attempt this).

Disposing of the Werewolf

Okay, so you were (hopefully) lucky enough to survive your encounter unscathed and uninfected, and your werewolf is finally down for the count. Your work isn't quite done, however. Now you must take mea-sures to ensure that the fallen lycanthrope doesn't get back up. In most cases, it has been reported that a mortally wounded werewolf returns to human form once regeneration has ceased. The werewolf appears to be dead. However, werewolves are nothing if not resilient.

Bark vs. Bite

The antiwerewolf methods that are discussed in this chapter are purely hypothetical, and all of the information provided in this chapter is intended for purposes of entertainment *only*. Please use your head and be realistic. Harming another human being, even one you may (for whatever reason) suspect of lycanthropy, will result in very real and serious consequences. Remember … this is all in good fun.

If the downed werewolf has not already been decapitated, this should be done immediately. The heart should also be removed. Once these measures have been taken, quickly gather up as much wood as you can and pile it high. Incineration is the only known method for ensuring that the werewolf will not "cease to be deceased," if you will. Burn the remains, including the head and heart, to ashes. Some sources say that the head and heart should be burned first. Others claim that the body should be the first thing tossed into the flames. Both sequences, however, agree that all of the remains should be incinerated. Any remaining bones should be buried. According to some lore, it is said that these bones should be buried in separate places. (This probably falls into the category of a "just in case" measure.)

The Least You Need to Know

- Silver is considered the most effective material for constructing antiwerewolf weaponry.

- Never pull a weapon from a downed werewolf, as they are known to regenerate very quickly.

- Wolf's bane will not kill a werewolf, but it will supposedly keep one at bay.

- Removing and destroying a werewolf's heart and/or brain should take it down.

- Incineration is considered the only proper method of werewolf remains disposal, and any remaining bones should be buried.

- The information in this chapter is meant to be taken in fun. Do not let your imagination get out of hand. There's nothing fun about endangering the safety and well-being of others or yourself.

Chapter 17

Explanations for Werewolf Phenomenon

In This Chapter

- ◆ Hypertrichosis and its possible relationship to lycanthropic sightings

- ◆ Ergot poisoning and the werewolf phenomenon

- ◆ A closer look at porphyria and its possible connection to lycanthropy lore

- ◆ How rabies infections may have had a hand in ancient and medieval werewolf lore

- ◆ The possibility that werewolf sightings resulted from overwhelming bouts of hysteria

- ◆ An examination of the possibility that werewolves may be a species of humanoid cryptids

Do werewolves actually exist? There are many who insist that they do not. Since the Age of Reason, beliefs in creatures such as the werewolf have increasingly been dismissed as ludicrous impossibilities. Many believe that lycanthropy is nothing more than an extreme state of self-delusion, brought on by mental illness or some neurological defect. Others claim that ancient werewolf sightings were nothing more than superstitious explanations for unusual medical conditions. Perhaps these sightings were hallucinations, caused by a well-documented fungus from which LSD was first derived.

To cryptozoologists, however, it is thought that the werewolf might be some form of unidentified primate or humanoid. After all, it's often said that many human myths were originally based on some forgotten (but real) event. Is that the case with werewolves? Or does this ancient phenomenon have a rational explanation?

Hypertrichosis

Hypertrichosis is one of the rarest skin disorders in existence. It is a condition in which long, fine hairs grow on a person's body far beyond what is normal for the affected individual's age, sex, and ethnicity. There are two basic forms of hypertrichosis—general and localized. For those with generalized hypertrichosis, hair grows all over the body. With localized hypertrichosis, thick patches of hair may grow only in certain places on the body (such as the forehead or neck). The condition can be congenital, which means present at birth, or acquired, occurring later in life (most often during puberty). There have only ever been 50 recorded cases of hypertrichosis in the entire world. However, only the known occurrences can be recorded. The first recorded cases of hypertrichosis date all the way back to the Middle Ages, but the condition has probably been around since the dawn of humankind.

Congenital hypertrichosis is believed to be the result of a rare genetic abnormality. When humans are in the womb, a coat of long, light-colored hairs (called lanugo hairs) covers the entire fetus. This hair is normally shed by the fetus sometime around the eighth month in the womb and is replaced by smaller, finer hairs (called vellus hairs, more commonly referred to as "peach fuzz"). The lanugo hairs that are shed from the scalp are replaced with what are called terminal hairs. Babies who are born with congenital hypertrichosis, however, usually come out of the womb with lanugo hairs covering their entire bodies. For whatever reason, the genetic trigger that causes most fetuses to shed their lanugo hairs for vellus hairs either does not activate or simply does not exist in those who have congenital hypertrichosis.

The Curse

When one considers the story of King Lycoan from Chapter 3, it is possible to speculate about the truth that may have spawned the myth. For example, King Lycoan may have been suffering from acquired hypertrichosis. In the superstitious view of the ancient world, something as strange as a king's body suddenly becoming covered with a thick coat of hair could have been seen as a curse from the gods. Lycoan's flight from Arcadia could possibly be a metaphor for his expulsion from the city, likely by the priests of a temple devoted to Zeus (hence that god's role in the myth).

Acquired hypertrichosis, which occurs later in life, is often seen by doctors as a warning sign that one or more malignant, cancerous tumors are present in a patient's body. Sometimes, narcotics use or certain drug interactions can also trigger acquired hypertrichosis. Acquired hypertrichosis is usually localized and rarely causes thickened growth all over the body. However, it is not unheard of.

Before the times of reason and the advancement of medical science, individuals with hypertrichosis were often the victims of social stigma and/or violent persecution. From ancient times through the Dark Ages, a child born with an unusual amount of hair on the body was considered a bad omen at best. In some cultures, it was even believed that such children were werewolves (or even a demonic offspring). Sadly, this often resulted in the immediate abandonment of the child or, even worse, infanticide.

Ergot Poisoning

Ergot is considered one of the most potent hallucinogens that grow in the natural world. In fact, it is from ergot that the drug we now call LSD was first extracted by the pharmaceutical industry. And, interestingly enough, human beings have only been aware of the true nature of ergot for the last century and a half. However, they'd already been eating it for ages.

Beastly Words

Ergot is a disease that affects certain grain-producing plants such as rye. It is caused by the *claviceps purpurea* fungus and is one of the most potent hallucinogens to grow naturally. Ergot may be indentified by its brown or purple sacks, called sclerotia, which envelop the affected grain.

The ergot fungus can grow on any grain but is most common on rye. Before the 1850s, it had long been thought that the presence of ergot was just a normal part of rye grains. This was likely believed because its presence was so common. For hundreds of years, Europeans were ingesting ergot under the mistaken belief that it was a grain. (This would have resulted in widespread ergot poisoning across the continent.) In times of famine, people were even less likely to pick the ergot out of their grains (as a rare few are known to have done).

One doesn't have to be a rocket scientist to figure out what this means. Apparently, for much of human history, our ancestors were tripping out on a psychedelic hallucinogen … and they didn't even know it.

So you may be wondering what any of this stuff about ergot poisoning has to do with werewolves. Well, as anyone who has ever sampled LSD would likely tell you, psychedelic drugs can make it very difficult to keep a firm grip on reality. Such drugs can also cause lapses in one's ability to sense the passage of time. For example, a person suffering from ergot poisoning might look up and see a person he or she knows. Several minutes may pass, during which the other person walks away, but the poisoned individual is unaware that any time has passed. Then a wild dog or other animal passes by and somehow catches the attention of the affected person. To him or her, it would seem as if only a split second before there had been a person standing where the animal stands now when, in actuality, as much as an hour may have passed between these two events.

In addition to losing time, a person suffering from ergot poisoning experiences intense hallucinations that actually "amplify" reality (light, colors, sounds, etc.), often in ways that can become rather frightening under stress. This is commonly referred to by LSD users as having a "bad trip." Imagine if you will the effect that a sudden encounter with a wild dog (or even a wolf) would have on the mind of a person suffering from ergot poisoning. The dog would likely appear to the person as a monster with huge fangs. Any bark or yelp would sound like the bellowing growls of some demonic creature. In some cases, the poisoned individual might even hallucinate that he or she *is* a werewolf and go running, barking, and snarling through the village (scaring the crap out of the neighbors, who are probably also suffering from the hallucinogenic effects of ergot poisoning). Add to this mix the fact that the werewolf myth is already embedded in everyone's minds, and you have a recipe for absolute chaos and widespread lunacy.

The Savage Truth

Ergot poisoning can be fatal. It is called "poisoning" for a good reason. One would be *very* ill advised to experiment with the ingestion of this substance in any way, shape, or form. Doing so could result in irreversible damage to one's brain and/or spinal cord, (temporary or permanent) localized paralysis, a permanent state of psychosis, cardiac arrest, and even death. Any desired hallucinogenic or euphoric effects that one might expect to receive from swallowing ergot are most definitely not worth the serious health risks that it involves. Simply put, *do not ingest ergot.*

When one considers how widespread the occurrence of ergot poisoning must have been in ancient and medieval Europe, it is not hard to imagine how so many werewolf sightings occurred during these periods. It may be no small coincidence that sightings of werewolves and cases of lycanthropy have dropped off considerably since 1850, following the identification of ergot's hallucinogenic properties.

Porphyria

The condition known as porphyria is thought by some to be an explanation for some reports of werewolves. Porphyria is a condition that affects the blood and marrow. Those with porphyria have an inability to create porphyrin in the bone marrow. This leads to a discoloration of the skin that is reddish or purplish. Symptoms of porphyria are as follows:

- Severe photosensitivity (namely sensitivity to ultraviolet light).

- Hypertrichosis may develop on parts of the skin that are especially photosensitive.

- Teeth may turn a red or red-brown color.

- Skin lesions.

- Red- or brown-colored skin.

- Porphyria often attacks cartilage, causing mutilations and deformities of the eyelids, nose, mouth, and hands.

As a result of social expulsion, individuals with porphyria, especially during ancient and medieval times, may have grown up with little to no interaction with other humans. Their frightening appearances, coupled with their unsocial or "savage" behaviors, may have caused them to be mistakenly labeled as werewolves in the ages of the past.

Rabies

Rabies is an infectious virus that, once contracted, has the potential to attack the nervous system of most mammals (including wolves/canines and humans). There are two main types of rabies—paralytic rabies and "furious" rabies. When contracted by a human being, both types of rabies develop through the following three primary stages of infection:

Beastly Words

Rabies is a viral infection, often passed by the saliva through a bite, that attacks the brain and nervous system of warm-blooded animals. It is also thought to be a possible explanation for medieval reports of lycanthropy and certain parts of werewolf lore.

- **Stage One:** The individual is bitten by a rabies-infected animal, and a tingling sensation at the site of infection may be experienced.

- **Stage Two:** The infected person begins to experience fever, fatigue, nausea and loss of appetite, vomiting, diarrhea, migraine headaches, lung infection (similar to bronchitis symptoms), throat infection, and stomach pain.

◆ **Stage Three:** The infected individual becomes highly irritable, suffering from insomnia as well as extreme anxiety or paranoia. (This anxiety is usually irrational and unprovoked.) Near the latter part of the third stage of rabies infection, the infected person begins to suffer from severe depression and (mild to severe) hallucinations.

At the end of the third stage of rabies infection, the virus will take the form of either paralytic or "furious" rabies. By the time the rabies virus has reached the third stage, it is almost certainly too late to save the infected person. In all of known history, only three people have ever survived after being treated past the third stage of infection, and all of them lived out their lives with permanent physical damage. This is why it is so important to seek immediate medical attention when one has been bitten by any animal (especially mammals since rabies only affects warm-blooded animals). The sooner treatment is received, the less likely it becomes that one will suffer any permanent nerve or brain damage. However, once the symptoms of the third stage of rabies infection have been displayed, the virus is nearly 100 percent fatal.

After the third stage of infection, some human beings develop paralytic rabies. This form of the virus gradually paralyzes the infected person's muscles, starting from the site of infection (where the person was bitten) and working outward over a period of time until the entire muscular system (including the heart muscle and the diaphragm) has become paralyzed. In the end, the person will appear to enter a coma and remain comatose until his or her heart and lungs cease to function. While the paralytic form of rabies is not likely to have influenced werewolf lore, it would appear that the "furious" form of rabies may be responsible for a vast amount of it.

"Furious" rabies also occurs at the end of the third stage of infection. The symptoms and potential behaviors of a person suffering from "furious" rabies are as follows:

◆ Extreme dehydration/thirst

◆ Howling and growling

◆ Biting people

- Increasingly intense hallucinations

- Extreme hydrophobia (fear of water), a symptom that is so common and severe that rabies was long referred to alternatively as "hydrophobia"

Do any of the preceding symptoms sound familiar? They should. Most of these symptoms are also, according to the majority of werewolf lore, the primary symptoms of lycanthropic infection (which are discussed at length in Chapter 15). If one thinks about the occurrence of rabies in the ancient and medieval world, the relationship between rabies and werewolf lore makes perfect sense.

First of all, rabies infections are known to have occurred in a good number of canine breeds (including wolves and coyotes). These infections usually occurred when the carnivorous canine devoured a smaller, rabies-infected animal. In canines, any rabies viral infection had the potential to develop into the "furious" form.

During the Middle Ages of Europe, rabies infections were as rampant as occurrences of ergot poisonings. These occurrences were often thought to be cases of lycanthropy or some other work of the devil. During the Middle Ages, many of the people who were bitten by rabid animals, believing themselves cursed with lycanthropy, are known to have taken their own lives. Sometimes they were killed by the other villagers. Sadly, these may have been mercy killings since there was not yet a successful treatment for rabies infection.

The Savage Truth

The use of irons against werewolves probably originated from the practice of peasants carrying iron crosses, called the "Keys of St. Hubert," for protection against the curse of lycanthropy. Usually, these keys were inserted into the inner sides of house doors or were hung on house walls.

To combat these "curses," the bites were supposed to be immediately treated by being burned with hot irons. In many cases in which this method was put into practice, no further symptoms developed in those individuals. This may have led to the belief that iron was a potent element against werewolves and lycanthropic magic.

Bark vs. Bite

The success in some cases in which hot irons were applied likely had little to do with magic and more to do with medicine. Hot irons, if applied soon enough, would have cauterized and sterilized the bite. This would have minimized the infection or, in some cases, destroyed the infection completely.

Consider the following hypothetical scenario to understand how a rabies infection may have been viewed when it occurred in the ancient or medieval world:

A man went walking in the woods and came upon a rabies-infected wolf, coyote, or other wild dog. He was bitten during the encounter but survived to return home and tell the tale of his frightening encounter. The bite was bandaged, perhaps given a home-remedy salve of some sort by his wife, but was otherwise untreated.

Over time, the bitten man began to get sick, developing the symptoms of the initial three stages of rabies infection. His wife noticed that he was always getting nervous or angry about the silliest things. At other times, she noticed that he seemed to be staring in certain places for long periods, as if he saw something, when nothing was there.

Within a month (rabies can develop from the initial bite to its final form in anywhere from three to four weeks), the man's wife noticed that he always seemed to be thirsty. Soon enough, he began frothing at the mouth. The infected man then went mad and began growling and tearing at his clothes. He ran through the village, savagely biting anyone who attempted to restrain him. The man eventually disappeared into the forest and was never heard from again.

Shortly afterward, some of the people the man had bitten began to die under mysterious circumstances (those who developed paralytic rabies). Others, however, soon went as mad as the man who bit them. They also soon began to growl like animals, and many tried to bite their fellow villagers before they, too, ran off into the woods.

This situation, which we would now identify as a rabies outbreak, would have been considered a case of lycanthropy or demonic possession by most people who lived in the ancient or medieval world, where the unexplained was often labeled under superstitious terms.

Hysterical Beast Encounters

Hysteria is commonly defined as unusual or irrational behavior resulting from an experience of overwhelming fear, mental distress, or uncontrollable emotions. When it comes to werewolves, it is possible that some reports are actually nothing more than bouts of hysteria caused by a frightening encounter with a wild animal. This is especially the case when the encountered animal cannot be immediately identified by the individual.

Beastly Words

Hysteria is characterized by unusual and often irrational behavior by an individual suffering a mental break (often temporary but sometimes permanent) caused by an experience of overwhelming fear.

Hysteria from an encounter with a wild animal can occur as a result of diminished mental capacity (brought on by extreme panic or fear) or a limited knowledge of wildlife. For example, supposed sightings of a mythical vampire/lizardlike creature called the chupacabra have turned out to be nothing more than human encounters with inbred or mange-ridden coyotes. The animals were so horribly deformed by genetic inbreeding and mange that the individuals who encountered them could not identify that they were coyotes. As a result, the involved persons believed they had encountered a "monster" of some sort. Since the chupacabra was a part of their local or cultural lore, they ascribed the encounter as being with this creature. To this day, all claims to have killed or captured a chupacabra have turned out to be nothing more than coyotes … very *hideous* coyotes … but coyotes, nonetheless.

Hysteria from an encounter with a wild animal can also be caused when the animal is not one that would be expected in that region. For example, in recent years a winged "monster" was reported to have attacked a young boy in Florida, briefly lifting him off the ground with its sharp talons only to release him shortly after. Following an investigation of the descriptions and reported behaviors of the so-called "monster," wildlife officials came to the conclusion that an extremely large predatory bird (one normally indigenous to Africa) was responsible for the attack. Small primates are the most common prey for these large raptors, and the animal likely mistook the boy for food. It is also believed that human encounters with escaped, misplaced, or unidentified species of gorillas in North America (a region where gorillas are not thought to be indigenous) are the cause of many modern reports of werewolf and Sasquatch sightings.

Cryptids

The relatively young discipline of *cryptozoology* walks the sometimes blurry line between science and myth. Cryptozoologists are devoted to the study of special animals called *cryptids*, which are believed to be unidentified, undiscovered, or extinct species of animals that have often been mislabeled as "monsters." Cryptozoologists seek to either confirm or prove false the existence of cryptids through the use of scientific methods. Some argue that cryptozoology is not science but glorified "monster chasing." However, even mainstream science must admit that the discipline of cryptozoology has yielded some results.

Beastly Words

Cryptozoology is the study of special/rare animals called **cryptids**. Cryptids are believed (by cryptozoologists) to actually be unidentified, undiscovered, or extinct species of animals that have been mislabeled as "monsters" or "creatures." Perhaps the most globally known of the cryptids is the so-called "Loch Ness Monster," which has yet to be confirmed or concretely identified.

Cryptozoology scholars have successfully identified, and proven the existence of, a number of cryptids in recent years. In Indonesian New Guinea, there had long been a local legend about a race of short, hairy humanoids called the *bondegezou*, or "men of the forests." Cryptozoologists were able to uncover and examine a valid set of remains from one of these creatures that had been killed by a local hunter. The *bondegezou* turned out to actually be an unidentified species of unusually hairy tree kangaroo. These animals often move on two feet and have oddly flat faces, giving them the appearance of being humanoid if seen from any good distance.

As far as werewolves are concerned, the jury is still out. Cryptozoologists have werewolves listed among those cryptids that have yet to be either confirmed or disproven. There are some cryptozoologists who believe that werewolves are an undiscovered species of primate. Others in the field believe that werewolves may be an unidentified species of canine that has evolved to become bipedal. A very small number of cryptozoologists believe that werewolves, as well as certain other cryptids, are beings that come from alternate dimensions. Subscribers of this theory claim that such creatures temporarily pass over into our dimension from time to time, either purposely or accidentally, when temporal rifts (or portals) open up between our two dimensions.

The Least You Need to Know

- The rare condition of hypertrichosis, which causes long hair to grow all over a person's body, may have led to some werewolf legends.

- Ergot poisoning may have led to at least some of the reports of werewolves in the ancient to medieval world.

- The frightening appearance and behaviors of porphyria sufferers may have caused some of the older reports of werewolves.

- Many of the symptoms of rabies are identical to what are said to be the primary symptoms of lycanthropy.

- Hysteria caused by surprise encounters with wild animals may also be an explanation for some reports of werewolf encounters.

- In cryptozoology, werewolves are on the list of unconfirmed cryptids.

18

Werewolves and the Psyche

In This Chapter

- ◆ A close look at the phenomenon of clinical lycanthropy

- ◆ The "Lycanthropy Revisited" case studies by Surawicz and Banta

- ◆ "A Case of Lycanthropy" case study of Rostenstock and Vincent

- ◆ Several clinical lycanthropy case studies from the country of Iran

- ◆ A discussion of Sigmund Freud's *Wolf Man* case study

- ◆ The werewolf as an archetype of death/rebirth in Jungian psychology

Understanding what werewolves mean to the human mind is an important part of any study on lycanthropy. An examination into the significance of werewolves when it comes to the human psyche may offer answers to a number of questions. For example, why do some people fear the concept of lycanthropy while others seek to embrace it? Can psychological transformations be just as real as those of physical lycanthropy? Why do some cultures view wolves as hostile to the human way of life, while others seek to live in harmony with these wild ancestors of man's best friend? Why do some view lycanthropy as a curse while others view it as a gift?

The answers may be found by taking a closer look at how human beings have evolved in their understandings of the werewolf phenomenon. These answers often lead to new questions. Perhaps the simplest answer to the enigma of clinical lycanthropy is that, one might dare to say, some people just go a little bit crazy ... or a lot crazy.

The Truth about Clinical Lycanthropy

The most popular explanation for werewolves is a condition of mental illness now referred to by the psychiatric community as clinical lycanthropy. (Sometimes it is also called psychological lycanthropy.) Clinical lycanthropy is commonly defined as a mental disorder identified by a strong belief in the delusion that the afflicted individual can, is, or has at some time transformed into a wolf or werewolf. Though the condition is named after lycanthropy, it is in no way considered to be of supernatural origin.

The Savage Truth

One of the oldest cases of clinical lycanthropy may come from the Bible. Written in the Book of Daniel is an account of how King Nebuchadnezzar suffered from a bout of serious depression. Nebuchadnezzar's condition grew steadily worse. Eventually, the king went stark raving mad and, for a period of seven years, roamed the wild under the delusion that he had become a wolf.

Clinical lycanthropy is a wolf-specific form of a broader category of mental disorders referred to as *zoanthropy*. Zoanthropy is an umbrella term for states of mental delusion in which the afflicted individual harbors the belief that he or she can assume the form of an animal. In some cases, the person may even believe that he or she *is* an animal (and will behave accordingly).

In recent years, cases of zoanthropy and clinical lycanthropy have come to be viewed as secondary manifestations of some other underlying mental illness or neurological defect. For example, nearly all of the known recorded cases of clinical lycanthropy were discovered to be caused by long-term psychedelic drug use, an onset of *schizophrenia*, some other previously unidentified brain defect, or bouts of extreme mental distress (such as clinical depression). These delusions of lycanthropy are viewed as a specific manifestation of a patient's *lunacy*.

Beastly Words

Zoanthropy is a term used in psychology for states of mental delusion in which the afflicted individual harbors the belief that he or she can assume the form of an animal.

Schizophrenia is a mental illness commonly thought to be caused by neurological damage or defect and characterized by hallucinations, paranoid delusions, physical restlessness, and hearing voices.

Lunacy is defined as insanity, extreme foolishness, or a display of foolish behavior. It literally means something like "in the state of the moon" and actually originates from the Latin *luna,* or "moon." In ancient times, bouts of insanity were thought to be influenced by the lunar cycle. Despite the insistence of science to the contrary, many people still believe that the full moon influences humans to behave strangely.

Cases of clinical lycanthropy have been more widely identified and documented over the last century, with occurrences as recent as 2006. Sometimes cases of clinical lycanthropy involve unusual, but still relatively harmless, behaviors such as howling, growling, walking on all fours, or running around naked. Sometimes the person may engage in another common (yet rather creepy) behavior of persons suffering from clinical lycanthropy—sleeping in (or running naked through) graveyards. Clinical lycanthropy is considered to be a symptomatic condition, not a diagnostic one, since cases exhibit similar symptoms but with differing causes. The most common symptoms of clinical lycanthropy are as follows:

◆ Extreme anxiety

◆ An obsessive urge to frequent and/or sleep in graveyards

- Socially inappropriate displays of nudity (usually under the delusion that he or she has transformed)

- An obsessive urge to roam in woods

- Bestial sexual compulsions and/or exhibitions of sounds or postures that mimic animal sexual behaviors

- Belief/fear in the patient that he or she is demon possessed or in some way controlled by the devil

- A preoccupation with eyes and/or a belief that he or she has been cursed/haunted by an "evil eye"

Unfortunately, some extreme cases of clinical lycanthropy have violent manifestations, leading the delusional person to engage in any number of horrifying acts such as rape, cannibalism, and murder. Had the truth about clinical lycanthropy been understood in times past, it would likely have been applied to many of the disturbed individuals discussed in Chapter 6.

Two Clinical Werewolves ... Revisited

Dr. Frida Surawicz and Dr. Richard Banta are well known for their 1975 analysis of two similar case studies involving clinical lycanthropy, entitled "Lycanthropy Revisited." Their findings were first published as an article in the *Canadian Psychiatric Association Journal*. Since the publication of "Lycanthropy Revisited," others in the mental health profession have disclosed their own experiences with cases of clinical lycanthropy.

The male subjects of both case studies published by Surawicz and Banta were kept strictly anonymous in the printed article, and both have since been identified only by the pseudonyms Mr. H and Mr. W. Though both subjects were shown to have suffered from clinical lycanthropy, the causes, manifestations, and end results of their conditions differed in certain unique ways.

The Vices of Mr. H

The first case study presented by Surawicz and Banta is that of Mr. H, a 20-year-old male with a long history of heavy drug abuse. Mr. H was admitted for psychiatric treatment when he professed the belief that he was a werewolf. Mr. H had formerly served in the Army, and even during that time he was a heavy drug user. According to Mr. H's testimony, while stationed at a military installation in Europe, he took a hiking trip into a nearby forest. While there, he dropped multiple hits of *LSD* and *strychnine*.

> **Beastly Words**
>
> **LSD,** commonly referred to as "acid," stands for lysergic acid diethyl-amide. LSD is an extremely potent psychedelic drug that affects both the mood and perception of the user, causing hallucinations, disorientation, mood swings, paranoia, and other delusions.
>
> **Strychnine** is considered a fatal poison, but it is sometimes used as a heavy stimulant when taken in small doses.

The drugs didn't take long to do their thing, and according to Mr. H, he watched in horror as fur/hair began to grow rapidly all over his body and face (a hallucination caused by LSD). He then claimed to have been overwhelmed by animal compulsions and immediately began to chase, capture, and devour wild rabbits. It is unclear whether or not Mr. H actually did eat raw wild rabbits or if this was just another LSD-fueled hallucination. Mr. H remained in the woods in a drug-induced state of frenzy for a number of days before finally returning to his duty station. For some time after this experience, it would appear that Mr. H lived under the delusion that he was a werewolf.

Under professional psychiatric care, Mr. H was first gradually broken of his serious drug addiction. (The rehab methods suggest he was so physically dependent on drugs that going "cold turkey" might have killed him.) Mr. H's drug rehabilitation took a period of about nine months for him to achieve a relative state of sobriety. In drug rehab, Mr. H still expressed his belief that he was a werewolf. During this time, Mr. H frequently complained that he was hearing voices. He also reported seeing horrifying visions (which were usually satanic or demonic in theme). In addition to being a werewolf, Mr. H vehemently claimed that he was demon possessed and told doctors he had been endowed with a number of supernatural powers. (Apparently, however, he was unable to successfully demonstrate any of them for doctors or staff.)

At first it was thought that Mr. H suffered from some form of schizophrenia or even toxic psychosis (a mental condition resulting from extreme or long-term drug abuse). All of his tests were supportive of these hypotheses. Mr. H was prescribed a psychopharmacological treatment of antipsychotic drugs. The drugs brought him (relatively) back to his wits, which is rather ironic when one considers the fact that it was the use of drugs that put him in this sad condition to begin with.

After showing significant improvement while taking antipsychotics for a period of time, Mr. H was finally referred to an outpatient program. His first outpatient visit seems to have been unremarkable. By Mr. H's second outpatient visit, however, it became obvious that he had stopped taking his meds. Mr. H never showed up for his third visit, and all attempts to contact or locate him were unsuccessful. His current condition and whereabouts are unknown (though it would be a safe bet to say that any search for him should probably start in the local woods).

The Ailing Brain of Mr. W

The second clinical lycanthropy case study of Surawicz and Banta is that of Mr. W, a 37-year-old male patient who had been admitted for psychiatric treatment after multiple public incidents in which he had exhibited highly unusual behaviors. For example, Mr. W is reported to have not cut or cleaned his hair or beard (meaning he was covered almost head-to-toe in hair) in quite some time and had been seen sleeping in graveyards, howling at the moon, and lying down in the middle of a highway (even as cars were speeding past him).

What sets Mr. W apart from his counterpart, Mr. H, is that he had no known history of drug abuse (or even mild drug use). Mr. W had been in the Navy, and an IQ test from his military records showed that, during his service at least, he was found to be of "average intelligence." After his time in the Navy, Mr. W had briefly worked as a farmer. Little else is reported in the study regarding the specific events of Mr. W's life during the time between his military service and his psychiatric treatment.

Mr. W may have been of average intelligence during his naval service. However, new tests found that he was now far below the average intelligence for his age. Mr. W's mental maturity was found to be equal to that of a child of no more than 10 years of age. Under care, Mr. W's state of *dementia* only worsened with each passing day. It was concluded that a brain biopsy would be required to determine whether the cause was neurological or psychological.

Beastly Words

Dementia is a state of delusional madness usually marked by extreme disorientation, bouts of irritability, and an erratic/infirm grasp of one's current time and/or location. Clinical lycanthropy is considered a specified manifestation of dementia.

During his neural biopsy, it was found that Mr. W's brain tissue was in a state of heavy deterioration, a condition commonly referred to as "walnut brain." His condition was declared the result of neurological deterioration, and he was diagnosed with an unspecified but chronic syndrome of the brain. The causes of Mr. W's condition were never found. Like Mr. H, Mr. W was prescribed a treatment of antipsychotic drugs. Mr. W, once under treatment, ceased to exhibit the symptoms of clinical lycanthropy. He was soon after referred to an outpatient program. Though his behavior was no longer as disturbing as previously, during each outpatient visit Mr. W exhibited increasingly shy and childlike behavior, often mumbling and almost never making eye contact with others.

The Case of Mrs. L's Lycanthropy

Dr. Harvey Rostenstock and colleague Kenneth Vincent published their collaborative article, "A Case of Lycanthropy," in *The American Journal of Psychiatry* in October of 1977. This article followed Surawicz's and Banta's case studies by only two years and offered an entirely unprecedented manifestation of clinical lycanthropy. Rostenstock's and Vincent's subject was a female with no history of drug or alcohol abuse who also displayed no evidence of any neurological defects or other brain disorders.

The 49-year-old patient, whom will be referred to in this section only by the name "Mrs. L" (she was not given any such pseudonym in the official case study), was first admitted for psychiatric evaluation when she professed the belief that she was a wolf and frequently felt like a beast with claws. However, this would be only the beginning of Mrs. L's unusual behavior.

Of course, it might be far more likely that she was admitted due to the fact that, only a week before, she had torn off all of her clothes while at a family gathering. Then in front of God and everyone, Mrs. L had gotten down on all fours and presented herself (in the sexual sense) to her own mother, basically assuming the position commonly referred to as "doggy style." According to the case study, Mrs. L continued with this behavior, ignoring the pleas of her family members, for about 20 minutes.

On the night following this disconcerting incident, just after having sexual intercourse with her husband, Mrs. L began to growl, scratch, and bite at the bed. At first this might have even seemed normal to her husband (you never know). After she continued this behavior for roughly two hours, however, "Mr. L" must have realized that his wife was no longer quite right in the head.

Upon initial examination, Mrs. L was found to display a high degree of unprovoked anxiety. She also professed to hearing voices and admitted that she had struggled with compulsions of adultery, homosexuality, and bestiality throughout her 20-year marriage. She constantly expressed that she felt as though she could not control herself and the belief that her actions and thoughts were no longer her own.

According to the case study, Mrs. L had long harbored an extreme, and increasingly unhealthy, preoccupation with wolves. She claimed to have always thought about wolves, desired to be around wolves, and constantly dreamt about wolves. Mrs. L, much like Mr. H from the Surawicz and Banta case, often verbalized the belief that she was demon possessed, and she claimed that the devil would take over her body and transform her into a wolf. She also complained of hearing voices (also a similarity found in the 1975 case of Mr. H). However, unlike Mr. H, Mrs. L's experiences were not the result of drug or alcohol abuse. After this evaluation, it is not surprising that she was immediately committed for inpatient psychiatric treatment.

Mrs. L was prescribed antipsychotic medication, along with daily therapy sessions, as part of her inpatient treatment. During the first three weeks of her treatment, progress was slow. Mrs. L suffered a number of relapses into her wolf obsessions. She would often claim that she assumed the form of a wolf at night and the form of a woman during the daytime. On one occasion, it was recorded that Mrs. L was frightened by the sight of her own reflection. She confessed that it was her own eyes that had terrified her. She claimed that one of her eyes was her own but the other was the eye of a wolf. She also said that her "wolf eye" wanted revenge on her "normal eye." On several occasions, Mrs. L would explain during therapy sessions how she would look in the mirror and, instead of seeing herself, would see her body in differ-ing states of wolf metamorphosis. During such episodes, the case study explains that Mrs. L would growl, snarl, and howl. These episodes were also frequently followed by overwhelming homosexual and bestial impulses for Mrs. L as well as chronic masturbatory compulsions.

In the fourth week of Mrs. L's treatment, the antipsychotic drugs seemed to take effect. Mrs. L reported during therapy sessions that the wolf eye was no longer present when she looked in the mirror.

On the night of the full moon, Mrs. L did experience one very brief relapse. She was asked to write down her experience. In one very inter-esting passage from her writings, which hints of similarities to the case of Mr. W, Mrs. L proclaimed, "I will haunt the graveyards for a tall, dark man that I intend to find."

After nine weeks, Mrs. L was finally discharged to outpatient status, continuing her treatment of antipsychotic drugs.

The Case of Mr. A

In 2000, the *Canadian Journal of Psychiatry* published another clinical lycanthropy case study in an article that was collaboratively written by Drs. J. Arturo Silva, M.D., Dennis Derecho, M.P.H., and Gregory Leong, M.D. In this case, the patient is referred to by the pseudonym "Mr. A."

According to the case study, at the time of his diagnosis and treatment, Mr. A was 46 years old. He was admitted for care due to a series of hours-long delusional episodes in which he believed that he could feel and see hair growing all over his body or in specific places (usually his face and arms). During some episodes, Mr. A was able to recognize that despite the sensation, what he was experiencing was not real. Other times, however, he was overcome by this delusion to such a degree that he accepted it as reality.

In addition to his delusions regarding hair growth, Mr. A would also experience delusions in which he believed that his face would deform and that lesions were appearing on his skin. He claimed that these disfigurements would happen in seconds and last for several hours.

What makes this case interesting is that Mr. A claimed that his delusions made him *look* like a wolf. Whenever these hair growth and face disfigurement delusions occurred, Mr. A would look in the mirror and believe that he looked somewhat like a wolf. However, what makes his case different is that Mr. A also verbally stated that he did not believe he *was* a wolf. He also did not exhibit the delusion that his mind was under the influence of some evil force, as is common in cases of clinical lycanthropy.

Mr. A was eventually diagnosed with an unspecified psychotic disorder. He was treated with antipsychotic drugs and eventually released for outpatient treatment.

A Clinical Lycanthropy Case in Tehran, Iran

In April 2004, a clinical lycanthropy case study, entitled "Lycanthropy in Depression," was published in the *Archives of Iranian Medicine*. This case was recorded and documented by Dr. Ali-Reza Moghaddas, M.D., and Dr. Mitra Nasseri, M.D. This particular case occurred in the Middle Eastern region of Tehran, Iran.

The patient in this case was a 20-year-old male from a lower class family in the suburban Kazeroon region. The young man in question is left unidentified in the article (and not given a pseudonym). He had exhibited a serious stuttering problem since the age of 12 and for years had suffered with bouts of depression. He was admitted for psychiatric treatment when he verbalized complaints of having turned into a wolf. The young man claimed that, during these transformations, he gained superhuman strength. On several occasions, he had even gone so far as to attack and bite other people (sometimes even removing chunks of flesh and swallowing them).

The Curse

Many psychiatrists have pointed to the fact that symptoms of clinical lycanthropy seem to occur more commonly among patients from lower socioeconomic backgrounds. While this would indeed seem to be true, it is in no way exclusive to patients of these backgrounds. Take, for example, the case of Mrs. L, who was from a middle- to upper-class background.

The triggers for his delusions were sometimes psychological or emotional. He reported that they would manifest at times when he was experiencing extreme anxiety, loneliness, or fear. Other times, they occurred at particular times, such as in the early morning hours and at night. These experiences would last as long as three hours, and he would recover from them as one would from unconsciousness. The patient reported that he felt disoriented, afraid, and light-headed after these episodes, and often suffered from headaches for hours.

There is one rather interesting and unique delusional element to this case. The patient reported that at times he would experience delusions that the people around him, even friends and family, had transformed into wolves or other animals. In these situations, he would feel overcome by paranoid anxiety, believing that they were going to attack and even try to kill him. Afraid that he might harm someone, the patient would then run from people and confine himself in an isolated space until the experience passed.

The patient also experienced hallucinatory symptoms in addition to clinical lycanthropy. For example, he would sometimes suffer from delusions that insects were crawling all over his skin, or even inside of his body. He would hear sounds that were not there, and complain of smells that no one else could detect. Often, he would wake and complain of ghostly visions during his sleep.

CT scans and other tests were conducted, and it was concluded that the patient did not suffer from any neurological defects. An IQ test revealed that he had somewhat lower than average intelligence. In the end, the causal diagnosis for his lycanthropy symptoms was identified as extreme and delusional depression. He was treated with both antidepressant and antipsychotic drugs. Over a period of two years, the patient's symptoms of lycanthropy and other hallucinations began to decrease. He eventually made a full recovery.

A Unique Case of Clinical Lycanthropy

This particular case also comes out of Iran. The case study was recorded and documented by Dr. Toofani and Dr. Ali-Reza Nejad of Beheshti Hospital, and was published in July 2004 issue of the *Acta Psychiatrica Scandanavia*. This case deals with an integration of clinical lycanthropy with the symptomatic condition called Cotard's Syndrome. Cotard's is a rare symptomatic condition in which the person suffers from *nihilistic* delusions of immortality. Cotard's patients are often under delusions that they are physically dead but still animated— basically, that they are "undead."

Beastly Words

Nihilism is usually defined as a self-centered belief that one is somehow exempt from all rules and social/religious/moral restrictions. In a more broad sense, it refers to a philosophical belief that life has no point and that human rules are valueless. Someone suffering from this rejects the validity of any truth aside from one's own.

The patient in this case was a 32-year-old male from the southern Iranian city of Kerman. He was married with three daughters. He was also poorly educated, having dropped out of school in the ninth grade.

He was referred for psychiatric treatment by his family after refusing to go to work for nearly two weeks. His symptoms, however, had increased gradually over a period of roughly two years. In the last two weeks, they had reached an extreme level and began to interfere with his work and daily life.

During his initial evaluation, he explained that no one paid any attention to him and that people avoided him. The reason for this, he claimed, was because he was dead, but alive. He went on to explain that he had once experienced a sensation like an electric shock, and ever since then had felt that his body had been transformed into something that was dead but still moving. He insisted that he was no longer human, and told doctors "I speak, breathe, and eat, but I am dead."

When asked what he thought had caused him to become this way, the patient claimed that he believed this was punishment for living a sinful life. Basically, he claimed that he was being punished by God. He claimed that God had cursed him with a dead immortality, and would not allow him to be killed. He then voiced a paranoid delusion that many of his friends and family members had already tried to poison him by putting cyanide in his tea, but because of his divine curse/ protection he did not die. He also claimed that his wife and three daughters were also dead and immortal as he was.

When asked about his delusions of lycanthropy, he voiced a belief that both he and his wife were sometimes transformed into dogs. His daughters, he said, were transformed into sheep. He claimed to have discovered this when he realized that his daughters' urine smelled like sheep urine (which leads one to wonder why in the world he was sniff-ing urine).

The man also expressed a fear that he might be overcome by sexual urges. He suffered from insomnia because of this, and slept in a room that was separated from his wife and daughters because he feared that he might (involuntarily) sexually assault any of them if he did not.

Tests ruled out any neurological defects, and he was found to be of average to slightly above average intelligence. The patient was treated with antipsychotic drugs and electroconvulsive therapy for two weeks. After this treatment, all delusional and hallucinatory symptoms had subsided.

The Curse

The patient in this case was thought to have misinterpreted his own delusion that he was a dog and his daughters were sheep. He mistook his condition as that of a werewolf, but upon inquiry claimed that he felt more like a dog than a wolf. Dogs, you see, are the protectors of sheep, whereas wolves are their predators. Therefore, this delusion may have been a metaphor for his subconscious fears about his ability to protect his daughters. The man expressed a certain amount of guilt about not properly providing for his family.

The Condition of "Reverse Clinical Lycanthropy"

Reverse clinical lycanthropy is a rare but related symptomatic condition in which the patient suffers from the delusion that he or she has the power to transform others into wolves (and sometimes into other animals). One recent case of this, also out of Iran, was reported in a case study by Dr. Ali-Reza Nejad. The patient was an 18-year-old male suffering from delusional episodes and bipolar disorder. He was unmarried and without children. He was also poorly educated, having dropped out of school in the tenth grade, and from a poor, lower class background.

After a physically traumatic experience in which he was badly burned across his legs and backside with boiling water, the patient began to feel that he had somehow been changed. He began to voice delusions that he had transformed his own mother into a wolf on several occasions. No amount of reasoning from his mother could convince the young man of anything to the contrary.

When asked what he thought had caused him to become this way, the patient explained that he believed he was cursed by Shahe Parian, the "King of the *Jinn*" in Arabic mythology. When asked to elaborate about this, he claimed that he had somehow injured the King Jinn's daughter when he'd accidentally burned himself with boiling water. Because he had done this, the patient claimed, the King Jinn was taking revenge on him by giving him a power that he could not control— basically, by giving him a power that caused him to accidentally transform his beloved mother into a wolf.

Beastly Words

Jinn is the plural form of Jinni (Jinniyah in feminine form), a group of magic spirits in Middle Eastern folklore. The term is often misspelled in English as "genie." After the spread of Islam, Jinn came to be viewed as a malevolent class of demons or fallen angels.

It is important to note that this is not a traditional case of clinical lycanthropy. This case is altogether unique because of the fact that the patient's delusions regarding transformations are not directed at himself, but at those around him. Some have begun to refer to this sort of case as "reverse clinical lycanthropy," but further research will need to be done before an official label can be decided.

There are some in the psychiatric fields who reject the idea that this case is evidence of a new condition. These individuals point out that the case bears the elements of megalomania, a psychiatric disorder in which patients suffer from delusions of possessing great or superhuman powers. Megalomania can also manifest in delusions that one is in an important role which does not exist. One example of this form of megalomania would be a homeless man who suffers from delusions that he is in fact a secret agent.

However, there is one element of this case that differs from the condition of megalomania. Megalomaniacs often voice that they are in control of their powers, roles, or abilities. Megalomania is very much a condition of delusional grandeur, an element which this case would not seem to exhibit.

The Soul-Eater and His Runaway Devil

One of the most horrific crimes in recent years is considered by some to have been a case of clinical lycanthropy gone violently wrong. Some argue, however, that it is simply a case of a disturbed young man's obsession with murder. In either case, the story is worthy of mention in regards to this study of clinical lycanthropy.

In April of 2006, in the quiet Canadian town of Medicine Hat, 23-year-old Jeremy Allan Steinke and his 12-year-old girlfriend murdered the young girl's entire family.

According to the testimonies of several of the accused man's acquaintances, many of which were released by the press, Steinke often insisted that he was actually a 300-year-old werewolf. He was said to have been fond of referring to himself as a "lycan," a popular shortened version of the word "lycanthrope."

Steinke was often described as the kind of guy who wore almost entirely black clothes. He is also said to have enjoyed putting safety pins through his flesh. He was known for always wearing a black bandana around his neck, and he would sometimes pull it up to cover his face. Steinke was commonly seen wearing dark eyeliner and spiked dog collars. He is also said to have worn a small vial around his neck, which he proudly boasted was filled with human blood. A one-time roommate of Steinke's claimed that the disturbed young man once sliced his own hand open with a knife and began licking blood from the fresh wound.

Steinke's behavior had grown increasingly bizarre following a breakup with his girlfriend. However, at an all-ages punk show, he met and began a romantic relationship with an underage girl. In court records, the girl is referred to only by the name "J. R." Because of her status as a minor, the girl's identity has never been released. On one social website, the girl used the handle of "Runaway Devil." On the same website, Steinke used the name "Soul-Eater." Their conversations on the vampire-themed site led many media outlets to wrongly report that the two had met on the site, which was later learned not to be the case.

In December of 2008, a jury in Calgary, Canada, deliberated for only 11 hours before returning with a guilty verdict. Steinke, now 25 years old, was unanimously convicted on three counts of first-degree murder. Mr. Steinke showed no reaction when the verdicts were read. He was later sentenced to life in prison, with a possibility for parole in 25 years.

Steinke's underage girlfriend was later convicted of the same charges. However, she was also deemed mentally unfit to stand trial. She was placed in the care of a state mental health facility. All later court hearings regarding her mental state have been the same, and she remains confined to a high-security mental health facility in Canada.

Freud's *Wolf Man*

Technically, Sigmund Freud's *Wolf Man* case study cannot be classified as true clinical lycanthropy as it is now defined. Freud, however, could be credited with identifying the sexual aspects that later came to be associated with the condition. Freud first published this case study in his 1918 collective work (originally in German) entitled *Aus der Geschichte Einer Infantilen Neurose,* or "From the History of an Infantile Neurosis." Freud referred to his patient as the "Wolf Man" for the sake of anonymity. However, the man later identified himself as Russian aristocrat Sergei Pankejeff and even wrote a book about his experiences with Freud.

From Freud's writing, it cannot be said for sure whether Pankejeff's condition was delusional or simply a dream manifestation. The case was so-named because of a particular dream analysis. Pankejeff was suffering from extreme anxiety, manifesting in bouts of severe depression as well as physical symptoms that were harming the man's health and well-being. For example, it was written that Pankejeff could not have bowel movements without the aid of a rectal enema.

Freud's treatment of Pankejeff was concentrated heavily on a particular recurring dream the man had experienced during his childhood, most frequently during the winter season. In this dream, Pankejeff would be lying in bed with his feet pointed toward his bedroom window. Outside the window was a row of walnut trees. The window would open quite suddenly, as if on its own. Then Pankejeff would see seven white wolves sitting in the branches of the trees. Terrified that the wolves were going to eat him, Pankejeff (then a young boy) would wake up screaming. The young boy's nanny would then spend hours coaxing him back to sleep. Pankejeff's testimony about this dream was very clear on the point that it always felt just as real to him after he awoke.

Freud is known for his belief that all psychological disorders were caused by some sort of sexual issue, a point which caused many of his colleagues and students to break with him later. True to form, Freud concluded that Pankejeff's dream was caused by him having witnessed his parents having sex when he was extremely young. Basically, Freud argued that the young boy's mind would have perceived the act as "primal" in nature because his parents were probably having sex in the from-behind position (once again, the "doggy style" position). He claimed that this caused Pankejeff to associate sex with animals, a concept that his mind had displaced, in his dream at least, from his parents onto the white wolves.

Werewolf as Jungian Archetype

Carl Jung began as a student of Freud but would later break with his mentor due to disagreements between them regarding the nature of human motivational drives. Freud believed that drives originated with sex. Jung disagreed, stating that sex was only one of many drives. Jung believed that these drives were often expressed in myths and dreams in the form of symbolic figures, which he called *archetypes*.

Beastly Words

In the works of Jung, **archetypes** are inherited symbols, concepts, or thought modes that stem from the collective experiences of the human race. He believed these were passed on in the unconscious of all human beings.

Jung viewed the werewolf as one symbolic manifestation of a broader "death/rebirth" archetype. The werewolf represented, according to Freud, primarily the sexual transformation humans undergo in young adulthood, as well as a young female's initial fears regarding sexual intercourse or a male's fear that his own lustful urges may lead him to a terrible death or eternal damnation. In myth, the werewolf often has to be overcome by some magical or ritualistic device in order for a character to experience an "ideal" or "pure" form of love.

Jung first explained this concept of the werewolf archetypes in his work *Four Archetypes* by offering a myth about a beautiful princess whose lover has been transformed into a werewolf by some enchanter's spell. The princess has to consult a wise old sage, who instructs her to build a fire and place above it a cauldron of tar. He then tells her that she must place within the tar her most beloved possession, a white lily flower (which symbolizes virginity). He then tells her that, when her lover passes by in his wolf form, she must pour the contents of the cauldron over his head. The princess does as the sage tells her. Once she has completed her task of pouring the "lily-blessed" tar over her lover's head, he is freed from the spell and returns to human form. The two are then able to pursue their life together, the man having been "transformed" and the princess being "reborn" into her new life as part of a married couple (symbolized by the sacrifice of her treasured "virginity lily").

The Least You Need to Know

- Clinical lycanthropy is a mental disorder in which the affected person believes that he or she is, can, or at some point has turned into a wolf or werewolf.

- Clinical lycanthropy is a manifestation of symptoms but not a diagnosis.

- In recent years, an increasing number of clinical lycanthropy cases have occurred in Iran.

- Some argue that so-called "reverse clinical lycanthropy" is actually just a form of megalomania.

- Freud's *Wolf Man* is not considered a case of clinical lycanthropy, but it did serve to identify certain sexual aspects associated with the dream symbolism of wolves.

- Jung viewed the werewolf as a death/rebirth archetype, symbolic of a fear of sexual intercourse (the "death" of one's virginity) or of being killed and/or damned as a result of one's lustful desires.

Appendix

Glossary

What follows is a list of useful terms used throughout the book. This glossary has been provided in order to allow for an at-a-glance, user friendly reference.

alpha   In the animal world, the alpha animal is the lead animal in charge of a particular social group (such as a lion pride or wolf pack).

Anasazi   An American Indian term with multiple translations, depending on a tribal group's usage. It is commonly translated to mean "the ancient enemy." However, it can also mean, "ancient ones," or "enemy of the ancestors." The Anasazi are thought to be almost extinct. However, it is believed that a small number of them remain.

anime   A Japanese term that means "animation" and generally refers to cartoon series that are most frequently adapted from previously well-received manga (comics/graphic novels).

anthropomorphism   A term that refers to figures that embody both human and nonhuman traits.

archetypes   Originally a part of Jungian psychology, archetypes are inherited symbols, concepts, or thought modes that stem from the collective experiences of the human race. Jung believed these were passed on in the unconscious of all human beings.

Aswang   A term in Tagalog, the common language of the Philippines, that refers to an evil supernatural being that feeds upon human flesh. One type of Aswang, the "fake beast," is known to be an able shapeshifter.

bakemono   A Japanese term that roughly translates as "monster" or "demon."

bastet   *See* were-cat.

Benandanti   Originally an ancient religious order of northern Italy, primarily responsible for performing rites that ensured agricultural fertility. A number of accused werewolves claimed to be Benandanti members, and probably picked the name since they were claiming to protect farms from thefts by witches and demons.

berserker   A Norse/Germanic term that roughly translates as "bear skins," but really means something like "one who acts as a bear."

Berserkersgang   A class of ruthless and frenzied warriors feared by all who faced them. Among the berserkers was a more specific class called the *ulfheðnar*.

bouda   (Sometimes spelled *buda*.) An African term that has come to mean "were-hyena," though it is very likely that it originally could have had a different meaning. In Ethiopia, this term is sometimes used by Christians to refer to Ethiopian Jews, though not always with the "were-hyena" connotation.

bruxsa   A Portuguese word that refers to a creature possessing the powers and attributes of both a werewolf and a vampire, though legends vary on just which creature it started out being. The term *cucubuth* can be used interchangeably.

bultungin   In the dialects of the Nigerian state of Borno, this term literally means "I become a hyena." However, the term commonly refers to a person who shapeshifts into a hyena.

caul   A soft membrane that covers and protects the heads of embryos that are high vertebrates (such as primates and humans). This membrane is usually shed during delivery, slowly rubbed off and torn away as the infant travels down the tight birth canal. Many ancient and medieval cultures assigned certain omens (good and bad) to babies that were born with the caul still wrapped over their heads.

clinical lycanthropy   (Also called psychological lycanthropy.) A symptomatic psychological disorder (meaning it is a symptom of one or more main causal conditions) that is commonly identified by a strong delusion that one can, is, or has at some time transformed into a wolf or werewolf. However, it is important to note that no actual physical transformations are involved.

cryptids   Cryptids are believed (by cryptozoologists) to actually be unidentified, undiscovered, or extinct species of animals that have been mislabeled as "monsters" or "creatures." Perhaps the most globally known of the cryptids is the so-called "Loch Ness Monster," which has yet to be confirmed or concretely identified.

cryptozoology   The study of special/rare animals called cryptids.

cucubuth   *See* bruxsa.

dementia   A state of delusional madness usually marked by extreme disorientation, bouts of irritability, and an erratic/infirm grasp of one's current time and/or location. Clinical lycanthropy is considered a specified manifestation of dementia.

Dragoons   Specially trained soldiers that were once a common element of European armies. They were trained to fight on foot as well as horseback and were schooled in cavalry tactics. In the beginning, members of such units were commonly armed with "dragon" muskets.

enchanted lycanthropy   A form of lycanthropy that is achieved through the use of magic rituals or enchantments, or by using/wearing magical clothing, amulets, or other enchanted objects.

ergot   A disease that affects certain grain-producing plants such as rye. It is caused by the *claviceps purpurea* fungus and is one of the most potent hallucinogens to grow naturally. Ergot may be indentified by its brown or purple sacks, called sclerotia, which envelop the affected grain.

familiar   Refers to an idea, widely created by church propaganda, that witches (and, in this particular case, a werewolf) kept demonic spirits to assist them in their work. In order to avoid being discovered, church authorities claimed that these demon servants remained invisible in the presence of others, assumed the forms of household animals (the most popular being cats, especially black cats), or just possessed the bodies of animals that were already in their masters' homes.

graphic novel   A comic-style, illustrated book that typically has a more complex, full-length story than is usually found in comic books. It usually is created for a more mature reading audience.

hellhounds   Demonic hounds that come from hell. This idea likely originated from an ancient myth, such as that of the giant, three-headed dog named Cerberus that guards the gates of the underworld (the domain of the death god Hades) in Greek mythology. These dogs are often described as black, sometimes resembling shadows, with glowing red eyes.

hydrophobia   An irrational and debilitating fear of all water. Many pieces of werewolf lore state that lycanthropes have an unnatural aversion to water.

hypertrichosis   A rare skin disorder that is characterized by the growth of long, fine hairs on the affected individual's body far beyond what is normal for the person's age, sex, and ethnicity. The condition can be congenital, starting at birth, or acquired, occurring later in life. It can also occur all over the body or only in specific, localized areas.

hysteria   A condition that is usually characterized by unusual and often irrational behavior by an individual suffering a mental break (often temporary but sometimes permanent) caused by an experience of overwhelming, emotionally or mentally traumatizing terror.

inquisitor   A church title for an official member of the Ecclesiastical Court of the Inquisition, which was charged with rooting out enemies of Christianity, such as heretics, witches, devil worshippers, and quite often just about anyone else that the church deemed undesirable.

Jinn   A group of magic spirits in Middle Eastern folklore. The term is often misspelled in English as "genie." After the spread of Islam, Jinn came to be viewed as a malevolent class of demons or fallen angels.

kitsune   A Japanese term that can be used to refer to a normal fox. However, it is often used to refer to a Shinto "fox spirit."

lais   (Spelled *lays* in English.) Once a very common form of romance poetry, used especially in medieval England and France. One relatively well-known lai is "The Franklin's Tale," from Geoffrey Chaucer's fourteenth-century work *The Canterbury Tales.*

Layak (Also spelled *Leyak*.) A mythical shapeshifting being in Indonesian lore. Some lore claims that a Layak is an evil spirit, while others claim that a Layak is actually a human witch with dark powers. So the next time you meet a Layak, you should ask it about this.

libido A Freudian term for the human sex drive. Newly infected lycanthropes are often said to experience a sudden and extreme increase in sexual appetite and endurance.

LSD Commonly referred to as "acid," stands for lysergic acid diethylamide. LSD is an extremely potent psychedelic drug that affects both the mood and perception of the user, causing hallucinations, disorientation, mood swings, paranoia, and other delusions.

lunacy A term currently defined as insanity, extreme foolishness, or a display of foolish behavior. In ancient times, bouts of insanity were thought to be influenced by the lunar cycle. Despite the insistence of science to the contrary, many people still believe that the full moon influences humans to behave strangely.

lycanthropy The technical term for the state of being a werewolf. A person who is inflicted with or practices lycanthropy is called a lycanthrope.

manga A Japanese term that literally translates as "involuntary sketches." However, manga is now used in reference to a popular genre of book-length, black-and-white Japanese comics. The term is believed to have first been coined in 1814, when a Japanese artist named Hokusai created a book of impromptu black-and-white sketches, many of which had elements of storytelling, which he called manga.

Mark of the Beast A belief from medieval werewolf lore that has sometimes also been used in pop culture and werewolf cinema. It states that werewolves are marked (usually on the hand) with the mark of a pentagram or the numbers "666."

necrophilia A condition in which a person becomes unhealthily obsessed with corpses. This strange condition often leads to unusual behaviors such as stealing corpses and frequenting graveyards. It can also manifest in sexual ways.

nihilism   A term usually defined as a self-centered belief that one is somehow exempt from all rules or social/religious/moral restrictions. In a more broad sense, it refers to a philosophical belief that life has no point, that human rules are valueless, and rejects the validity of any truth aside from one's own.

O-Guchi no Magami   Japanese name that translates as "Great-mouthed Pure-Kami," an ancient wolf deity in the Shinto nature religion of Japan.

O-kami   In Japanese, O-kami is generally used to mean "wolf." Literally translated, however, it actually means "great deity."

pagan   This term originally comes from the Latin word *paganus*, which means "rustic" or "country person." During the rise of Christianity in the Roman Empire, the word came to refer to the "uncivilized" people who continued to practice polytheistic or pre-Christian religions. The word later took on a negative connotation and came to be associated with dark arts, devil worship, evil, etc. In recent years, the term has begun to shed this negative connotation as more people have begun to practice these old religions openly, now that they can do so without fear of harm.

pastoral   Refers to something related to the lifestyle, work, and activities of shepherds or their livestock. The word *pastor*, which is now a popular religious title, originally referred to a shepherd.

penny dreadful   A popular nineteenth century form of fiction known for its lurid and sensational content. The name comes from the fact that these were cheap (usually costing only a penny), relatively short, paperback-bound stories that usually involved "dreadful" plots of crime, murder, and a fair amount of sexual content. As one might imagine, these books were primarily sold to the younger male members of England's vast working class.

physical lycanthropy   Also called "cursed lycanthropy" or "viral lycanthropy," this refers to lycanthropy received as a result of being bitten by a werewolf.

porphyria   A rare condition that causes an inability in the body to create *porphyrin* in the bone marrow. This leads to a discoloration of the skin that is reddish or purplish, as well as extreme physical deformities (especially in the face and hands).

pulp fiction   Refers to inexpensive magazines or novels written for a mass market audience. Such works often contained violent or sexual material. The moods of such stories were generally melodramatic in dialogue and sensational in tone.

quicksilver   An obsolete term once used to refer to mercury. In ages past, mercury was believed to be a liquid form of silver.

rabies   A viral infection, often passed by the saliva through a bite, that attacks the brain and nervous system of warm-blooded animals. It is also thought to be a possible explanation for medieval reports of lycanthropy and certain parts of werewolf lore.

Rosicrucian Order   A seventeenth-century group of scholars, philosophers, and aesthetics who studied and collectively shared knowledge related to the secret arts of mysticism, metaphysics, and alchemy.

schizophrenia   A mental illness commonly thought to be caused by neurological damage or defect and characterized by hallucinations, paranoid delusions, physical restlessness, and hearing voices.

Shinto   The indigenous nature religion of Japan. For a time, it was the officially recognized Japanese state religion.

spirit lycanthropy   Lycanthropy that is achieved through spiritual rites, such as those used by the Native American tribes of the Pacific Northwest.

strychnine   Commonly considered a fatal poison, but sometimes used as a heavy stimulant when taken in small doses.

succubus   A female demon commonly known for seducing men as they sleep. A succubus is, for the most part, a female "sex demon" that has intercourse with men as they sleep. This likely originated from a demonic female figure from Judaic folklore, known as Lilith. In the Judaic tradition, men are not supposed to sleep alone in order to avoid encounters with Lilith.

tengu   In the Japanese nature religion of Shinto, a clever, mischievous, and sometimes destructive nature spirit, usually found in the mountains and described as having wings and a beaked face.

ulfheðnar   A specific class of berserkers. The word roughly means "wolf wearers," but really means something like "those who become wolves."

Valkyries   In Norse myths, these are beautiful female warrior spirits tasked with retrieving from battlefields the souls of fallen warriors who had died bravely and with honor. They would then escort the soul to Valhalla, a heavenly utopia of food, drink, sex, and battle, which was reserved only for the brave.

Vargamor   Roughly translates as meaning "wolf-crone." The term refers to the members of a prehistoric northern European nature cult, predominantly made up of women, who practiced magic wolf-rites. With the rise of Christianity, they came to be thought of as evil witches.

Wendigo   A term that literally translates as "cannibal." Originally, the term referred to those who had been possessed by the Wendigo, meaning they had resorted to cannibalism in order to survive. Over time, inhabitants of the region have claimed that the Wendigo is, in fact, a very real creature that looks somewhat like a Sasquatch/Bigfoot with antlers.

were-cat   Sometimes used interchangeably with *bastet*, this is a term commonly used to refer to a human with the power to assume the form of a large cat (usually some predatory cat, such as a lion or tiger) or some form of cat-human hybrid.

werewolf   A common term for one who is in the state of lycanthropy.

zoanthropy   A term used in psychology to refer to a state of mental delusion in which the afflicted individual harbors the belief that he or she can assume the form of an animal.

Appendix B

Further Reading

There are thousands of books available that deal with the subject of werewolves. These many works range from reference books to horror fiction, from horror-romance to psychology and sociology. If you would like to continue your study of lycanthropy, or just want to find some enjoyable fiction reads with werewolf characters, the following list of titles is definitely a good place to start.

Suggested Nonfiction/Reference Books

Anderson, Sarah. *The Cold Counsel: The Women in Old Norse Literature and Myth.* New York: Routledge, 2001.

Ashley, Leonard. *The Complete Book of Werewolves.* New York: Barricade Books, 2001.

Baring-Gould, Sabine. *The Book of Werewolves.* Scotts Valley: IAP, 2009 (originally published in 1865).

Bourgault du Coudray, Chantal. *The Curse of the Werewolf: Fantasy, Horror, and the Beast Within.* New York: I.B. Taurus, 2006.

Cybulski, Angela. *Fact or Fiction? Werewolves.* Farmington Hills: Greenhaven Press, 2004.

De Blecourt, Willem. *Werewolves*. New York: Hambledon Continuum, 2005.

Douglas, Adams. *The Beast Within: Man, Myths, and Werewolves*. New York: Orion, 1993.

Glut, Donald. *True Werewolves of History*. Rockville: Sense of Wonder Press, 2004.

Godfrey, Linda. *Hunting the American Werewolf*. Boulder: Trails Media Group, 2006.

Godfrey, Linda, and Rosemary Guiley. *Werewolves*. New York: Checkmark Books, 2008.

Guiley, Rosemary. *The Encyclopedia of Vampires, Werewolves, and Other Monsters*. New York: Checkmark Books, 2004.

Hamel, Frank. *Werewolves, Bird-Women, and Other Human Animals*. Dover: Dover Publications, 2007.

Hirschmann, Kris. *Mysterious Encounters—Werewolves*. New York: KidHaven Press, 2006.

O'Donnell, Elliot. *Werewolves*. Rockville: Wildside Press, 2008.

Otten, Charlotte F. *A Lycanthropy Reader: Werewolves in Western Culture*. New York: Dorset Press, 1990.

Pipe, Jim. *In the Footsteps of the Werewolf*. East Sussex, UK: Copper Beech, 1996.

Sconduto, Leslie. *Metamorphoses of the Werewolf: A Literary Study from Antiquity Through the Renaissance*. Jefferson: McFarland, 2008.

Senn, Harry A. *Were-Wolf and Vampire in Romania*. Columbia: East European Monographs, 1982.

Steiger, Brad. *The Werewolf Book: The Encyclopedia of Shape-Shifting Beings*. Canton: Visible Ink Press, 1999.

Summers, Montague. *The Werewolf in Lore and Legend*. Dover: Dover Publications, 2003.

Suggested Literature/Fiction Books

In this list, please note that the classic literary texts already discussed in Chapter 10 have been excluded.

Andrews, Christopher. *Triumvirate: Of Wolf and Man*. New York: Rising Star Visionary Press, 2009.

Barlow, Toby. *Sharp Teeth*. New York: Harper Perennial, 2008.

Bergstrom, Elaine, and various. *Werewolves: Dead Moon Rising (Anthology)*. Calumet City: Moonstone, 2007.

Briggs, Patricia. *Alpha and Omega Saga*. New York: Ace Mass Market, 2008.

Cassidy, Dakota. *The Accidental Werewolf*. Berkeley: Berkeley Trade, 2008.

Douglas, Carole Nelson. *Dancing with Werewolves: Delilah Street, Paranormal Investigator*. New York: Juno Books, 2007.

Enck, Eric. *The Work*. Washington, D.C.: PublishAmerica, 2005.

Farago, Gina. *Ivy Cole and the Moon*. Randleman: NeDeo Press, 2005.

———. *Luna*. Randleman: NeDeo Press, 2008.

Half-Human, Half-Animal: Tales of Werewolves and Related Creatures. Bloomington: Authorhouse, 2003.

Harris, Charlaine. *Dead and Gone*. New York: Ace Hardcover, 2009.

Harris, Charlaine, and various. *Wolfsbane and Mistletoe (Anthology)*. New York: Ace Hardcover, 2008.

Jones, Carrie. *Need*. London: Bloomsbury USA, 2008.

Kennard, Vincent. *The Wolf Chronicles*. Bloomington: Authorhouse, 2007.

MacInerney, Karen. *Howling at the Moon: Tales of an Urban Werewolf*. New York: Ballantine Books, 2008.

Nelson, S. M. *Hallowed Moon*. Washington, D.C.: PublishAmerica, 2008.

Salzman, Shawn W. *Order of the Wolf.* Bloomington: Xlibris Corporation, 2008.

Thompson, Ronda. *Confessions of a Werewolf Supermodel.* New York: St. Martin's Press, 2007.

Wedel, Steven E. *Call to the Hunt.* Massena: Scrybe Press, 2005.

Wilks, Eileen. *The World of the Lupi Series.* Berkeley: Berkeley Trade, 2004.

Index

Y-Z

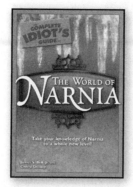
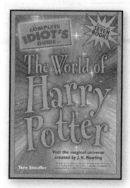